Fauquier County, Virginia's Clerk's Loose Papers

A Guide to the Records 1759–1919

by
Joan W. Peters, C.G.R.S.

HERITAGE BOOKS
2012

HERITAGE BOOKS
AN IMPRINT OF HERITAGE BOOKS, INC.

Books, CDs, and more—Worldwide

For our listing of thousands of titles see our website
at
www.HeritageBooks.com

Published 2012 by
HERITAGE BOOKS, INC.
Publishing Division
100 Railroad Ave. #104
Westminster, Maryland 21157

Copyright © 2001 Joan W. Peters

Back cover illustration: from the Clerk's Loose Papers, Land Records, 1815–008 Oversize. A Treasury Warrant from Governor James Monroe to John Mauzey dated May 6, 1802 in an Ejectment Land Dispute styled Horner v Utterback.

All rights reserved. No part of this book may be reproduced or transmitted in any form or by any means, electronic or mechanical, including photocopying, recording or by any information storage and retrieval system without written permission from the author, except for the inclusion of brief quotations in a review.

International Standard Book Numbers
Paperbound: 978-1-58549-689-1
Clothbound: 978-0-7884-9479-6

Fauquier County, Virginia's Clerks Loose Papers: A Guide to the Records 1759-1919

FOREWORD

I have written this guide for two reasons. First, I wanted to raise public awareness of these important sets of records, which are now available in some Virginia courthouses. Second, I wanted to persuade those researchers with Virginia roots or an interest in local history to think about re-visiting the courthouses here to look at these records, if available. Whenever I ask public researchers whether they have seen these records, they invariably reply, "Oh, I've already done my court house research." "Not," I want so badly to say, "if you haven't been to Virginia since 1993!"

So, what are Clerk's loose Papers? They are exactly that: loose papers, filed during a Clerk of Court's term. The papers are tri-folded, tied with red tape and filed by year and customarily stored in basement vaults in Virginia's courthouses. They may be found in old metal or wooden woodruff drawers or they may be some other non acid-free storage display.

The records could pertain to almost anything with which the Court dealt. There are sheriff and constable bonds. There are Chancery records. There are Court records of debts to merchants and other lenders. There are criminal causes for theft, arson, burglary, murder, malicious wounding, and the like. Files could include a host of free Negro and slave records, including free Negro apprenticeships. Land records like deeds and leases and court records of land disputes like trespass or ejectments are found throughout the Clerk's loose Papers.

There are some very interesting coroner's inquests in these drawers. Researchers looking for military appointments, discharges, land warrants and pensions should look carefully at the military records in the Clerk's loose Papers. In addition, there are mill, road, and ordinary applications, which provide understanding of the county's early growth patterns.

Local history records, found in the Clerk's loose Papers, relating to a county jail and Courthouse, often give added awareness of the growth of the local infrastructure. Declarations of intent and naturalization papers may reveal an emigrant ancestor. Overseer of the Poor records give a picture of the county's poor whose presence is often hard to find in other court records. Probate records like wills, plats and surveys of divisions, and inventories, not found in the General Index to Wills, may be found in the Clerk's Loose Papers.

Schoolmaster suits for non-payment of fees from students' families and other early school records add an additional fillip relating to the early education of the county's elite. Sheriff records will often give lists of prisoners and convey awareness to the enforcement of the criminal and civil code of the times. Fauquier's tax and fiscal records in the Clerk's loose Papers may rewrite the early history of the county since they include little known and inaccessible colonial tithable lists and a hitherto unknown 1785 state census of the county.

Finally, there are vital records in these papers. Thirty-four 1784 marriage bonds were newly discovered sandwiched between Administrator and Executor Bonds filed in the vault. These "new" marriage bonds may prove useful in proving revolutionary war descent. There are also early births and deaths in these vital records, especially as they relate to free Negroes and slaves.

The variety and diversity of this record base underscores the importance of these records to professional researchers, architectural and local historians, surveyors, title examiners, attorneys and paralegals, genealogists and family historians. In short, any one who frequents the courthouse doing genealogical or title research can benefit from the accessibility of records from the Clerk's loose Papers.

Unfortunately, these records are not readily accessible in many of Virginia's courthouses. Clerks of Court may claim a legitimate ignorance to the presence of these records. They may cite fire and the deprivations of invading union troops to explain why the Clerk's loose papers are no longer extant. Indeed, Fauquier had two such fires. The records escaped destruction only because they were housed in a separate Clerk's office.

*Dedicated to Mr. William Harris, Mrs. Gail Barb,
and our volunteers Bill, Lisa, Margaret, Paula and Starr.*

ACKNOWLEDGMENTS

Many people, on both the state and local level, have been helpful with the three preservation grants to Fauquier County that enabled the Clerk's Loose Papers of the early County records to be preserved and made accessible for research. **These members of the State Library of Virginia** helped to set the first grant up and see it through, way back in 1993: **Glenn, Paul, John and Paige. Amy** later stepped in and ably oversaw the second and third phases to completion. Thanks to the all of you, for your support and especially for your patience when answering the seemingly endless questions we had about the records and the Chancery index forms.

In our first grant, Karen, Dave and I would never had been able to complete the project without the aid and support of **the Fauquier County Library Board, Fauquier County Librarian Maria Del Rosso and Library facilities coordinator Ava Lee. Butch Farley and Clerk of Court William Harris** was especially helpful in finding a site for the second grant to continue **and Gail Barb and Hunton Tiffany Jr.** were equally helpful in finding a site for the last grant phase.

I would also like to acknowledge **Mary Rephlo and the Modern Archives Institute training program** for Archivists. I took this two-week intensive training in Archival methodology and preservation in January 1998. This is a "must" for anyone interested in archival work.

Thanks also go to my co-workers**: Dave Martin, Karen White**, who worked with me on the first grant. On the second grant, **Jane Pearson** was the very competent archivist who assisted in the preservation of the Ended Chancery records.

The grant process began under the County Clerkship **of Mr. William Harris** in 1993; the last grant was completed by his successor, **Mrs. Gail Barb.** I was indeed fortunate to have both of these clerks' dedication, encouragement, and enthusiastic support during the entire length of this preservation project.

Finally, there were the volunteers**: Bill, Lisa, Margaret, Paula and Starr**. These devoted and dedicated people spent hours and hours working on the indexes for the Clerk's Loose Papers and entering data for the state-mandated Chancery Index. I was extremely fortunate to have such dependable and enthusiastic volunteers whose endless willingness to enter large amounts of data into an insatiable index made it possible to meet grant deadlines.

COVER ILLUSTRATIONS

The front cover is from the Land Records and Disputes Record Series of the Clerks Loose Papers. The Deed from George and Martha Washington to nephew Robert Lewis for a tract in Fauquier County is found in 1799-011 Hickerson v. Blackwell.

The back cover is also from the Land Records and Disputes Record Series. It is a Treasury Warrant from Governor James Monroe to John Mauzey for 25 ½ acres on Cedar Run in Fauquier County. It was an exhibit in the 1815-008 Ejectment suit styled Horner v. Utterback.

Fauquier County, Virginia's Clerks Loose Papers: A Guide to the Records 1759-1919

In Virginia, the Civil war played havoc with county courthouse throughout the Commonwealth. Nearby Prince William County lost its marriage bonds before 1853 and large portions of their probate records along with some of the land records. Stafford County lost so many of their colonial land and probate records during the civil war that the county has been dubbed a "burned county". Many of Virginia's seventeenth and eighteenth century General Court records were lost when victorious union troops took Richmond in April 1865.

Despite these setbacks to accessibility, there may still be Clerk's loose papers stored in basement vaults. Clerks simply may not be aware of their existence.

As the last decade of the twentieth century opened, the State Library of Virginia became aware of the importance of preserving these records. They offered grants to preserve the Clerk's loose papers and to separate them into record categories for ease of access.

Then, in 1994 the State Library had a change in policy. They decided that separating the Clerk's loose papers into record categories was a too costly and time-consuming process. Instead, the State Library decreed that only chancery records were to be culled from among the Clerk's loose papers.

Library archivists would then prepare a Chancery Index form to enter information into seven searchable fields. These fields are 1) The suit's index number, 2) the old docket number, 3) the primary plaintiff and 4) the primary defendant, 5) surnames of those found in the suit papers and depositions, 6) whether there were plats and surveys in the suits and 7) the name, date and residence for those men and women leaving wills.

So today, while some of the counties have preserved **all** of their Clerk's loose papers, others have preserved only the Chancery records.

There are two related challenges here. One is to those who regularly conduct courthouse research. It concerns the accessibility of those loose papers. Have they been preserved and arranged so that the researcher can look at them?

The second challenge lies in finding financial support for such a project. The preservation, arrangement, storage and indexing of these papers requires funding that is often outside the means of a county Clerk or county budget item.

In Virginia, the State Library has undertaken the task of chancery preservation through grants to county Clerks for this process. No funds from the state legislature have been used; instead, a portion of the recording fees of Court documents from each court is "put into the pot", so to speak, and is used to fund chancery preservation grants to individual counties who apply to preserve their early records.

The ultimate challenge, of course, lies with the researcher and the research public at large. It depends on whether researchers want to become active in the preservation process and advocate for funding the conservation and safeguarding of the Clerk's loose papers. It is contingent upon whether these same researchers are interested in becoming those who work on the preservation of the records by encouraging their county clerks to apply for a preservation grants for these papers.

Only when the research public becomes pro-active, fully involved and totally committed to document preservation, will these important papers be preserved for the use of future generations.

Fauquier County, Virginia's Clerks Loose Papers: A Guide to the Records 1759-1919

PREFACE

1. Background

David Martin and I became aware of the Library of Virginia's Preservation Grants in late summer, 1993. After a visit to Shenandoah County to see a County Circuit Court preservation grant in progress, we thought we might like to try a similar project for Fauquier County.

We both felt that we brought complimentary skills to a preservation grant project. Dave's company Computer Archives Technology is an electronic publisher of family genealogies, journal compilations and Civil War History. He also had extensive genealogical roots in the county that dated back to the mid eighteenth century; thus he had a general idea of the record base with which we would be working.

As an historian, I brought three very pragmatic skills to the project: an exhaustive and wide-ranging knowledge of the local Court record base, a practical skill in reading, transcribing and abstracting eighteenth and nineteenth century handwriting, and a comprehensive knowledge of the legal terminology found in the records

After some consultation, we decided to ask Karen White, then the co-founder of the Afro-American Historical Association of Fauquier County, to work with us. Karen was a knowledgeable African American family historian and had a broad range of computer skills we could utilize to set up a variety of index-capable databases for the project.

In late winter 1993, the three of us approached Fauquier County's Circuit Court Clerk, William D. Harris, with a proposal to set up an archives for the County's Loose Papers stored in the Circuit Court basement vault, dating from 1759-1832. Mr. Harris enthusiastically endorsed the idea of applying for a Library of Virginia grant that would preserve and store the county's earliest Court records in an acid-free environment.

2. The Preservation Grants: The Clerk's Loose Papers Grant (1759-1832)

Ten months later, in September 1994, Mr. Harris applied for and received a sixteen-month grant from the Library of Virginia to do this, following LVA preservation guidelines and training procedures. Once the grant process was completed, the Court could then open these records to the public. Historians, title examiners, public researchers and genealogists would be able to see these documents for the first time.

During this grant term, we separated the Clerk's loose papers into nineteen LVA-approved records series. This meant when we unwrapped a record relating to Mills, for example, we flat filed the record, mending as necessary, and placed it into a folder with an index number and information about the mill in question. We then put the folder into an acid free document box entitled Mills. We did the same for other records as well: documents relating to Chancery Records, Free Negro/Slave records, Military Records, Roads, Land Disputes, Overseer of the Poor records, Probate records, and Tax and Fiscal records.

By the end of the grant, we found that we had flat filed, mended, preserved and made accessible more than 300 storage boxes of Clerk's Loose Papers between 1759-1832. All of the records had been placed into their appropriate record category while strictly adhering to the LVA preservation guidelines. At the same time, we were able to put together our own indexes for most of the records and designed inventories for the remaining series.

3. The Preservation Grants: Ended Chancery and Clerk's Loose Papers (1832-1919)

By 1997, Karen and Dave had gone on to other activities so I decided to apply for a grant to preserve, flat file, store, index and make accessible the Ended Chancery suits in the courthouse basement. These suits were folded into three parts, bound by red ribbon and housed in metal woodruff drawers. Mr. Harris received that grant in September 1997.

When processing these suits, it didn't take me long before I realized that I needed help. Their sheer volume was overwhelming. Fortunately, I was able to find not only an experienced archivist to share the workload but a very competent volunteer to help with the indexing. Jane Pearson worked for a year on the project and Bill Scales, my volunteer, took up the slack by taking over the indexing chores.

When we finished, we had more than 300 boxes of Chancery causes. These included Ended Chancery, County Court Chancery (found in the Clerk's Loose Papers 1832-1904), 1866 and 1868 Dropped Chancery and something the court termed "Lost" Chancery. These were chancery suits which attorneys had taken from the court and never returned. We also completed a Chancery index according to State Library standards.

By the end of the second grant, all of the County's Clerk's Loose papers had also been processed. Several more boxes of record groupings for Negro records, Local History, Land, Military, Probate and Tax records were added to our Clerk's Loose Papers. These boxes were then indexed and made accessible to the public for the first time.

Meanwhile there were changes afoot in the basement vault. The staff removed the old metal cabinets and woodruff drawers, previously the home of the 1759-1904 Clerk's Loose Papers and Ended Chancery suits from 1832-1919. New, acid-free metal shelving replaced the old woodruff drawers and cabinets; now, row upon row of brown archival boxes house the Chancery records and Clerk's Loose Papers. The new shelving had an additional benefit: they allowed for the Clerk's Loose Papers to be arranged according to their record grouping. This meant easy access for the staff when the public wished to see these records.

4. The Preservation Grants: Consolidation of Ended and County Court Chancery and the Circuit Superior Court/Circuit Court Chancery Grant

In the summer of 1999, the State Library approached the Court to apply for a grant to update and consolidate all of Fauquier County's Chancery records into one set of records and one indexed database. This meant that the Chancery suits in the Clerk's Loose Papers between 1759-1904 would be consolidated with the rest of the Chancery causes. The State Library also agreed to allow us to pull chancery records that might be found in the nineteenth century Circuit Superior Court records along with the mid-nineteenth century Circuit Court records housed in the basement vault.

Once the Circuit Superior Court records (1832-1854) and the Circuit Court records (1854-1910) had been examined, *all* of Fauquier County's chancery would be indexed, accessible to the public and available for research.

Mrs. Gail Barb, the new Clerk of the Circuit Court, received this chancery consolidation and indexing grant in late October 1999. While there are no Clerk's Loose Papers associated with this grant, the consolidation of the early Chancery found in those papers, the Dropped Chancery and the "lost" chancery with the Ended Chancery and the remaining Circuit Superior/Circuit Court Chancery has significantly altered the numbering system. The old index created for the Chancery in the Clerk's Loose Papers is no longer valid; indeed the index created by the State Library for the Chancery preservation grant is one that will be used for *all* the counties that have separated their chancery suits from the rest of their county's loose papers.

Now there will be one consistent searchable data base that will give the principal parties, surnames of those involved in the suit or those giving depositions, an indication as to whether there is a plat and survey filed with the suit and the name, date and county of residence of those leaving wills. Slaves are identified; so are businesses. The index is concise and elegant in its form.

Now that the preservation projects for the Clerk's Loose Papers and Chancery have been completed, it is my hope that these papers uncovered in these three grants will help fill in the gaps in knowledge relating to past generations. These records are our bridge to the past.

                                                 Joan W. Peters, C.G.R.S.
                                                 Broad Run, Virginia

TABLE OF CONTENTS

Pages

ACKNOWLEDGEMENTS

FOREWORD

PREFACE   i-ii

TABLE OF CONTENTS

LIST OF PLATES

Chapter 1. Introduction	1-7
Plates 1-3	8-10
Chapter 2. An Introduction to the Records	11-14
Plate 4	14
Chapter 3. Bonds, Oaths & Commissions	15-16
Plates 5-7	16-18
Chapter 4. Chancery Records	19-27
Plates 8-15	27-34
Chapter 5. Dead Papers, Ended Causes & Judgments	35-40
Plates 16-19	41-44
Chapter 6. Free Negro & Slave Records (after 1865: Negro Records)	45-51
Plates 20-24	52-56
Chapter 7. Land Records & Disputes	57-66
Plates 25-35	67-76
Chapter 8. Medical Records	77
Plate 36	78
Chapter 9. Military Records	79-81
Plates 37-43	82-88
Chapter 10. Mills, Roads & Bridges	89-91
Plates 44-57	92-104

TABLE OF CONTENTS

	Pages
Chapter 11. Miscellaneous Records	105-106
Plates 58-77	107-126
Chapter 12. Ordinary Records	127-129
Plates 78-83	130-136
Chapter 13. Overseers of the Poor/Churchwarden Records	137-140
Plates 84-89	141-146
Chapter 14. Oversize Records	147
Plates 90-92	148-150
Chapter 15. Probate/Fiduciary Records	151-152
Plates 93-100	153-160
Chapter 16. School Records	161
Plate 101	162
Chapter 17. Sheriff's Records	163
Plate 102	164
Chapter 18. Tax & Fiscal Records	165-168
Plates 103-107	169-174
Chapter 19. Vital Records	175-176
Plates 108-111	177-180
Quick Reference "Pointers"/Index	181-182
Name Index	183-202

LIST OF PLATES

Plate 1.	Land Disputes 1799-011.	Page 1 of Augustine Washington's Will	8
Plate 2.	Chancery 1808-024.	Cover of Benjamin Banneker's 1796 Almanac	9
Plate 3.	Land Disputes 1769-001 OS.	Proprietary Grant from Lady Fairfax to Mary Mauzy	10
Plate 4.	Bonds, Oaths & Commissions 1811-001.	Richard Tyding's Minister Bond	14
Plate 5.	Bonds, Oaths & Commissions 1789-001.	Original Young's Oath to support the Constitution	16
Plate 6.	Bonds, Oaths & Commissions 1762-001.	Justice of Peace Commission signed by Francis Fauquier	17
Plate 7.	Bonds, Oaths & Commissions 1800-002.	Richard Rixey's Coroner's Bond signed by James Monroe	18
Plate 8.	Chancery 1798-018.	Memorandum to Judah Levy regarding a Certificate issued James McGraw, killed in Beaufort's defeat in the Revolutionary War	27
Plate 9.	Chancery 1798-018.	Page 1 of Chancery Bill in Levie + wife v. Blackwell	28
Plate 10.	Chancery 1783-004.	Edward Burgess' Will	29
Plate 11.	Chancery 1796-011.	Plat & Survey of Captain George Neavill's 24 Acre tract on Cedar Run	30
Plate 12.	Chancery 1798-022.	Threatening letter from Thomas Helm in his Divorce case	31
Plate 13.	Chancery 1811-039.	Affidavit by Joseph Bailey in Bailey v. Bruce	32
Plate 14.	Chancery 1853-033.	Page 1 of a Mutual Assurance Society of Virginia Plat for four buildings on the north Side of Main Street in Warrenton	33
Plate 15.	Chancery 1855-008.	Peter Hitt's Inventory in Hitt v. Smoot	34
Plate 16.	Ended Causes – Commonwealth Causes.	1798 Grand Jury Presentments	41
Plate 17.	Ended Causes 1786-016 folder.	Bond & Receipt in Stuart v. Minter	42
Plate 18.	Ended Causes 1786-013 folder.	A Declaration in Lee v. Blackwell for Trespass On the Case	43
Plate 19.	Ended Causes 1786-013 folder.	Capias and an Account in Lee v. Blackwell	44

List of Plates

Plate 20.	Free Negro/Slave 1838-008.	Catharine Stephenson's Certificate of Importation of Slaves	52
Plate 21.	Free Negro/Slave 1832-021.	A Patroller Account	53
Plate 22.	Free Negro/Slave 1832-037.	William C. Ashby's List of Free Negroes who were delinquent in their 1831 Taxes	54
Plate 23.	Free Negro/Slave 1837-001.	Maria Harrison's May 5, 1837 Free Register	55
Plate 24.	Negro Records 1920-001.	Page 1 of William Frederick Oliver's World War 1 Military Service and photo	56
Plate 25.	Land Disputes 1815-005.	Cover of Marshall v. Arnold, a suit to collect back rent	67
Plate 26.	Land Disputes 1815-005.	Replevin Bond in Marshall v. Arnold, A suit to collect back rent	68
Plate 27.	Land Disputes 1815-001.	Motion to grant Letters of Administration On Denny Fairfax's Estate to James M. Marshall in Fairfax's Exor. v. Payne, &c.	69
Plate 28.	Land Disputes 1815-001.	Court's Opinion in Fairfax's Exor. v. Payne &c.	70
Plate 29.	Land Disputes 1760-001	Plat & Survey in Stone v. Stevenson, a suit In Ejectment	71
Plate 30.	Land Disputes 1790-007.	Instructions for "Serving the Ejectment"	72
Plate 31.	Land Records 1801-007.	Henry Hooe's letter to the Clerk Requesting a record search for land devised in a forged will	72
Plate 32.	Land Disputes 1767-003.	Edward Ball's Inventory & Appraisement in Duling v. Ball, &c.	73
Plate 33.	Land Disputes 1790-007.	1726 Proprietary Grant from Thomas, Lord Fairfax to Jeremiah Murdock in Withers v. Jett Ejectment suit.	74
Plate 34.	Land Records, Deeds 1724-001.	1724 Proprietary Grant from Robert Carter, as agent to Lord Fairfax, to Michael Meldrum	75
Plate 35.	Land Disputes 1799-001.	Declaration of Fanny McBee, "a poor distresed [sic] widow... left with seven small children..." in McBee v. Clarkson	76
Plate 36.	Medical Records 1813-004.	Coroner's Inquest on Henson Foster	78

List of Plates

Plate 37.	Military Records 1821-006.	Warner Sullivan's Military Commission As Ensign, 44th Regiment	82
Plate 38.	Military Records 1793-002.	Benjamin Taylor's Pension Warrant	83
Plate 39.	Military Records 1803-002.	List of 1802 Revolutionary Pensioners for Virginia	84
Plate 40.	Military Records 1809-001.	Heirs-at-Law of Joshua Jenkins, a Revolutionary War soldier, killed at the Battle of Brandywine 9/11/1777	85
Plate 41.	Military Records 1812-001.	Mary Kern's 1812 Pension Certificate	86
Plate 42.	Military Records 1887-001.	J. M. Moore's Confederate Pension Application as member of Co. K., 31st Regiment, Virginia Volunteers, Early's Brigade, Jackson's Division	87
Plate 43.	Military Records 1900-004.	Page 1 of Confederate Soldiers Claims approved by the Fauquier County Pension Board	88
Plate 44.	Mills 1764-003.	Charles Duncan's Mill Petition	92
Plate 45.	Mills 1764-003.	Viewer's Report for Charles Duncan's Mill Petition for a Mill on Summerduck Run	93
Plate 46.	Mills 1769-001.	Plat & Survey for George Neaville's Mill	94
Plate 47.	Mills 1787-001.	Daniel Harris' Mill Petition	94
Plate 48.	Mills 1792-001.	Plat & Survey for Thomas Fallis' Mill	95
Plate 49.	Mills 1806-004.	"Representation of Mill Seats" on Summerduck Run and Wolf Trap Branch	96
Plate 50.	Mills 1813-004.	John & James Marshall's Mill Petition	97
Plate 51.	Roads & Bridges 1761-001.	Joseph Palmer's Agreement to build A Bridge over Deep Run	98
Plate 52.	Roads & Bridges 1761-001.	Joseph Palmers' Bond to build a Bridge over Deep Run	99
Plate 53.	Roads & Bridges 1762-002.	Culpeper County Residents' Petition for a Road from William's Ford to Falmouth	100
Plate 54.	Roads & Bridges 1762-002.	Culpeper County order regarding residents' Petition for a Road from William's Ford to Falmouth	101

List of Plates

Plate 55.	Roads & Bridges 1773-005.	Viewers' Report for road from the Manor Road to the Bridge over Carter's Run At Pickett's Mill and back into the Manor Road	102
Plate 56.	Roads & Bridges 1786-010.	John Mauzey's Account with Fauquier County For setting 7 sign boards at Cross Roads	103
Plate 57.	Roads & Bridges 1794-007.	David Gibson &c. Road Petition	104
Plate 58.	Misc. Records, Citizenship 1819-001.	John R. Callow's Alien Report	107
Plate 59.	Misc. Records. Citizenship 1821-002.	Michael Rusie's Alien Report	108
Plate 60.	Misc. Records. Citizenship 1826-004.	Dennis McDermott's Alien Report	109
Plate 61.	Misc. Records. Naturalizations 1834-001.	Peter McPhelin's Alien Report	110
Plate 62.	Misc. Records. Naturalizations 1836-001.	Ann Jenkins' Alien Report	111
Plate 63.	Misc. Records. Naturalizations 1853-001.	Joseph Bear's Declaration of Intent	112
Plate 64.	Misc. Records. Naturalizations 1854-006.	Patrick Sullivan's Declaration Of Intent	113
Plate 65.	Misc. Records. Naturalizations 1866-002.	Louis Lion's Declaration of Intent	114
Plate 66.	Misc. Records. The Jail 1767-001.	William Pickett's Bond to build a Prison	115
Plate 67.	Misc. Records. The Jail 1771-001.	Prison Bounds Survey	116
Plate 68.	Misc. Records. The Jail 1793-001.	Three Jail Work Accounts	117
Plate 69.	Misc. Records. The Jail 1809-001.	Plat & Survey of Prison Bounds	118
Plate 70.	Misc. Records. The Courthouse 1759-001.	Close Writ Ordering Court to be Adjourned from William Jones' House to John Duncan's House	119
Plate 71.	Misc. Records. The Courthouse 1817-002.	Order Summoning Justices to Consider building a new Courthouse	120
Plate 72.	Misc. Records. Interesting Finds 1771-001.	John Pickett's Arrest Warrant	121
Plate 73.	Misc. Records. Interesting Finds 1800-005.	An Early Search Warrant	122
Plate 74.	Misc. Records. Interesting Finds 1822-003.	A Counterfeit $50.00 Bank Note	123
Plate 75.	Misc. Records. The Courthouse 1840-001 County Court Papers	Plan of Change in Courthouse Floor Plan	124

LIST OF PLATES

Plate 76.	Misc. Records. The Courthouse 1848-001. County Court Papers	Diagram of brick wall to enclose Courthouse and Clerk's Office	125
Plate 77.	Misc. Records. The Courthouse 1853-002. County Court Papers	Proclamation of Govern Johnson Johnson regarding the destruction Of the Courthouse by fire	126
Plate 78.	Ordinary Records 1759-004.	Martin Hardin Ordinary Bond	130
Plate 79.	Ordinary Records 1762-001.	George Neavill's Ordinary Bond	131
Plate 80.	Ordinary Records 1782-001.	Thomas Maddux's Ordinary Bond	132
Plate 81.	Ordinary Records 1788-001.	Commonwealth v. Mary Neale for selling liquor without a License (pages 1-2)	133-134
Plate 82.	Ordinary Records 1796-001.	List of Ordinary Licenses for Grand Jury August 1792-November 1794	135
Plate 83.	Ordinary Records 1796-003	Commonwealth v. Henry Datree and Alexander Sampsell for Unlawful Gaming	136
Plate 84.	O.P. Apprenticeships 1792-001. O.P. Apprenticeships 1792-002.	Edward Newgent to Archibald Duncan William Griffith to Isaac Johnson	141
Plate 85.	O.P. Apprenticeships 1810-001.	William Nelson to Aaron Bise	142
Plate 86.	O.P. Apprenticeships 1822-001.	Joseph Thompson to Henry Turner	143
Plate 87.	O.P. Misc. Records 1788-011	List of the Poor in District #7	144
Plate 88.	O.P. Misc. Records 1809-001	Commonwealth v. Levi Pickerail, alleged Father of Nancy Carrol's bastard child	145
Plate 89.	O.P. Misc. Records 1839-028.	List of Clothing Provided Paupers in Poor House In 1839	146
Plate 90.	Oversize Records. Land Disputes 1799-011.	Page 1 of Augustine Washington's Will from Hickerson v. Blackwell Trespass Suit Papers	148
Plate 91.	Oversize Records. Land Disputes 1794-005.	Escheat of Manor of Leeds to the Commonwealth	149
Plate 92.	Oversize Records. Signature 1763-002.	John and Jeffrey Johnson's Bond	150
Plate 93.	Probate Records 1771-001.	Mrs. Ann Green's Dower Allotment	153
Plate 94.	Probate Records 1793-006.	Page 1 of Peter Waggoner's Will	154
Plate 95.	Probate Records 1799-002.	Peggy Norris' Relinquishment of Administration Of Estate of Thaddeus Norris	155

List of Plates

Plate 96.	Probate Records 1810-002.	Page 1 of William Smith's Inventory & Appraisement	156
Plate 97.	Probate Records 1818-005.	Page 1 of Charles Duncan's Sales Account	157
Plate 98.	Probate. Admr & Exor. Bonds 1759-005.	John Shadrack's Extrx. Bond	158
Plate 99.	Probate. Guardian Bonds 1807-002.	Margaret & Elizabeth Mauzey's Guardian Bond	159
Plate 100.	Probate. Guardian Bonds 1817-022.	Rebecca Sallard's Guardian Bond	160
Plate 101.	School Records 1828-001.	Josiah Fishback's Schoolmaster Account from a Tuition suit styled Fishback v. Ball's Admr.	161
Plate 102.	Sheriff's Records 1770-002.	An Escape Warrant for Runaways	164
Plate 103.	Tax & Fiscal Records 1759-001.	Page 1 of Thomas Marshall's 1759 List Of Tithables	169
Plate 104.	Tax & Fiscal Records 1785-005.	Leeds Manor, Fauquier County State Census (pages 1-2)	170-171
Plate 105.	Tax & Fiscal Records 1809-001.	A page from Thomas Robinson's 1809 Personal Property Tax List	172
Plate 106.	Tax & Fiscal Records 1809-001.	List of Free Negroes found in Thomas Robinson 1809 Personal Property Tax List	173
Plate 107.	Tax & Fiscal Records 1825-001.	A page from Stephen Chilton's 1825 Land Book	174
Plate 108.	Vital Records 1784-007	Marriage Bond & Consent. 2/16/1784 Aquilla Davis to Isabella Briggs	177
Plate 109.	Vital Records 1784-017	Marriage Bond & Consent. 10/16/1784 Judith [Judah] Levy to Mary McGraw	178
Plate 110.	Vital Records 1787-001.	Jesse Brown's Birth Record	179
Plate 111.	Vital Records 1803-001.	Rev. William F. R. Davis' Minister Returns for February 1801 to January 1803.	180

Fauquier County, Virginia's Clerks Loose Papers: A Guide to the Records 1759-1919

CHAPTER 1 INTRODUCTION

1. The Clerk's Loose Papers

In 1994, the Clerk of the Fauquier County Circuit Court applied for and received a grant to preserve, flat file, arrange and index the County's Clerk's Loose Papers from 1759-1832. These records were stored in metal woodruff drawers in the basement vault. The papers, folded into three parts and bundled together with ribbon, covered a wide gamut of areas of interest to genealogists, family historians, title searchers, historians, and other members of the research public.

Minister and Public Officials' Bonds, Chancery records, Deeds, Land Disputes, Mill Applications, Road Applications, Probate records, Overseer of the Poor records, Military Records, and records relating to Free Negroes and Slaves were among the records housed in these drawers.

The records filed in these drawers were arranged by year and Court session. The drawers were labeled as "Ended Causes" followed by the months and year. For example, a drawer's label might read something like this: " Ended Causes: 1765 June-August".

In 1997, the Clerk applied for and received another grant to preserve, flat file and arrange the Chancery Records found in the Ended Chancery Causes in the basement vault. While the focus was on the Ended Chancery, the Clerk's loose papers were also culled and records of a purely local interest were separated and placed in to the appropriate Loose Papers categories.

In 1999, the Clerk applied for and received a third grant to consolidate and update the Chancery records from the Ended Chancery files and the causes found in the County Court files of the Clerk's Loose Papers. At the same time, the Superior Court records were culled for any further chancery records. At the end of this grant, **all** of the Chancery records in Fauquier would be available for examination by the public.

At the end of the three preservation grants, there were more than 500 document boxes of records relating to the Clerk's Loose Papers newly available for the research public. In addition, nearly 400 more document boxes of Chancery records had been preserved and indexed in a new Library of Virginia Chancery index.

- **Fauquier's Historical Residents**

George and Martha Washington lived here. So did George's father Augustine; George's nephew, Robert Lewis; Catharine, Lord Fairfax and her son Thomas; as did Thomas Ludwell and Molly Lee; Colonel Richard Henry and Ann Lee; Governor Henry Lee; Charles and Landon Carter; Gawin Corbin; Thomas Marshall and son John; Benjamin Bannaker; President James Monroe.

Court records signed by these individuals, along with suits and documents from a host of lesser-known folks have rested quietly in the vault in the basement of a rural Virginia county's circuit court. Stored in dusty bundles in black metal woodruff drawers, these documents lay forgotten for more than two centuries.

- **Learning the New...**

With the grant monies in hand, the preservation team (called P.A.I.R. for Preservation And Inventory of Records) began a fascinating process of discovery that still excites us today. These papers give an entirely new feel for the history of the times that is unparalleled. At times, the reader is there; one could almost see, in the mind's eye, the stir caused by a slander case or by a particularly graphic eyewitness account to a killing in a tavern found in a deposition. Just think of the excitement created when Joseph Hickerson triumphantly produced in court a Deed from the late President of the United States to Robert Lewis in his 1800 trespass suit against Samuel Blackwell.

Fauquier County, Virginia's Clerks Loose Papers: A Guide to the Records 1759-1919

The difference in the way eighteenth century and nineteenth century paper felt sent the team scurrying to find reference articles and preservation texts about papermaking. We found out how ink was made and the hazards nineteenth century Clerks encountered when experimenting with ink. Some experiments worked; some didn't. The failed ones produced burns in paper caused by too much or too little gall, ink migration and an unfavorable reaction between the acid in the paper and the acidity of the ink.

- **... And Discovering the Old**

We have chuckled over some of our eighteenth century Clerks and their assorted doodling on court records; we have found ourselves wholeheartedly relating to Charles Marshall's random drawings, verses, and doodling on various Court documents. You see, Mr. Marshall was the Commonwealth Attorney. Evidently, he found doodling more attractive than note taking at particularly boring Court hearing and trials. After all, who would know? No one... at least not for another two hundred ten years or so!

Then, there was the overzealous Clerk of Court who set about to "organize" the basement vault and some of its woodruff drawers. This took place in the mid twentieth century. Among the records he separated from their original bundles were eighteenth and nineteenth century Guardian bonds and early nineteenth century Administrator and Executor bonds. In the middle of the drawer he labeled Administrator bonds, we found thirty-four previously unknown 1784 marriage bonds.

Our document "finds" in these papers have been almost overwhelming! We have nearly a dozen grants, deeds and wills that pre-dated the formation of the county in 1759. Our earliest record is a copy of a 1716 will.

There are records from counties that border Fauquier – Stafford, Prince William, Loudoun and Culpeper. There are deeds and wills from two of Virginia's "burned" counties – Stafford and King George. There are plats of Mount Vernon in a late nineteenth century chancery suit. There are court papers from the Superior Court in Haymarket, Virginia in session from 1800 to 1809.

Chancery Court records cover those in the Fauquier County Chancery, and the Superior Courts of Chancery in Fredericksburg and Winchester. We have found additional court records from the district court at Dumfries and from courts in Fairfax and Spotsylvania.

2. The "Signature Series" in the Clerk's Loose Papers

There are so many documents signed by well-known historical personages from a Commonwealth and national perspective, we created a special "Signature" record series.

These include Lady Catharine Fairfax, her son Thomas, Lord Fairfax, George William Fairfax, Francis Fauquier, Thomas Ludwell Lee, Colonel Richard Henry Lee, Governor Henry Lee, Robert Carter, Charles Carter, Thomas Marshall, John Marshall and James Monroe.

- **The Washington Discovery**

I feel a special affinity towards the Washington documents because I was the one who happened to come across them. I don't think I'll ever forget that day! It was June 28th and I was alone in the office. It had been pretty much a run-of the-mill morning, filled with separating Court Judgments and flat filing them into our brown document boxes. The case "Hickerson v. Blackwell, In Trespass" looked routine.

As I flattened the papers, I noticed that a note on the outside of one of the documents had a notation about a Washington survey. "Hmmm", I thought. "I wonder if this is **George** Washington?"

Not expecting much, I turned over the document, which proved to be a deed. There, in the bottom right hand corner was George **and** Martha's signature! I jumped out of my seat and jumping up and down, kept saying "Ho-ly Cow! Ho-ly **Cow! Ho-ly Cow!**" It was wild! I had seen George's signature before. I just had never seen George and Martha's signature together on a record.

Fauquier County, Virginia's Clerks Loose Papers: A Guide to the Records 1759-1919

Then I realized there was no one in the office. I was going to have to tell *someone* this momentous news! Who should I tell first? Dave? No. He was in Maryland and a long distance phone call. Besides, he could be on his way her and I wouldn't be able to reach him. Karen? She also could be on her way to work and I did not have her car phone number. Gail, at the Clerk's Office? I tried. She wasn't there. (Isn't that always the way? You find out something great and then can't find anyone with whom to share it!) Clearly, I was dithering! So… I caught my breath, sat back down in my chair and tried to stop grinning.

At that moment, Karen came in. I jumped back up, grabbed her by the wrist and kept saying (Karen says "yelling") "Look at this! Look at this! Look at this!" When she saw the signatures, she sat down too. When she recovered all she could say was, "I don't believe it!"

- **The Augustine Washington Will in "Hickerson v. Blackwell"**

As it turned out, while George and Martha's Deed of Gift to their nephew Robert Lewis was an exciting find, the most significant historic discovery in this Trespass suit may well have been an 1800 certified copy of Augustine Washington's will.

Augustine's will was admitted to probate in King George County Virginia in 1743 and was recorded in the first King George County Will Book. Augustine's will was a matter of public record all during the remainder of the eighteenth century and the will book was an integral part of that county's records until the outbreak of the Civil War. During the war, this particular will book disappeared when Union troops looted the Court house.[1]

So, at the time of the 1800 Trespass suit, when Joseph Hickerson needed to establish his claim to the land in controversy, the recorded will was available to him. Augustine's will left his son George a one half share to a 4,360-acre tract, called the "Deep Run Tract". In 1800, this tract sprawled across Fauquier and Stafford Counties. This acreage made up the 1798 Deed of Gift to Robert Lewis. Lewis then sold small portions of the tract to Hickerson and others.[2]

It was not until after the Civil War that problems with Augustine's will or with the certified copies of the will began to surface. By that time, no one knew location of the *original* will; nor did anyone know the whereabouts of the King George Will Book, which housed the *recorded* will.

- **The Nineteenth Century Copies**

Between 1889 and 1918, two certified copies of Augustine's will surfaced. One copy of the will was certified by Harry Turner, Clerk of the King George Court in 1743 as a true copy and signed by him. This certified copy had been part of the manuscript collection housed at Mount Vernon when the Washington family still owned the estate.

The family gave permission to the National Museum in Washington D.C. to place this manuscript collection on exhibit early in 1889 which included Harry Turner's certified copy of Augustine's will, in preparation for sale at public auction in Philadelphia. In 1891, after the exhibit, Thomas Birch & Sons duly sold the Turner certified copy of the will to a private collector.

At the time of the 1889 exhibition, Washington family members also gave permission to transcribe some of these family records, including Augustine's will. A second copy, made in 1889, for Lawrence Washington became part of his own extensive private collection of Washington papers.

Thus, by 1891, the contents of this will had been largely erased from public consciousness. The will book had disappeared. The two certified copies were now in private hands and not available for public research.[4]

Fauquier County, Virginia's Clerks Loose Papers: A Guide to the Records 1759-1919

- **The Twentieth Century Transcript and the return of the Will Book**

As the twentieth century dawned, it appeared that the will might stay "lost" to the public. However, in 1918, Charles A. Hoppin, a prominent genealogist and record examiner, was given permission to go through Laurence Washington's papers. In 1926, he published, for the first time, a transcript of the Laurence Washington copy of Augustine's Will in Genealogies of Virginia Families, Volume IV, W-Y, in *Tyler's Quarterly*.[5]

That left the problem of the whereabouts of the King George Will Book #1, still unknown, in 1926. It was to take a little more than fifty years after Hopper's publication, before the will book was returned anonymously to its rightful owner, the King George county court.[6]

- **The significance of Fauquier's Copy of Augustine's Will**

What makes the discovery of the Fauquier county copy so exciting to us is that it is *also* certified by Harry Turner and is likely to be the *only other publicly certified copy* of Augustine Washington's will! As a transcribed copy, it is certainly *much* earlier than the 1889, 1891 and 1926 transcribed copies. It is very likely that the Fauquier copy may be the *only one available* outside King George. The irony? It has been in our vault all along!

3. The Importance of Land Disputes to Genealogists and Family Historians

George and Martha Washington's Deed of Gift and Augustine Washington's will were documents filed in a land dispute --- a trespass suit between Joseph Hickerson and Samuel Blackwell. Hickerson alleged that Blackwell had trespassed and cut down and carried away one hundred trees on his property.[7]

The suit papers contained documents supporting Hickerson's title to the property. Among those papers were three genealogical significant records: George and Martha's Deed to nephew Robert Lewis, the Augustine Washington will and an early plat and survey of the tract that showed neighboring land owners.

Many of the land disputes in the Clerk's loose papers contain substantial historical and genealogical information. Land disputes can be suits for trespass, breach of the close, a breach of contract involving land, back rent suits and Ejectments.

For example, there are twenty-three wills to be found in suit papers in the ten boxes of Land Disputes taken from the Clerk's loose papers. Wills recorded elsewhere in the Commonwealth often found their way into Fauquier's early land disputes. These can be genealogically significant, especially if the recorded copies have disappeared.

There are wills in land disputes that have been recorded in Prince William County, Stafford County, King George County, Lancaster County and Westmoreland County.

Joseph Welch, Sarah Welch, Richard Bullock, John Dagg and Benjamin Crump had their wills recorded in Prince William County. They were all involved in different land disputes filed in the Fauquier County Court.

Peter Mauzy, Mary Waugh and William Mountjoy resided in Stafford County in the mid eighteenth century. Their wills are also found in land disputes filed in Fauquier.

The importance of the Augustine Washington will has already been discussed. He was a resident of King George. At least three other residents of King George also have wills involved in Fauquier land disputes. They were Samuel Skinker, William Bernard and Richard Bernard.

John Bell's will, recorded originally in Lancaster County is found in a land dispute; so is Thomas Shadrick of Westmoreland County. Another of George Washington's documents is involved in another land dispute, this time in 1812. There is a copy of his will in those suit papers.

There are also a variety of other probate records in these suits. Plats and surveys, divisions, dower allotments, administrator appointments, executor accounts, inventories and appraisements to be found in the exhibits filed in these disputes.

Keep in mind that Prince William lost portions of their will books and land books during the Civil War. The courthouses of Stafford and King George were both thoroughly looted. Original or recorded probate records disappeared. These depravations make the records filed in Fauquier's Land Disputes even more significant as they may be the only existing copy of original records that are no longer extant.

In addition to the probate information contained in the land disputes, there are also five boxes of Deeds of Bargain and Sale, Lease and Releases, Articles of Agreement, Deeds of Gifts, Leases and other land records. Genealogists and family historians should look at these records as well as they supplement the county's Grantee and Grantor indices.

4. Fauquier County's Free Negro/Slave and Negro Record Series

There are sixteen document boxes of records relating to Free Negroes and Slaves from 1759-1865 and an additional sixteen boxes for these records after 1865. This record series contain suits and records as diverse as those involving improper treatment of hired Negro slaves, Churchwarden and Overseer of the Poor Apprenticeships for free Negro children, Freedom suits instituted by slaves who believed they were held illegally in slavery and free Negro Certificates of Freedom.

There are copies of wills, inventories and appraisements in which slaves were either emancipated or distributed to heirs. There are copies of Emancipations, Certificates of Importation, Bills of Sale and Deeds for land to free Negroes taken from other record series within the Clerk's loose papers.

Whenever we found a record in another series, like Land or Probate, for example, mentioning a slave by name, we placed the original in that series and a copy of the record in the Free Negro/Slave series. When we found a case in our Ended Causes Record series involving a recovery of a debt involving a slave who was named we placed the original in this record series. We did the same for records suits from Ended Causes involving free Negroes.

There is one other important record series associated with the Free Negro/Slave and Negro record series. Those records relate to the Overseer of the Poor. There are lists of the poor in residence at the county's poor houses as well as various bills submitted to the county for providing food, medical care, and transportation to the poor. Names of old and infirm slaves as well of free Negroes before 1865 are found through out the Overseers of the Poor records. After 1865, names of there are also names of poor Negroes and Apprenticeship of poor Negro children whose families were subsisting on the poverty level.

- **The Bannaker Almanac Find**

Chancery records that have names of free Negroes or slaves before 1865 have been copied to our free Negro/Slave series. One of our most notable "finds" in Chancery, which related to the Free Negro/Slave records, involved a copy of a Benjamin Bannaker 1796 Almanac. We have placed that copy in our "signature" series.

Benjamin Bannaker, grandson of a freed slave, was born in Maryland in 1731. A self-taught mathematician and astronomer, he was appointed in 1789 by President Washington to be a member of commission to build the nation's capital. Between 1791 and 1793, Bannaker helped survey the future city of Washington D.C

He is most well known for his *Pennsylvania, Delaware, Maryland, Virginia Almanac and Ephemeris*, published annually between 1792 and 1802. He sent his original manuscript for the 1792 edition to Thomas Jefferson, then Secretary of State in the Washington administration.

Along with the Almanac, Bannaker also dispatched a letter to Jefferson opposing slavery and questioning Jefferson's claim that whites were intellectually superior to blacks. Nineteenth century abolitionists were to go one step further: they used Bannaker's *Almanac* as proof of the intellectual capabilities of blacks.[8]

The presence of this 1796 *Almanac* in a Chancery suit in the Clerk's loose papers [9], compiled by such a well-known eighteenth century free African American, underscores the importance of separating Chancery records *along with* other records to form a Clerk's loose papers record series.

- **The importance of the Free Negro/Slave and Negro Records series to Virginia African-American Research**

The documents found within the Free Negro/Slave and Negro record series, and to a lesser extent, the Overseers of the Poor record series will significantly benefit scores of African-Americans researchers. These two record series are among the most important research tools for African-Americans with Fauquier county heritage.

5. Reaping the Benefits: The Value of the Records

This brief overview illustrates the types of records that are available in the Clerk's loose papers. There are records here that are valuable in explaining an ancestor's "historical present". The time frame in which an eighteenth or nineteenth century ancestor lived is far different than the one in which we live today. There was an "inter-connective ness", if you will, between families, their land, their homes, their churches, their communities.

- **From discovering an Ancestor's "Historical Present"…**

An eighteenth or nineteenth century ancestor's trip to town or to the Court called for some specific planning: how to get there, where to stay, thinking about what other activities that could be accomplished while there. It meant a visit to a merchant for the wife, an overnight stay at friends or relatives, picking up supplies to take back home. It could mean a stop over at a nearby gristmill to drop off grain or to put in an order for plank or board at a sawmill. It meant keeping an eye on road conditions. It meant thinking about the condition of the bridge over the run.

Records about Court days, merchant accounts, ordinary records, mills, roads, bridges are *all* found in the Clerk's loose papers. These records help explain an ancestor's "historical present" in terms of the times in which he lived. These records are of inestimable value in bringing an ancestor's time back to life.

- **… To reaping the genealogical value of the records**

The Clerk's loose papers are filled with information about a family's genealogical heritage. Military Records contain pension applications, heirs of veterans, military appointments and discharges, Bounty Land Warrants and Court Martials. Pension applications and depositions provide a glimpse into what war was *really* like. These records often contain information about family and economic status. By 1832, there is enough information on family members of a veteran that it often reaches into the third or even fourth generation. Some applications give locations for out of state heirs.

Tax and Fiscal Records are another set of records that have great genealogical value. Early personal property tax records often contain the names of free tithes between 16-20. Male family members of a household can often be found in these tax records. Other eighteenth century personal property tax records contain complete lists and ages of slaves owned by the head of household. There are lists of free Negroes in the back of some of the early nineteenth century personal property tax records. Insolvent tax lists often indicate county residents who have moved west.

One of the most valuable historical finds in the tax records of the Clerk's loose papers was the 1785 State Census, an enumeration of the names of heads of households, number of tithes in their family units and the size and number of buildings on their property. Utilizing the data in these lists, historians will know much more about *who* was here and the types of structures they built to house their families.

Fauquier County, Virginia's Clerks Loose Papers: A Guide to the Records 1759-1919

The genealogical nature of the land records has already been discussed. There are also probate records in the Clerk's loose papers – 50 boxes of them! That means this record series has even *more* records to examine: more wills, inventories, dowers, appraisements, administrator accounts, executor accounts, bonds, guardian accounts.

Truly, the Clerk's loose papers and their associated record series are a veritable genealogical treasure chest of records. Think of the missing links that might reside in these records in the form of a missing will, a missing deed of gift, a missing mill or ordinary application. Their genealogical value is immeasurable!

End Notes
1. Hoppin, Charles A. "The Will of Augustine Washington Sr. (Father of George Washington)" in *Tyler's Quarterly: Genealogies of Virginia Families*, Volume 4, page 289. Hoppin was succinct in his treatment of the disappearance of the King George Will Book. The will book, he said was "known t be in existence… in a northern state."
2. *Fauquier County Virginia Deed Book 14*, page 129. 6/10/1798 Robert Lewis to Joseph Hickerson.
3. Hoppin, page 289.
4. *Ibid.*, pages 289-290.
5. *Ibid.*, pages 290-293. This is a complete transcript of the certified copy signed by Harry Turner, Clerk.
6. Information from LVA Archivist Paul Hunter Shelton.
7. *Fauquier County Chancery 1799-011* **"Hickerson v. Blackwell". An Action in Trespass.**
8. Bannaker, Benjamin, "*Microsoft Encarta 1996 Encyclopedia* Copyright 1993-1995 Microsoft Corporation. Funk & Wangles Corporation. (For more information, see the small "j" on the Encyclopedia's tool bar.)
9. *Fauquier County Chancery 1808-023 White's Admr. v. White's Exor.*

Fauquier County, Virginia's Clerks Loose Papers: A Guide to the Records 1759-1919

> In the Name of God. Amen I Augustine Washington of the County of King George Gent. being Sick and Weak but of Perfect and Disposing Sence and Memory do make my Last Will and Testament in Manner Following hereby Revoking all former Will or Wills whatsoever by me heretofore made Imprimis I Give unto my Son Lawrence Washington and his Heirs forever All that Plantation and Tract of Land at Hunting Creek in the County of Prince William Containing by Estimation Five Thousand five Hundred Acres with the Water Mill Adjoining thereto or lying near the same AND all the Slaves Cattle and Stocks of all kinds whatsoever and all the Houshold Furniture whatsoever now in or upon or which have been Commonly Possessed by my said Son Together with the said Plantation Tract of Land and Mill Item I Give unto my Son Augustine Washington and his Heirs forever all my Lands in the County of Westmorland Except such only as are herein after otherwise Disposed off Together with Twenty five head of Neat Cattle, Forty Hoggs and Twenty Sheep and a Negro Man Named Frank besides those Negroes formerly Given him by his Mother Item I Give unto my said Son Augustine three Young Working Slaves to be Purchased for him out of the first Profits of the Iron Works Item I give unto my Son George Washington and his Heirs the Land I now live on which I Purchased of the Executrys of Mr William Strother Decd and One Moiety of my Land lying on deep Run and ten Negro Slaves Item I Give unto my Son Samuel Washington and his Heirs my Land at Chotank in the County of Stafford Containing about Six hundred Acres and also the other Moiety of my Land lying on Deep Run Item I Give unto my Son John Washington and his Heirs my Land at the head of Maddox in the County of Westmorland Containing about Seven hund. Acres Item I Give unto my Son Charles Washington and his Heirs the Land I Purchased of my Son Lawrence Washington Inhereon Thomas Lewis now lives Adjoining to my Sons Lawrence's Land above Devis'd Also Give unto my said Son Charles and his Heirs the Land I Purchased of Gabriel Adams in the County of Prince William Containing about Seven hundred Acres Item It is my Will and Desire that all the Rest of my Negroes not herein Particularly Devised may be Equally Divided between my Wife and my three Sons Samuel, John and Charles and that Ned, Jack, Bob, Sue and Lucy, may be included in my Wifes Part which Part of my said Wife after her Decease I Desire may be Equally Divided between my Sons George, Samuel, John, and Charles and the Part of my said Negroes so Devised to my Wife I Mean and Intend to be in full Satisfaction and

Plate 1. Scanned image of Page 1 of Augustine Washington's Will from Land Records & Disputes 1799-011. Hickerson v. Blackwell. In Trespass.

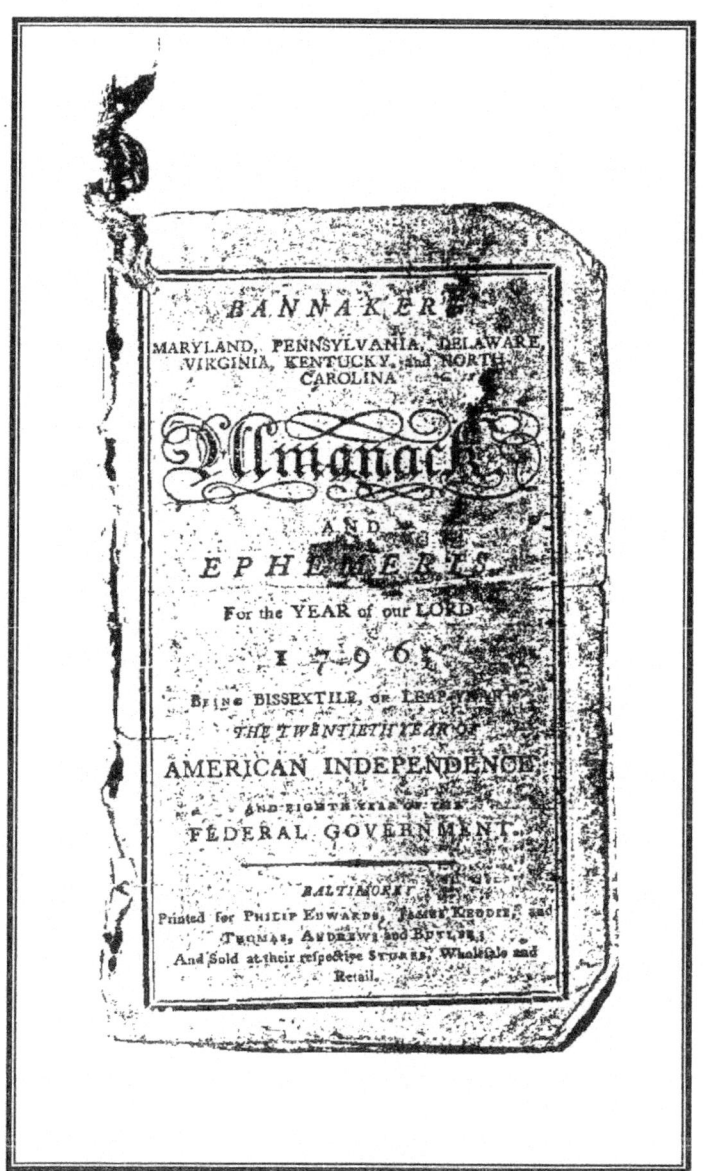

Plate 2. Benjamin Bannaker's Almanac from Fauquier County Chancery 1808-024. White's Admr. v. White's Exor.

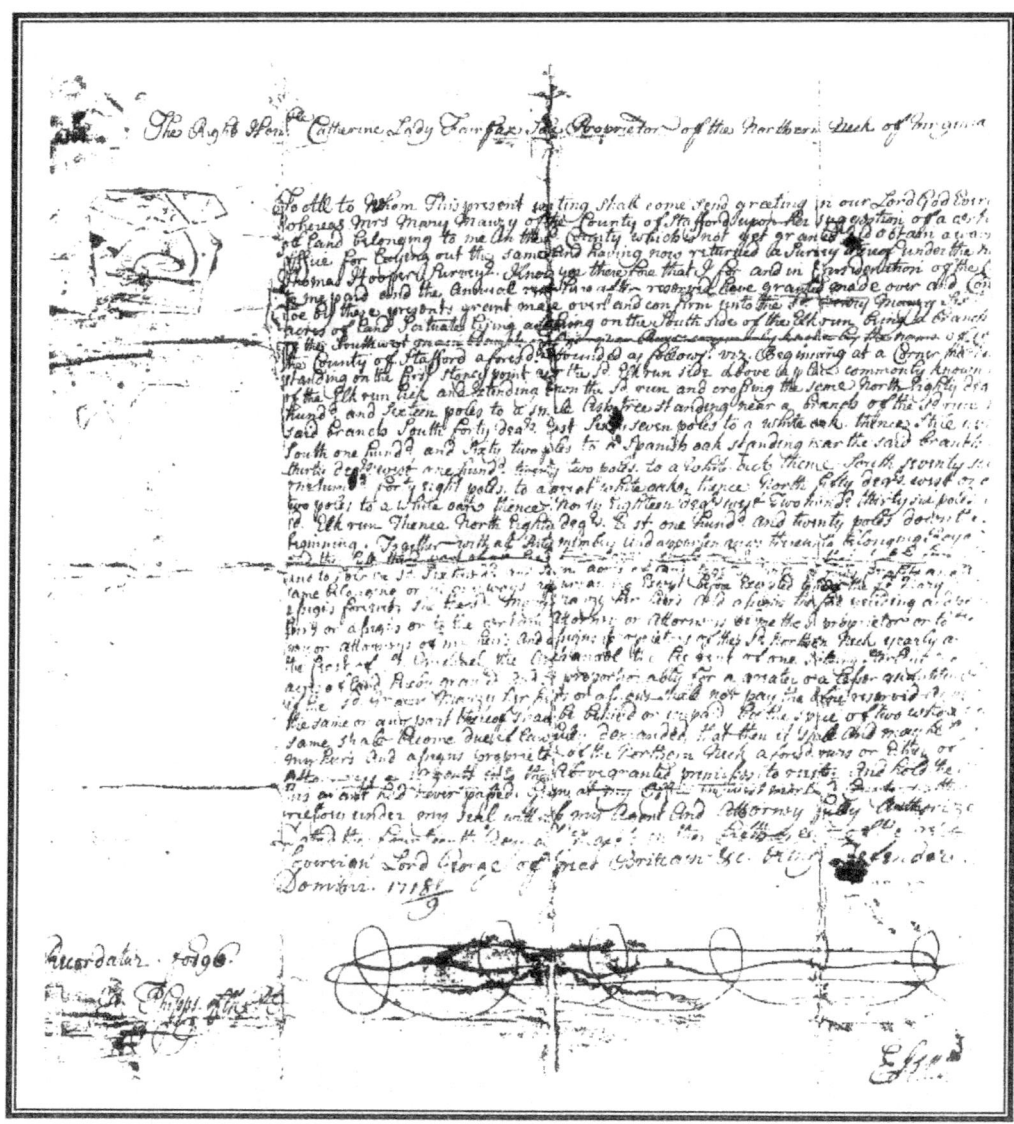

Plate 3. Scanned image of a 1718/19 Proprietary Grant: Catharine, Lady Fairfax to Mary Mauzy from Oversize Land Records & Disputes 1769-001 (Mountjoy v. Mauzey). This is the oldest record in the Clerk's Loose Papers

Fauquier County, Virginia's Clerks Loose Papers: A Guide to the Records 1759-1919

CHAPTER 2
AN INTRODUCTION TO THE RECORDS

1. **The Record Series**

   The Fauquier County Clerks Loose Papers consist of the following record series:

   1. Bonds, Oaths and Commissions
   2. Chancery
   3. Dead Papers, Ended Causes, Judgments
   4. Free Negro/Slave Records
   5. Land Records and Disputes
   6. Military Records
   7. Mills
   8. Miscellaneous Records
   9. Ordinary Records
   10. Overseer of Poor Records
   11. Oversize Records
   12. Probate/Fiduciary Records
   13. Roads
   14. Schools
   15. Sheriff Records
   16. Tax & Fiscal Records
   17. Vital Records

2. **The Folders**

The folders in all the record series have the same general format.

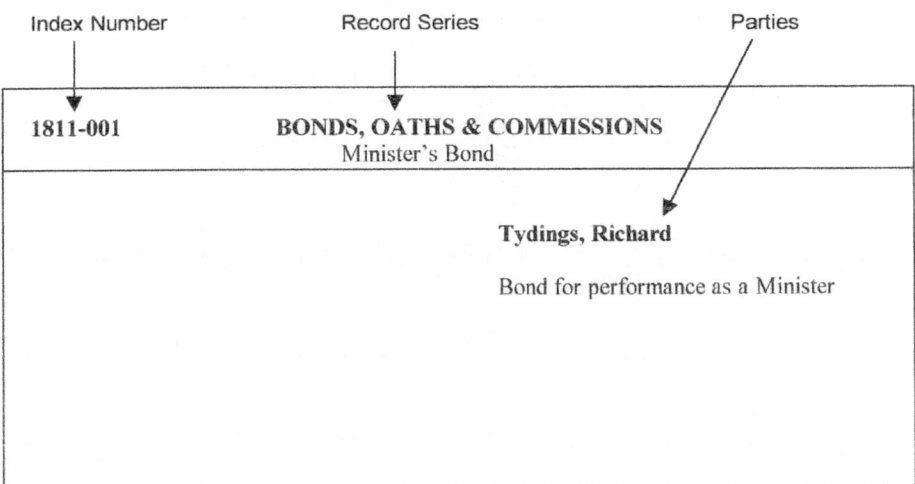

The index number, made up of the year and a three digit number (acting as a control number) will **always** appear in the upper left corner of a folder. The Record Series will **always** appear on the center top of the folder. The names of the parties involved will **always** appear on the folder below.

Fauquier County, Virginia's Clerks Loose Papers: A Guide to the Records 1759-1919

3. The Database – Indices and Inventories

Each of these record series has a database with either a *record* or a *name index* or an *inventory* associated with it.

Inventoried record series are 1) Military Records, 2) Mills, 3) Miscellaneous records, 4) Ordinary records, 5) Roads (after 1820), 6) School records, 7) Sheriff records and 8) Tax & Fiscal records. For the purposes of this guide, an inventory here is used as an actual number count of the records. They are filed by year and index number. Figure 1 below shows the fields in a **record inventory**.

INDEX #	BOX #	RECORD	# OF FOLDERS
1761-001 to 1799-002	1	Service Records and Pensions	28
1826-001 to 1832-009	2	Revolutionary War Pensions	28

*Figure 1. Sample **Record Inventory** from Military Record series*

Record series **indexed by records** are 1) Bonds, Oaths and Commissions, 2) Free Negro/Slave indexes and 3) Overseer of the Poor Miscellaneous records. These records are filed by year and index number. You may sort, filter or query the records by year, in record type, and parties. If you are looking for a particular surname, you may use the search and find feature of the database. Figure 2 shows the fields and contents of a sample record index database.

INDEX #	RECORD TYPE	PARTIES	REMARKS
1788-001	Commissioner of Revenue Bond	Maddux, Richard	Maddux replaced Elias Edmonds as Comr. of Revenue.

*Figure 2. Sample **Record Index** from Bonds, Oaths & Commissions*

Record series **indexed by names** are 1) Chancery, 2) Land Records and Disputes, 3) Probate/Fiduciary Records, 4) Free Negro/Slave Apprenticeships, 5) Overseers of Poor Apprenticeships, and 5) Vital Records—Marriage Bonds. **All** of these records series are filed by their index number. Figures 3 through 8 show a sampling of the contents of Name indices from these record series.

Chancery records are arranged by their index number. The LVA Index will allow you to sort, query, and filter the plaintiff, defendant, plat, and will fields. You may sort the surnames by form.

INDEX #	PLAINTIFF	DEFENDANT	SURNAMES	PLATS	WILL
1798-018	Levie, Judah &c.	Blackwell, Joseph	Levie, McGraw, Blackwell, Levy		
1809-056	Bailey, Carr	Tomlin, John & wife &c.	Bailey, Tomlin		Fauquier Co., Carr Bailey, 1771.

*Figure 3. Sample **Name Index** from the LVA Chancery Index*

Fauquier County, Virginia's Clerks Loose Papers: A Guide to the Records 1759-1919

Free Negro/Slave records Apprenticeships are arranged by their index number. You may sort, query, and filter these fields: "apprentice", "indentured to" and "to learn" fields. You may sort by the index # for a chronological arrangement of the records by a year. These records refer to poor or orphaned Free Negro children who the county bound out to learn a trade. Figure 4 illustrates a sample name index from Free Negro Apprenticeships.

INDEX #	APPRENTICE	INDENTURED TO	TO LEARN
1842-006	Johns, Bushrod	Stinson, Toliver	Farming
1846-001	Brown, Louisa	Withers, James O.	Housekeeping

*Figure 4. Sample **Name Index** from Free Negro/Slave Apprenticeships.*

Deeds are filed by their index number. You may sort, query or filter grantees and grantors in this index. Figure 5 shows the some of the sample fields in the Land Records Recorded Deeds database.

INDEX #	GRANTOR	GRANTEE	TYPE OF LAND RECORD
1725-001	Fairfax, Lord Thomas	Chambers, Joseph (of Stafford Co.)	Proprietary Grant
1728-001	Gooch, William	Edwards, John	Land Patent

*Figure 5. Sample **Name Index** from Land Records: Recorded and Clerk's Copies of Deeds*

Land Disputes are filed by their index number. You may sort, query and filter on the type of disputes and on the plaintiff and defendant fields. Figure 6 shows a sampling of the types of information you can find in the Land Records and Disputes index.

INDEX #	TYPE OF DISPUTE	PLAINTIFF	DEFENDANT
1763-001	Rent Suit in Manor of Leeds	Corder, Charles	Carter, Thomas
1766-005	Ejectment	Payne, Richard	Porter, Thomas &c.
1799-011	Ejectment	Hickerson, Joseph	Blackwell, Samuel

*Figure 6. Sample **Name Index** from Land Disputes*

Overseers of the Poor Apprenticeships are filed by their index numbers. They are set up exactly as the Free Negro/Slave Apprenticeships are. These records refer to poor children or orphaned children who were bound to tradesmen, artisans or farmers so they would not become a charge to the county. Both boys and girls were bound out. Figure 7 shows the information you can find in this index.

INDEX #	APPRENTICE	INDENTURED TO	TO LEARN
1826-001	Claxton, Robert	Pendleton, James A.	Tailoring
1835-002	Woolingham, Washington	Feagans, John	Farming

*Figure 7. Sample **Name Index** from Overseers of the Poor Apprenticeships.*

Fauquier County, Virginia's Clerks Loose Papers: A Guide to the Records 1759-1919

Probate/Fiduciary records are filed by their index number. You may sort, query and filter by the name of the person in this index. Figure 8 shows a sampling of the types of information you can find in this index.

INDEX #	NAME	INSTRUMENT	DATE	REMARKS
1759-001	Weaver, Tilman	Will	3/1760	
1762-001	Garner, John	Order to appraise Estate	7/1762	
1771-001	Green, Ann (Mrs.)	Dower Allotment in Slaves Slaves	1771	Ann Green was widow of Duff Green

*Figure 8. Sample **Name Index** from Probate/Fiduciary Records: Recorded Wills, Inventories &c.*

In addition to these computerized index/databases, there are separate printed databases either in the form of a record index or a name index or in the form of an inventory for all of these records except Ended Causes. There are also a bride and groom index for the thirty-four 1784 Marriage bonds.

Plate 4 below shows an example of a Minister's Bond in the Bonds, Oaths & Commissions Records Series of Fauquier's Clerks Loose Papers.

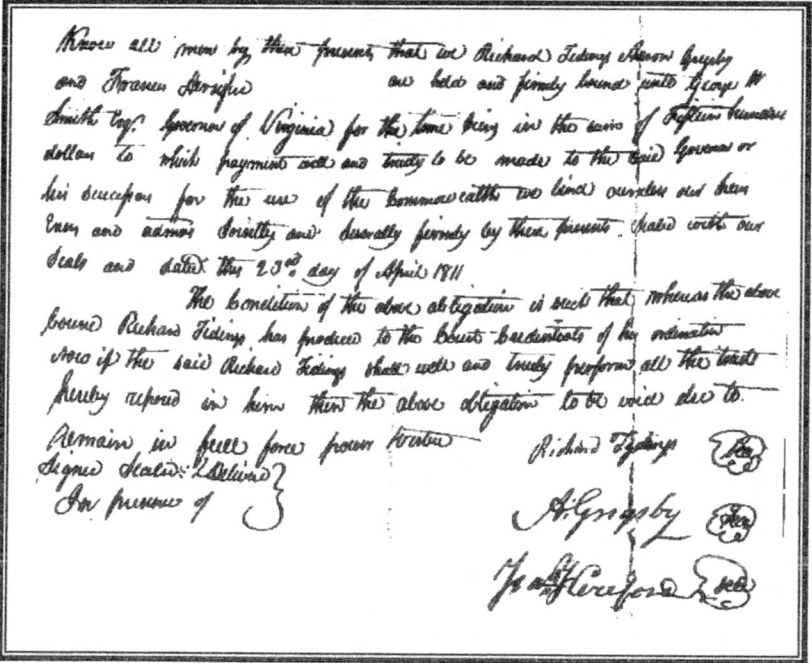

Plate 4. Scanned image of a Minister's Bond from Bonds, Oaths & Commissions 1811-001. Richard Tydings' Minister Bond

Fauquier County, Virginia's Clerks Loose Papers: A Guide to the Records 1759-1919

CHAPTER 3
BONDS, OATHS & COMMISSIONS

1. **Overview**

    In seventeenth, eighteenth and nineteenths century Virginia, public officials took out *bonds* to insure that they performed their civic responsibility. County officials took an *oath of allegiance* to the government, and an *oath of office* for the performance of their duties to the local jurisdiction. Officials could take an oath of allegiance to the colonial government, to the Commonwealth of Virginia or to support the United States Constitution.

    Commissions are authorizations granted to public officials by an appropriate governing agency or by a Court. Commissions allowed officials to perform certain duties, like the duties of a Justice of the Peace or the duties of a Magistrate. Commissions could also be an appointment to public office, like a Clerk of a County Court or Superior Court.

    There are several examples of bonds, oaths and commissions in this record series. There are bonds from Commissioners of Revenue who acted as tax collectors. There are bonds from Coroners. (Coroners held judicial inquiries regarding people who had suffered death in questionable circumstances.) There are bonds from Constables and bonds from Jailors. There is even a bond for the Clerk of the County Court.

    This record series also contains examples of oaths of allegiance and oaths of office. In 1789, for example Original Young, as High Sheriff of Fauquier County, took an oath of allegiance to support the new Constitution. (See Plate # 3 on page 12 for a scanned image of this document)

    One of the examples of a commission found in this record series is the commission appointing Berkeley Ward as the Clerk of the Superior Court of Law for Fauquier County. In this case, because this was a judicial appointment, the Judge of the 10th Judicial Circuit Court of Virginia authorized the selection.

2. **Finding Your Way Around Bonds, Oaths and Commissions**
    Series Title: Bonds, Oaths & Commissions
    Color Code: Orange Dot on Box
    Series Dates: 1753-001 to 1841-001 (Includes a No Date-001 and No Date-002)
    Series Extent: *1 Box. 68 Records. 5 linear inches.*
    Series Arrangement: Filed by Year
    Series Finding Aid: Index by Record

    Types of Records include
    - **Appointment of Officials**
    - **Commissions**
    - **Bonds for Public Officials**
    - **Minister Bonds**
    - **Oaths of Office for Public Officials**
    - **Oaths of Allegiance**

Fauquier County, Virginia's Clerks Loose Papers: A Guide to the Records 1759-1919

3. A Preview of the Records Index for Bonds, Oaths and Commissions

Figure 9 illustrates the types of documents you can find in the Records Index for Bonds, Oaths and Commissions. Remember, these records are filed by their Index number. If you are looking for a particular type of record or for a surname, use the Search and Find feature of the database.

INDEX #	TYPE OF RECORD	PARTIES	REMARKS
No Date –001	Justice of Peace List	List of Magistrates	List contains 14 names.
1753-001	Tax Collector's Bond	John Crump	Prince William County Bond
1762-001	Justice of Peace Commission	Thomas Harrison, Joseph Blackwell; Wm. Eustace &c.	Commission signed by Francis Fauquier
1789-001	Oath to U.S. Constitution	Original Young	Sheriff's oath
1800-002	Coroner's Bond	Richard Rixey; James Monroe	Coroner's Bond signed by Governor James Monroe
1811-001	Minister's Bond	Richard Tydings, Aaron Grigsby, Francis Hereford	

Figure 9. Examples of records from the Record Index for Bonds, Oaths and Commissions

Plates 5-8 on this and following pages contain scanned images of examples of the records found here.

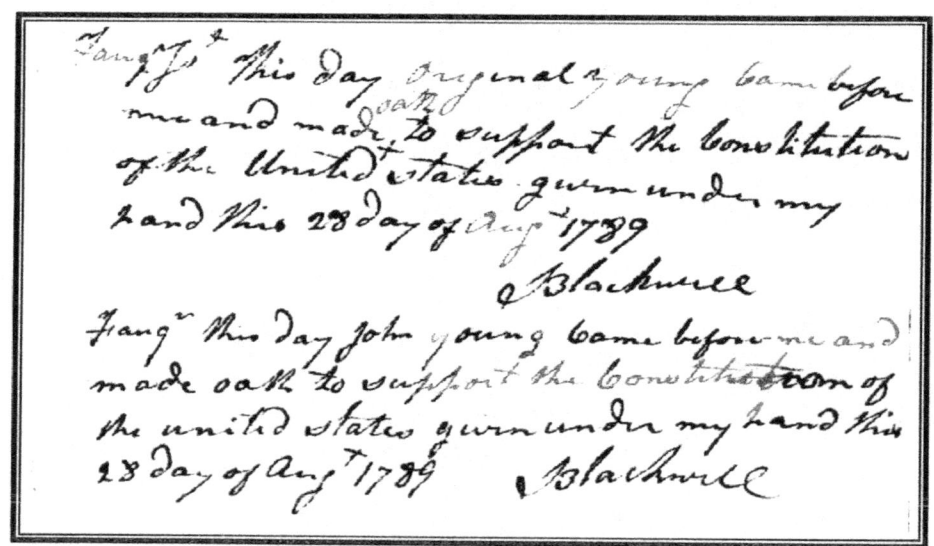

*Plate 5. Scanned image of an Oath from Bonds, Oaths & Commissions 1789-001
Original Young's Oath to Support the U.S. Constitution*

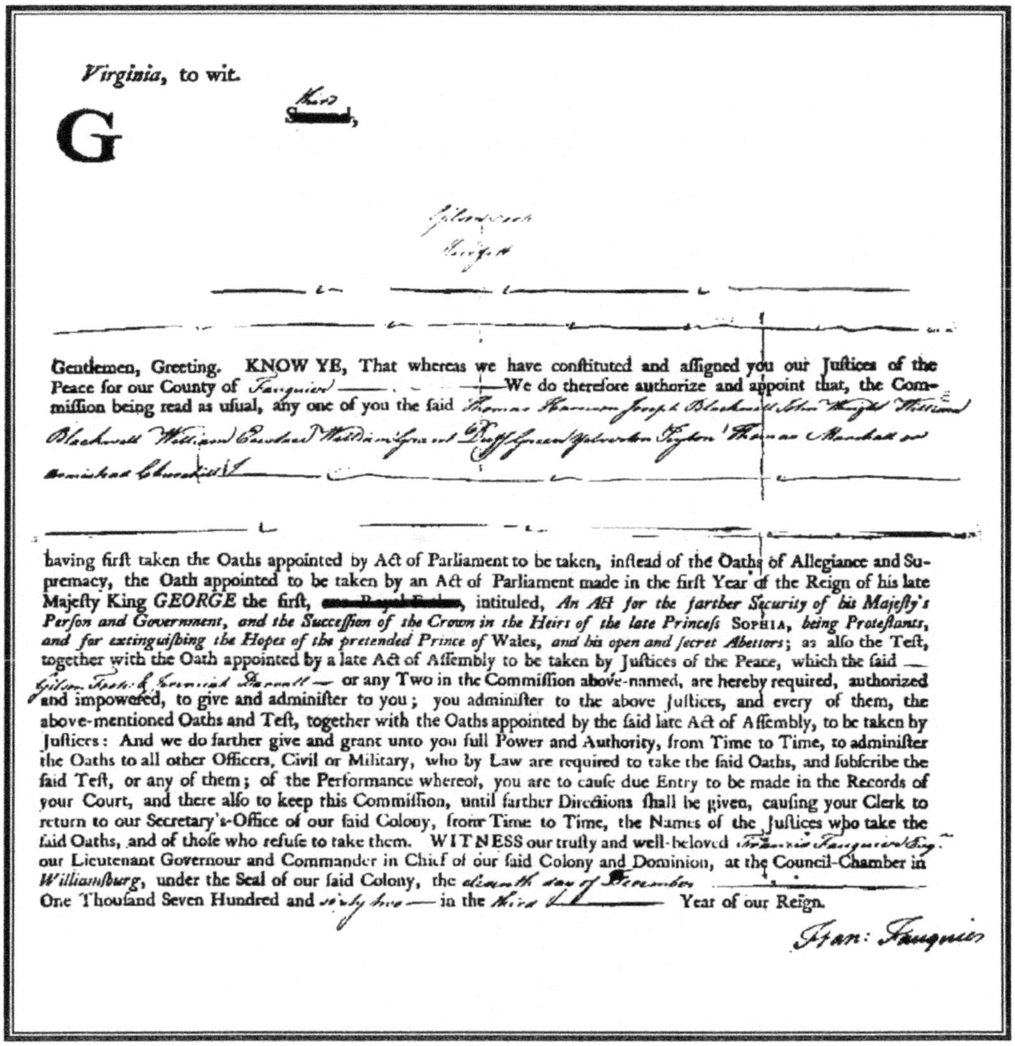

Plate 6. Scanned image of a Commission from Bonds, Oaths & Commissions 1762-001. Justice of Peace Commission signed by Francis Fauquier

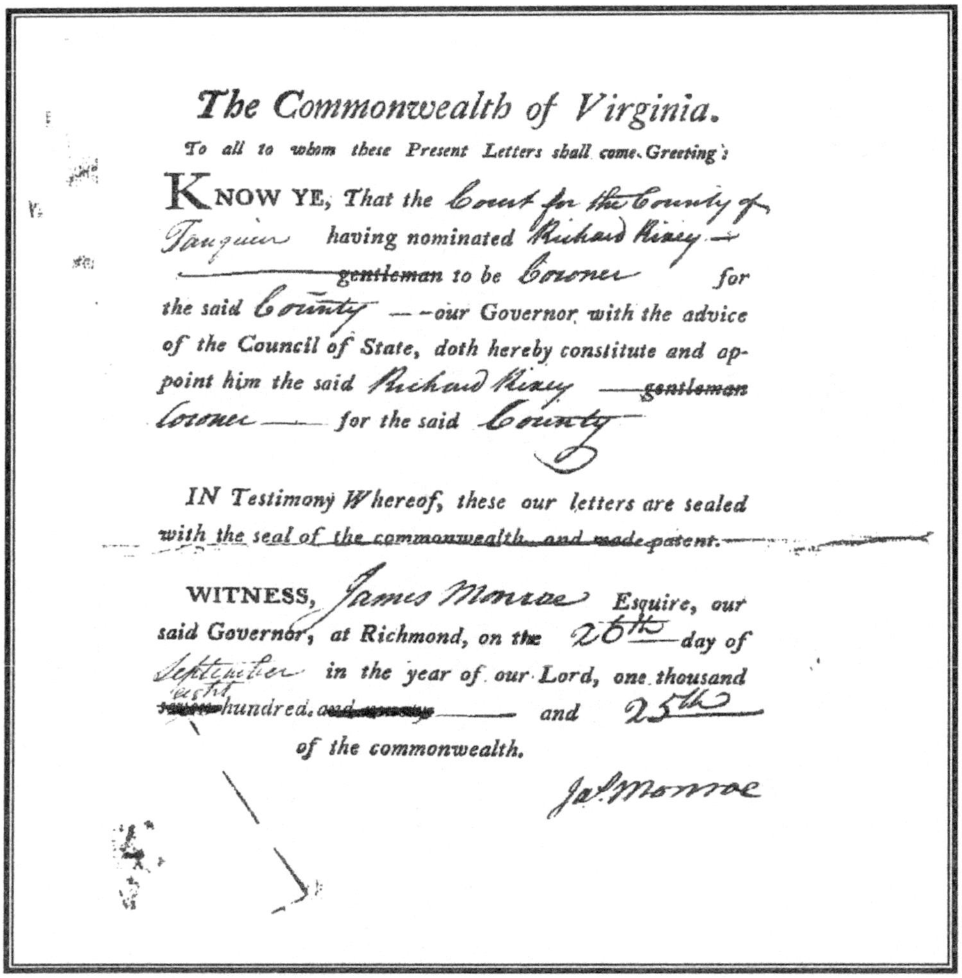

Fauquier County, Virginia's Clerks Loose Papers: A Guide to the Records 1759-1919

The Commonwealth of Virginia.

To all to whom these Present Letters shall come, Greeting:

KNOW YE, That the Court for the County of Fauquier having nominated Richard Rixey ———— gentleman to be Coroner for the said County ———— our Governor, with the advice of the Council of State, doth hereby constitute and appoint him the said Richard Rixey ———— gentleman Coroner ———— for the said County ————

IN Testimony Whereof, these our letters are sealed with the seal of the commonwealth, and made patent.

WITNESS, James Monroe Esquire, our said Governor, at Richmond, on the 26th day of September in the year of our Lord, one thousand eight hundred, and ———— and 25th of the commonwealth.

Ja^s Monroe

Plate 7. Scanned image of a Coroner's Bond from Bonds, Oaths & Commissions 1800-002. Richard Rixey's Coroner's Bond signed by Governor James Monroe

Fauquier County, Virginia's Clerks Loose Papers: A Guide to the Records 1759-1919

CHAPTER 4
CHANCERY RECORDS

1. Overview

Chancery is often abbreviated "Ch^y" in the Clerk's Loose Papers. These are Courts of Equity – that is, they deal with rules of fairness, rather than with points of law. Chancery cases are not heard by a jury and are not adversarial by nature. A Chancery Judge, who appoints a Chancery Commissioner to actually do the work, hears most cases. The Commissioner, having gone out and talked to the parties and gathered depositions, if needed, reports his findings to the Court. The Court then issues a ruling, in a decree, based on the Commissioner's findings. This means that Chancery courts reach their decisions based on what is fair and equitable to all the parties.

Chancery suits may be filed for any number of reasons. Among those are:
1) Suits by merchants or creditors. A merchant or individual may sue to collect monies owed by an account or a loan. There are many chancery suits from uncollectable "judgments" on debts rendered by the Court of Law. The person to whom the money is owed wants to get *something* back, so he goes to chancery to do so.
2) Suit to recover debts from a wife's separate estate. Women's husbands get into debt and, if the woman has a separate estate, creditors may bring a Chancery suit to collect the debt from *her* estate.
3) Suits to recover costs for sales of "damaged" property. If the purchase of property, like slaves or horses, turns out to be unsound, the party receiving the property in question, will go to Court to redress the wrong done them. For example, swapping an unhealthy horse for a sound one or purchasing a horse stipulated to be sound that turned out not to be, would bring new owners in to a Court of Equity VERY quickly!
4) Suits for Divorce – more common than you think in the nineteenth century. Men also sued for divorce. Common causes were, for women, cruelty and beatings; for men, adultery.
5) Suits to sell real estate and/or personal property to collect a debt.
6) Suits to divide or sell real estate of a deceased person, with proceeds to be distributed among heirs.
7) Suits to divide or sell personal property, like slaves, with proceeds to be distributed among heirs.

Many of the suits brought into Chancery Court deal with the distribution of property among the heirs-at-law of someone who has died. The *plaintiff* (the person bringing the suit), in those instances, may be an heir. He files a *bill* with the Court. The bill describes the reasons for the suit to the Court.

For example, a plaintiff's father-in-law may have died and left land, in a will, to the plaintiff's wife and to her brothers and sisters. Alternatively, there may not *be* a will; the plaintiff's wife and her siblings may want to divide their deceased father or mothers' estate among themselves. The plaintiff, in "right of his wife" would then ask the Court to divide that land among the heirs. (Remember, wives had few legal rights in the eighteenth and nineteenth century. So husbands often filed for a division of land in their behalf.)

The plaintiff requests the division of the estate, identifies his wife's brothers and sisters and any other parties that are involved in the suit in the bill. He then asks the court to make the brothers and sisters *defendants* in the suit. If some of the siblings are under 21, the plaintiff requests the court to appoint a *guardian ad litem* for those children. The guardian ad litem will then act in the best interest of the minor children as long as the suit is heard. The plaintiff does all of this in order to divide the land fairly among all the heirs.

If there *is* a will, then the plaintiff will file it as an exhibit, to "be taken as part of the bill".

The Court then sends out *subpoenas*, or summons, to the defendants named in the bill, so that they may respond to the bill. The subpoenas will tell you the names of <u>all</u> the parties in the suit. The widow may also be identified and can be either a plaintiff or a defendant, depending on the information within the Bill. Suits to divide land and slaves among heirs may include a dower allotment to the widow as well as the division of property among the children.

The defendants will file separate *answers* to the plaintiff's bill. The answer is exactly that: a defendant's response to the content of the bill. If the defendants have any legal documents they want filed with the suit, they will present them as part of the answer. These exhibits are all filed in the suit papers.

If needed, the commissioners will take *depositions* or *affidavits* from witnesses. These are sworn statements by friends, family members, neighbors and public officials. Depositions often contain background information about the family and are extremely useful in giving the reader insight into what the suit is all about.

After the Commissioner has heard all the evidence in the suit, he writes a *report* to the Court. He may cause a *plat* and *survey* to be made of the property. The Court uses this report as a basis for their *decree* in the suit. If the property, whether land or slaves, cannot be divided among all the heirs, the parties may want to sell it instead and divide the proceeds among themselves. Then the Court would decree a sale and the Commissioner would be responsible for seeing to it that the property was sold either at public auction or privately. Once this had been accomplished, the Commissioner would make a *report of sale* to the Court. The court would then make its ruling based on the conditions of sale and tell the Commissioner to draw up a deed with *special warranty* of title to the purchaser.

A word of caution here. Some Chancery suits are short and easy to read. Others are thick and a challenge to work you way through. Some of these suits went on for <u>decades</u>! Especially, after the Civil War and especially in the South, when land was plentiful and money was not!

So keep in mind the economic conditions of the time, when reading these suits. That knowledge will help in your understanding of the heirs' motivations in wanting to sell the land if that was what they believed was in their best interests. It helps, too, to have an understanding of the law and of the economic and political history of the time. It will be of inestimable assistance in guiding your grasp and awareness of the circumstances surrounding the actual Court process – from the filing of the Chancery bill through to the final decree ending the suit.

2. **A Glossary of Chancery Terms**

The glossary on the next two pages contains legal terms associated with Chancery suits along with a short explanation of the expression.

> *Bill* – The bill in a chancery suit gives the reasons for the suit. The **plaintiff**, the person who brings the suit, files the document. It often contains information about the plaintiff's family and others who are connected with the suit.
>
> It gives information about the parties in the suit along with the reasons for the suit. If the plaintiff is suing to prevent action from being taken, he files a bill of injuction, asking the court to enjoin the defendant from the action about to be taken. The Court usually grants a bill of injunction temporarily until the **defendant** can answer the allegations in the bill.
>
> *Answer* – This is the defendant's response to the bill. The defendants can either refute the charges made in the bill, admit the charges or demand proof of the charges.
>
> *Plaintiff* – the person or persons who sue. He files a **Bill** with the Court.

Defendant – the party or parties who "defend" the suit. Once the plaintiff files the bill, the Court sees to it that the defendants receive a **subpoena** or **summons** to answer the bill.

Subpoenas or Summons – A subpoena is sent to all the defendants in a chancery suit. It requires them to respond to the plaintiff's bill. In the Chancery suits in the Clerk's Loose Papers, the subpoenas and summons, if present, may be found in a folder called "Court Process".

Exhibits – Both the plaintiff and defendant may file exhibits that will make their case stronger with the Court. These exhibits are filed with the suit papers. Wills, Deeds, Trusts, Bonds, Promissory Notes, Articles of Agreements, Inventories, Appraisements, Accounts, Sales, Plats & Surveys, and Divisions are all examples of the types of exhibits that may be found in the suit papers. These records often contain information of a genealogical nature.

Guardian ad Litem or *"Next Friend"* – Guardian ad litem are appointed for minor children, called **infants**, in Court cases. Guardian ad Litems are appointed for defendants under legal age; "next friends" are appointed for minors on the plaintiff side. The guardian ad litem is expected to act in the best interest of the minor involved in the suit. The Court may also appoint "next friends" to act in the interests and behalf of women seeking a separation or divorce in chancery.

Infants – minor children under legal age

Decrees – A decree is a ruling of the Court. Once the Bill and Answer have been filed, the Court then makes a ruling on what it wants to do next. Usually a *commissioner* is appointed with specific tasks in mind. The Court will require a report when the Commissioner completes his assigned duties. When the **Commissioners Report** has been made, the Court makes another ruling on the report itself. There are often several decrees in Chancery, especially if there are **exhibits** like deeds, wills, inventories, trusts, or accounts, Commissioner reports and **depositions**. A chancery case ends when the Court makes a *final decree* or ruling.

Commissioner – Commissioners are appointed by the Chancery Court Judge to do a variety of tasks. They may be appointed to divide or sell property or land and then make a **report** to the Court. They may be appointed to take **depositions** from neighbors and friends of the parties. They may be appointed to allot dower to a widow or divide slaves among heirs. They may be appointed to make a financial report to the Court regarding monies paid out to the parties and others.

Commissioner Reports – Once the Commissioner has fulfilled his assigned task, he returns a report to the Court. There may be Reports of Sales, Reports of Divisions, and Receiver Reports along with the usual Report of Findings. Family historians often overlook them. These reports frequently have genealogical "nuggets" hidden in them.

Plats & Surveys – If there is a division or sale of real estate, there may be a plat and survey of the land involved in the suit. A **plat** is a one-dimensional "map" of the land and its boundaries and neighbors. The **survey** gives the **metes and bounds** of the land. The metes and bounds are points on the land – trees, mountains, roads, runs, creeks, mill races, neighbor lines and are given in terms of distance and compass direction.

Depositions and Affidavits – Depositions and affidavits make for some of the most interesting reading in a Chancery case. An affidavit is a written, sworn statement given by the witness before an authorized official. Depositions are also written statements under oath, to be used in Court. In depositions, both sides get to question the witness. They are common in any suit about property, land, divorce, and heirs.

Fauquier County, Virginia's Clerks Loose Papers: A Guide to the Records 1759-1919

3. Finding your way around Chancery Records

   Series Title: Chancery Records
   Color Code: Blue dots on Boxes
   Series Dates: 1759-001 to 1919-001
   Series Extent:
   Series Arrangement: Filed by Index number, there under by Cause.

   Series Finding Aid: Library of Virginia Chancery Index. No Cross Index.

   Types of Records include
   a. **Bill and Answers**
   b. 1) Bill of Complain/Bill of Injunction
      2) Answer
      3) Injunction Bonds
   b. **Decrees and Court Orders**
   c. **Commissioner Reports**
   d. **Subpoenas/summons** (Court "process)
   e. **Exhibits**
      1) Deeds
      2) Wills
      3) Inventories
      4) Sales Lists
      5) Accounts
   f. **Plats and Surveys**
   g. **Depositions and Affidavits**

4. **The Folders in Chancery: Small suits**

   Small suits (those that have only a few records and are complete in themselves) are filed in white folders and look like this:

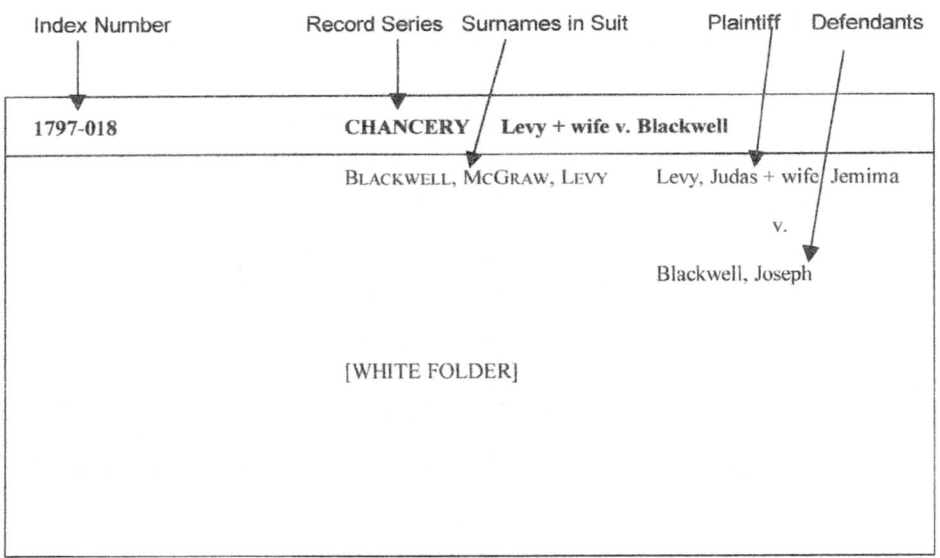

There is a definite arrangement for records in these suits. You will **always** find the *bill* and *answers*, if present as the first records in these suits. After the bill and answers, you will find 2) the decrees, 3) Commissioner Reports, 4) the court "process", 5) Exhibits, like accounts, deeds, trusts, agreements, wills; 6) Plats and Surveys, 7) Depositions. The papers in a Fauquier County Chancery suit are **always** arranged in that order.

5. Folders in Chancery: Large Suits

Larger suits are filed in white folders within brown folders. The brown folder suits are set up just like the small suit folders. The papers in the suit are each filed in separate white folders. The bills and answers are filed in a white folder; the decrees are filed in a white folder; the Commissioner Reports are filed in separate white folders; the Court "process are all filed together in a white folder; each exhibit is filed in a separate white folder; the plats and surveys have their separate white folder and depositions and affidavits are filed together in a separate white folder.

The Brown folder will look something like this folder for an 1823-029 Chancery suit.

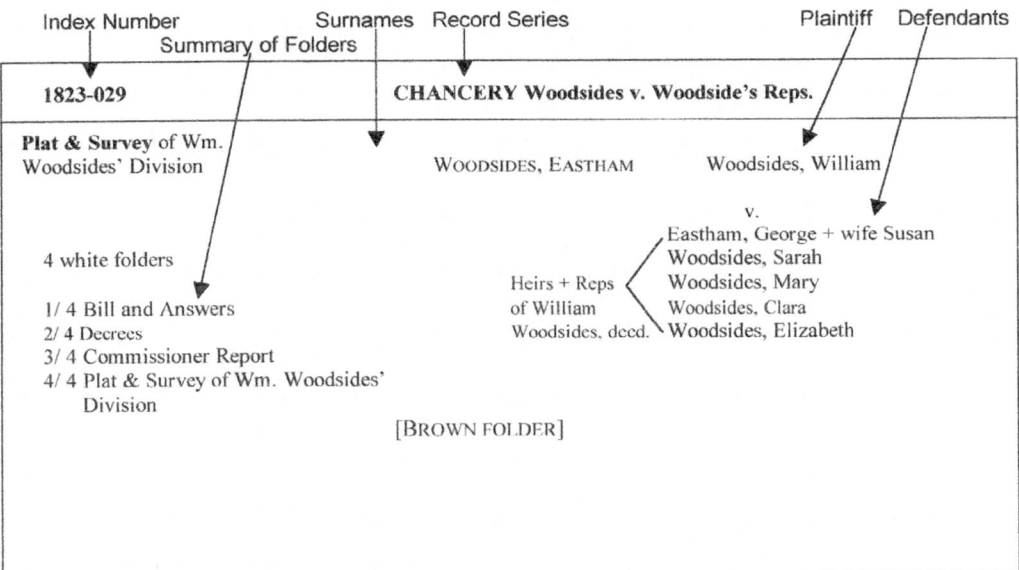

There is a definite *arrangement* in which suit papers are filed in the white folders within the brown one. The brown folder gives the essential information found in the suit papers. If there is a Plat & Survey, a Will or mention of free Negroes or Slaves in the Bill, this information will be found in the upper left hand corner of the brown folder.

The brown folder will also give information about how many folders are in the suit papers and a breakdown of folders of interest. In the example above, there are four white folders encased in this brown one. The first folder holds the Bill and Answers; the second white folder holds the decrees; the third white folder has a Commissioner's Report; the fourth white folder contains a plat and survey of Wm. Woodside's Division.

The brown folder also has all the parties in the suit, in this case a plaintiff and four defendants.

Fauquier County, Virginia's Clerks Loose Papers: A Guide to the Records 1759-1919

The white folders are arranged according to the example below.

FOLDER #1 **always** contains the Bill and/or Answers, if present. In this instance, both bill and answer were filed.

1823-029 Folder 1/ 4	**CHANCERY Woodsides v. Woodside's Reps.**
Bill and Answers [WHITE FOLDER]	

FOLDER # 2 in this suit contains the Decree and orders or rulings of the Chancery Court.

1823-029 Folder 2/ 4	**CHANCERY Woodsides v. Woodside's Reps.**
Decrees [WHITE FOLDER]	

FOLDERS # 3 in the Woodsides v. Woodsides suit papers holds the Commissioner's Report.

1823-029 Folder 3/ 4	**CHANCERY Woodsides v. Woodside's Reps.**
Commissioner's Report [WHITE FOLDER]	

FOLDER # 4 in these suit papers contains the Plat and Survey of Wm. Woodsides's Division.

1823-029 Folder 4/ 4	**CHANCERY Woodsides v. Woodside's Reps.**
Plat & Survey of Wm. Woodside Division [WHITE FOLDER]	

Neither the plaintiff nor the defendant filed exhibits with the bill or answers. If present, these records would come after the plat and survey and be filed in separate folders.

The above suit papers also did not contain depositions or affidavits. If the Court calls for depositions or affidavits, those records will be the last record filed, in a separate folder for large Chancery suits and the last record filed in the small suits.

6. The Library of Virginia Chancery Index

Fauquier County's Chancery suits are indexed according to the Virginia State Library Chancery Index database. Figure 10 illustrates how Fauquier's Chancery appears in this database.

INDEX #	PLAINTIFF	DEFENDANT	SURNAMES	PLAT	WILL
1761-003	Spilman, Jacob	Gent, Mary	Spilman, Gent, Fishback, Hoffman, Holtzclaw		
1762-001	Welsh, James	Freeman, James	Welsh, Freeman, Turner, Darnal		Prince Wm. Co., James Freeman, 1751.
1783-004	Readish, Joseph + wife	Burges, Garner &c.	Readish, Burgess, Burges		Stafford Co., Edward Burgess, 1759.
1796-031	Hathaway, James	Barnett, Ambrose	Hathaway, Barnett, Neavill	Y	
1797-018	Levy, Judas + wife &c.	Blackwell, Joseph	Blackwell, McGraw, Levy		
1798-022	Helm, Elizabeth	Helm, Thomas	Helm, Gunyon, Grayson		
1798-025	Grigsby's, Wm. Admr. &c.	Briggs, David	Grigsby, Obanion, Briggs, Tait, Hansford, Routt, Keith		

Figure 10. The LVA Chancery Index form for Fauquier's Chancery suits

Fauquier County, Virginia's Clerks Loose Papers: A Guide to the Records 1759-1919

As shown by Figure 10, the LVA Chancery Index has fields for the 1) Index number, 2) the plaintiff's name, 3) the defendant's name, 4) Surnames in the suit papers, 5) indication by a "Y" if a plat and/or survey is present, and 6) County, Name and date for a will, if present in the suit papers. Wives are not identified by given name. "Next friends" and men serving as a "guardian ad litem" are identified by surname in the surname field of the database.

The Chancery Index was prepared using Microsoft Access 97. You may sort, filter and query the plaintiff and defendant fields. You may sort, filter and query the names in the Will field. You may filter the plat field to see how many plats are filed in Chancery papers.

7. Abbreviations found in the LVA Index
There are several abbreviations associated with the index:

- *Admr., Adm.* = Administrator; Administrators

- *Alexander Lithgow & Co]* = In the plaintiff or defendant field, the square bracket after the name indicates that this is a business or merchant concern. Businesses and merchants are entered by their given name and then their surname as indicated above. All other plaintiffs and defendants are entered surname, given name.

- *[Alexander Lithgow & Co]* = In the surname field, square brackets before and after the name show that this is a business or merchant.

- *Dev., Devs.* =Devisees

- *&c* = and others

- *Exr., Exrs.* = Executor; Executors

- *Gdn* = Guardian

- *Grigsby's, William Admr. or Exr.* = the way all administrator and executor suits are entered into the index.

- *Hrs* = Heirs

- *Reps* = Representatives

- *Trst., Trsts.* = Trustee; Trustees

- *~ Following a given name: for example, Billy ~* = A tilde indicates a lack of a surname and typically refers to either a slave or free Negro, whose surnames are not found in suit papers.

Fauquier County, Virginia's Clerks Loose Papers: A Guide to the Records 1759-1919

8. A Reminder

We ask that you return the records into the folders following the form already given. For the small suits in white folders, please remember to place the bills and answers in the front of the folders. For the larger suits in brown folders, please remember to place the records in the folders as they are marked.

Remember, the first folder in the large suits is *always* for the bill and answers. Each white folder within the brown folder will tell you what the record is in that folder. **Just be sure to put the record back in the correct folder.**

Plates 8-15 on the following pages illustrate examples of records found in Chancery causes.

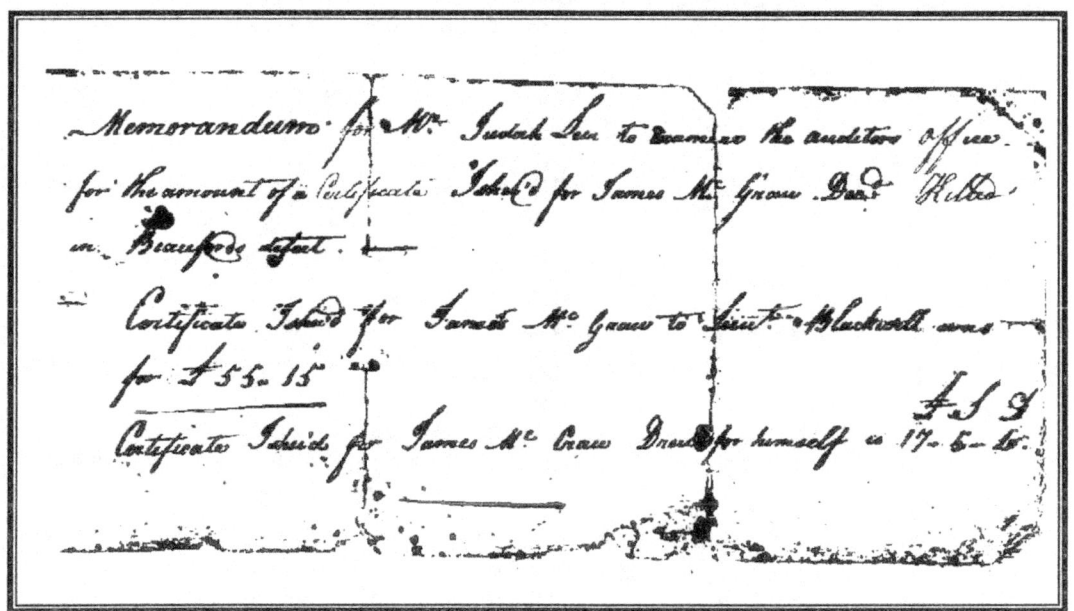

Plate 8. Scanned Image of Exhibit in Chancery 1798-018 Levie + wife v. Blackwell.
Memorandum to Judah Levi to examine Auditor's office for amount of Certificate issued James McGraw,
killed in Beaufort's Defeat in the Revolutionary War.

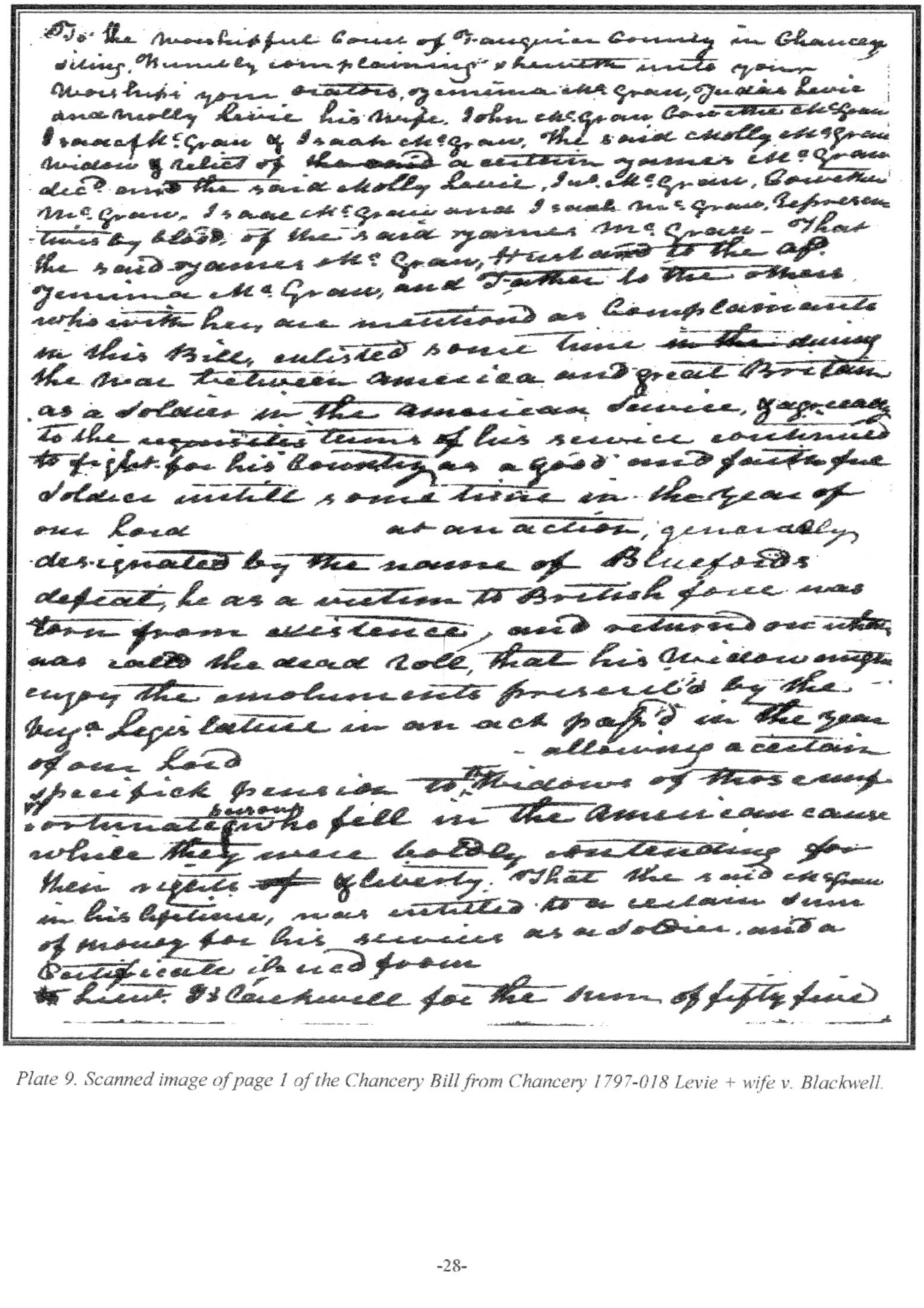
To the worshipfull Court of Fauquier County in Chancery
sitting, Humbly complaining sheweth unto your
worships your orators, Jemima McGraw, Judias Levie
and Molly Levie his wife, John McGraw, Corothie McGraw
Isaac McGraw & Isaah McGraw, the said Molly McGraw
widow & relict of ~~the said~~ a certain James McGraw
dec^d. and the said Molly Levie, Jno. McGraw, Corothie
McGraw, Isaac McGraw and Isaah McGraw, Representatives by blood, of the said James McGraw - That
the said James McGraw, Husband to the afs.
Jemima McGraw, and Father to the others
who with her are mentioned as Complainants
in this Bill, enlisted some time ~~in the~~ during
the war between America and great Britain
as a soldier in the american Service, & agreeably
to the requisites terms of his service continued
to fight for his Country as a good and faithful
soldier untill some time in the year of
our Lord   at an action, generally
designated by the name of Bluefords
defeat, he as a victim to British force was
torn from existence, and returned on what
was called the dead roll, that his widow might
enjoy the emoluments prescrib'd by the
Virg^a. Legislature in an act pass'd in the year
of our Lord   - allowing a certain
specifick pension to the widows of those unf-
ortunate persons who fell in the American cause
while they were boldly contending for
their rights ~~of~~ of liberty. That the said McGraw
in his lifetime, was entitled to a certain sum
of money for his services as a soldier, and a
Certificate issued from
Lieut. Blackwell for the sum of fifty five

Plate 9. Scanned image of page 1 of the Chancery Bill from Chancery 1797-018 Levie + wife v. Blackwell.

January the Ninth day in the Year of our Lord one Thousand Seven Hundred & fifty nine I Edward Burge being Sick & weak of body but of perfect mind & memory, thanks be to God therefore & Calling to mind the mortality of my body Knowing it is appointed for all men once to Die do make & ordain this my last will & Testament. And as it has Pleased God to bless me in this Life I give & dispose of the same in the following manner & form. — IMPRIMIS I give to my wife Margaret Burge the whole & sole Executrix of all my Estate during her Natural Life & after my wife Decease. Item I give & bequeath to my Daughter Mary Burge one Feather Bed & furniture & one Cow & Calf. Item I give & Bequeath to my Sons Edward, Moses, & Reubin Eight Pounds Each to be raised out of my Estate, & after my wifes Decease my Land Negroes Goods & Chattles to be sold & Equally to be Divided among all my Children & I also appoint my Sons Gardener & William Burge to be Executor of this my last will & Testament in Witness thereof I put my hand & Seal ———

Signed in the presence of
Joel Anchorum
Anne Amerson

Edward Burge

Plate 10. Scanned Image of a copy of Edward Burgess's Will, recorded in Stafford County May 8, 1759 and exhibited in Chancery 1783-004 Readish + wife v. Burgess &c.

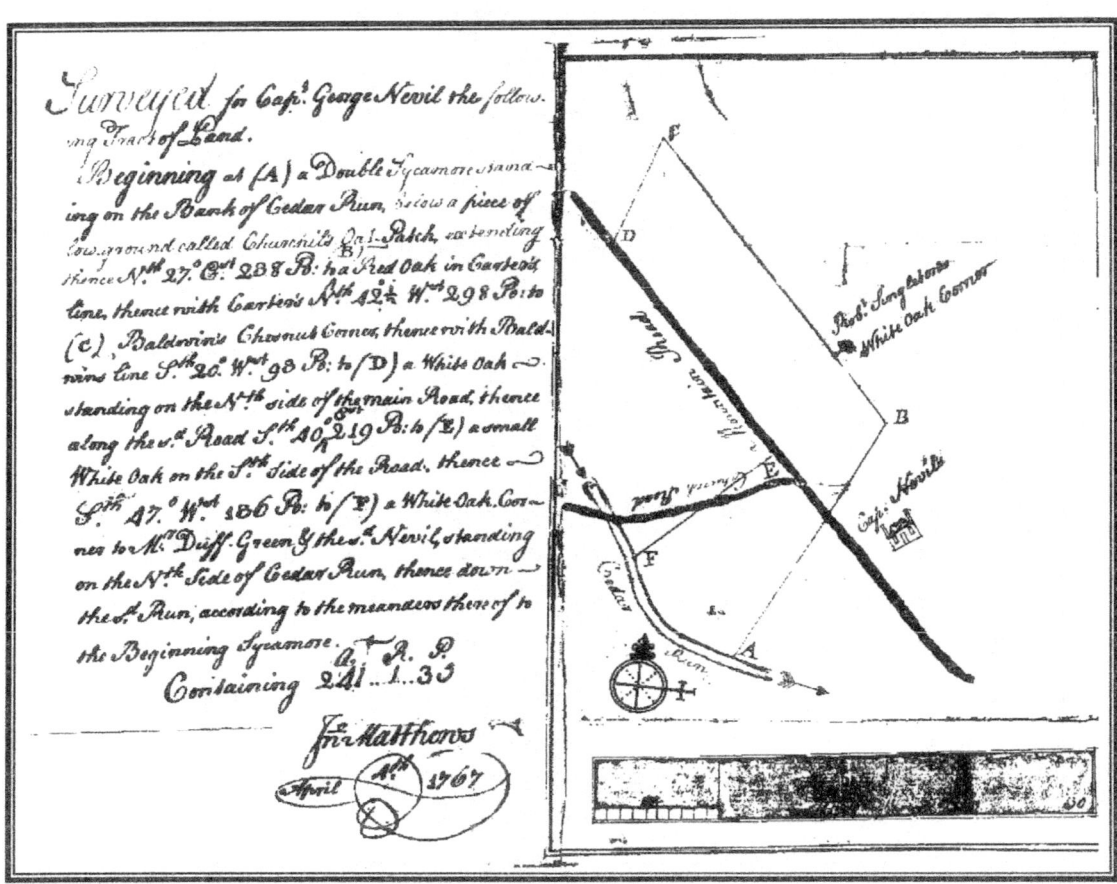

Plate 11. Scanned image of a Plat & Survey of Captain George Neavill's 241-acre tract on Cedar Run from Chancery 1796-031 Hathaway v. Barnett

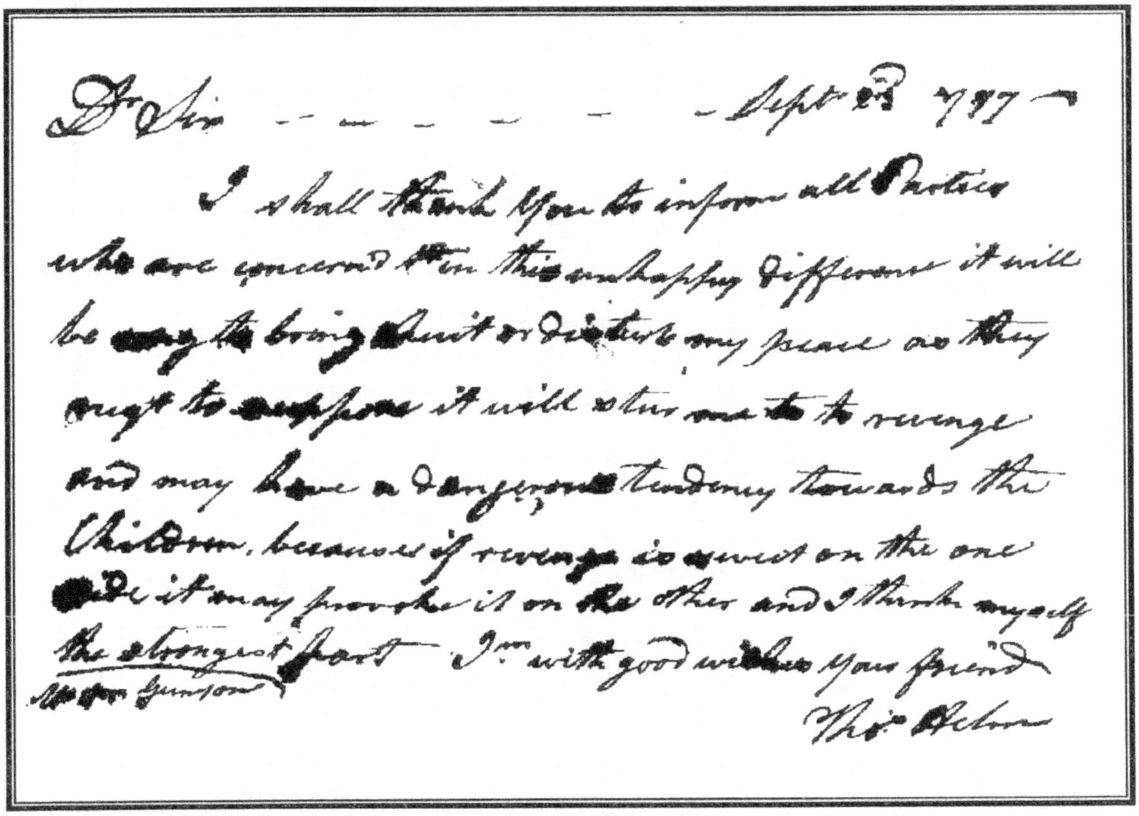

Fauquier County, Virginia's Clerks Loose Papers: A Guide to the Records 1759-1919

Plate 12. Scanned image of a threatening letter from a suit for divorce in Chancery 1798-022 Helm v. Helm

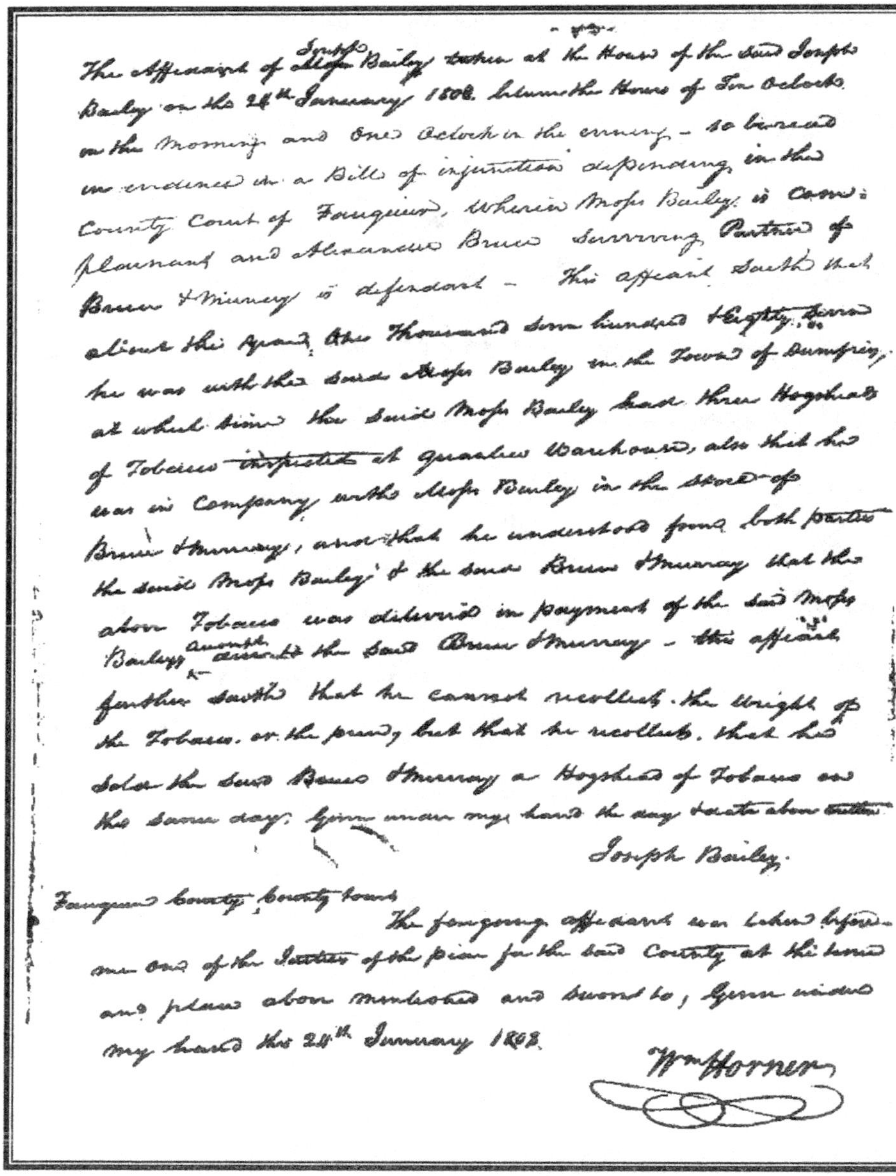

The Affidavit of Joseph Bailey taken at the House of the said Joseph Bailey on the 28th January 1808, between the Hours of Ten Oclock in the Morning and One Oclock in the evening — to be read in evidence in a Bill of injunction depending in the County Court of Fauquier, Wherein Moses Bailey is complainant and Alexander Bruce Surviving Partner of Bruce & Murray is defendant — This affiant Saith that about the year One Thousand Seven hundred Eighty two, he was with the said Moses Bailey in the Town of Dumfries, at which time the said Moses Bailey had three Hogsheads of Tobacco inspected at Quantico Warehouse, also that he was in Company with Moses Bailey in the Store of Bruce & Murray, and that he understood from both parties the said Moses Bailey & the said Bruce & Murray that the above Tobacco was delivered in payment of the said Moses Baileys account to the said Bruce & Murray — this affiant further saith that he cannot recollect the Weight of the Tobacco, or the price, but that he recollects that he sold the said Bruce & Murray a Hogshead of Tobacco on the same day. Given under my hand the day & date above written.

Joseph Bailey

Fauquier County, County to wit
    The foregoing affidavit was taken before me one of the Justices of the peace for the said County at the house and place above mentioned and sworn to, Given under my hand this 28th January 1808.

Wm Horner

Plate 13. Scanned image of an Affidavit by Joseph Bailey in Chancery 1811-039 Bailey v. Bruce

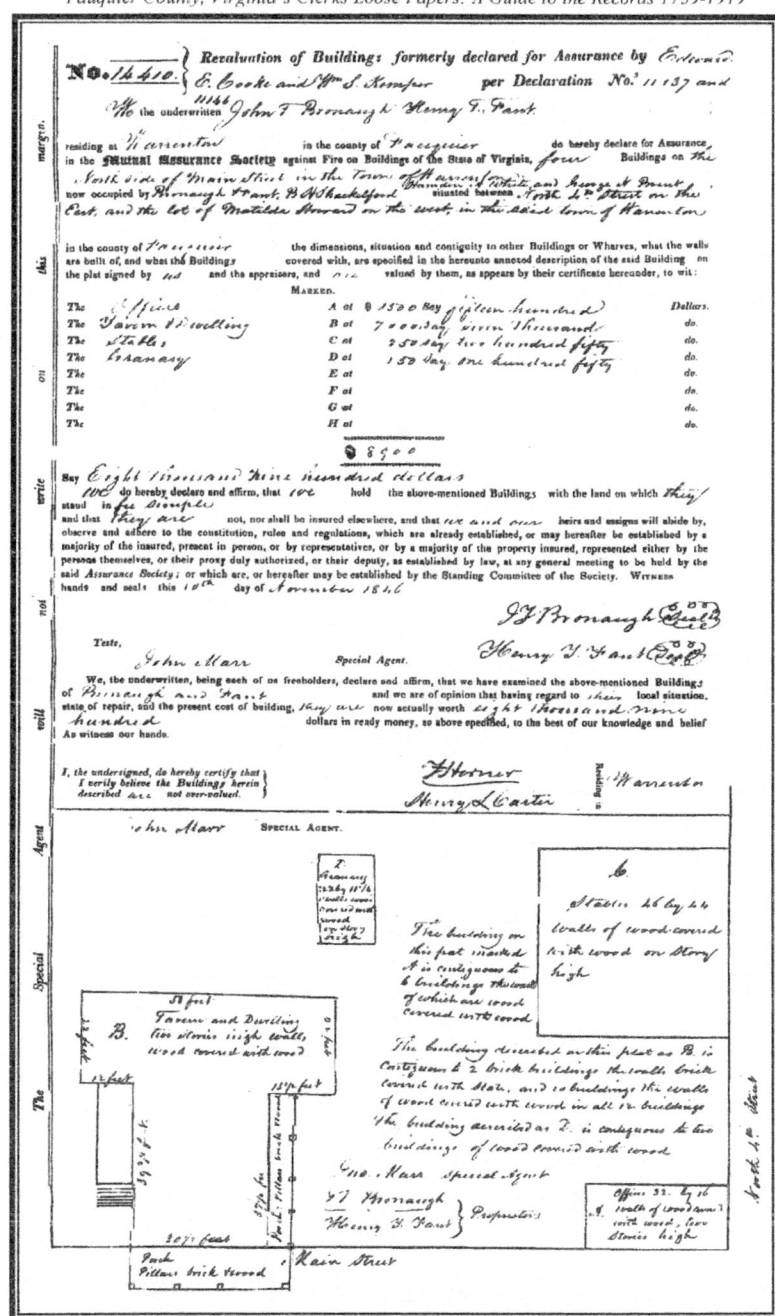

Plate 14. Scanned Image of page 1 of a Mutual Assurance Society of Virginia Plat for four buildings on North side of Main Street, Warrenton occupied by John T. Bronaugh and Henry T. Fant, and exhibited in Chancery 1853-033 Mutual Assurance Society v. Alexander Baker &c.

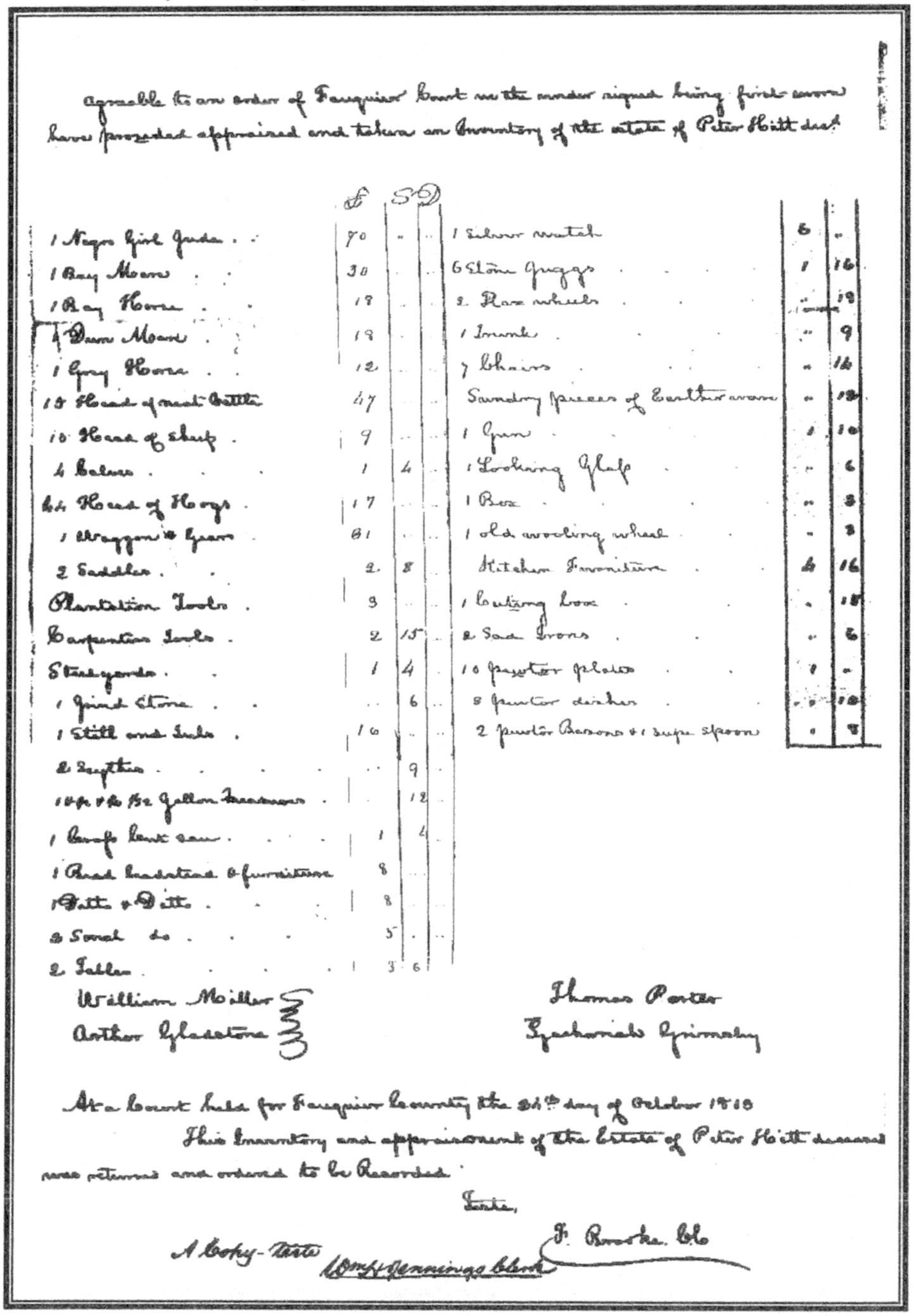

Agreeable to an order of Fauquier Court we the under signed being first sworn have proceeded appraised and taken an Inventory of the estate of Peter Hitt decd.

	£	S	D
1 Negro Girl Juda	70	..	..
1 Bay Mare	30		..
1 Bay Horse	18	..	..
1 Dun Mare	18	..	
1 Grey Horse	12	..	..
18 Head of neat Cattle	47		..
10 Head of Sheep	9	..	..
4 Calves	1	4	..
44 Head of Hogs	17	..	..
1 Waggon & Gear	81	..	..
2 Saddles	2	8	..
Plantation Tools	3	..	..
Carpenters Tools	2	15	..
Steelyards	1	4	..
1 Grind Stone	..	6	..
1 Still and Tubs	16	..	..
2 Scythes	..	9	..
1 ½ & ¼ & 1/2 Gallon measures		12	..
1 Cross cut saw	1	4	
1 Bed bedstead & furniture	8	..	
1 Ditto & Ditto	8		
2 Small do	5	.	..
2 Tables	3	6	

1 Silver watch	5	..
6 Stone Juggs	1	16
2 Flax wheels	..	19
1 Trunk	..	9
7 Chairs	..	16
Sundry pieces of Earthen ware	..	12
1 Gun	1	10
1 Looking Glass	..	6
1 Box	..	3
1 old wooling wheel	..	3
Kitchen Furniture	4	16
1 Cutting box	..	15
2 Sad Irons	..	6
10 pewter plates	1	..
8 pewter dishes	..	10
2 pewter Basons & 1 Soup spoon	..	5

William Miller
Arthur Gladstone

Thomas Porter
Zachariah Grimsley

At a Court held for Fauquier County the 21st day of October 1803
This Inventory and appraisement of the Estate of Peter Hitt deceased was returned and ordered to be Recorded.

Teste,
F. Brooke. Clo

A Copy - Teste Wm H Jennings Clerk

Plate 15. Scanned Image of a copy of Peter Hitt's Inventory recorded in October 1803 exhibited in Chancery 1855-008 Hitt v. Smoot

Fauquier County, Virginia's Clerks Loose Papers: A Guide to the Records 1759-1919

CHAPTER 5
DEAD PAPERS, ENDED CAUSES & JUDGMENTS

1. Overview

There are more records in Dead Papers, Ended Causes and Judgments than any other record series in Fauquier County's Clerks Loose Papers. Ended Causes and Judgments concern civil and criminal law suits. A judge, magistrate, Justice of the Peace or jury could hear the cases. They would then make a ruling based on points of law. The series is called "dead papers" because these suits were "dead"; that is, a judge or jury made a judicial ruling, involving points of law that ended the suit.

2. The Steps in A Civil Action: Moving a civil case through the Court.

Civil actions at law were brought by an individual to recover monetary damages for injuries to the person, his property, his pocketbook, or his reputation. Each case had at least two parties – a plaintiff and a defendant. Two of the most important kinds of civil actions at law involve contract suits and something called a *tort*. A tort is an injury cause d by something other than a breach of contract. A plaintiff can seek monetary damages for the injury or a court order called an *injunction* to enjoin the defendant from doing any further wrong. Examples of *tort* actions are *assaults, assault and battery, trespass, misrepresentation* and *defamation*.

Step 1. **The Court issued a Writ of Summons or a Capias.** A summons was a order notifying the defendant to appear before the court to answer a complaint. The Clerk of Court, at the request of the plaintiff or his attorney, issued the writ under the Court's authority.

The Court directed the Sheriff, deputy Sheriff or Constable to serve the summons on the defendant. The serving officer could leave the summons with the defendant or an adult member of his family. The officer produced the summons, informed the defendant of its contents and left a copy. The sheriff then made out a return, usually on the back of the original writ, stating where, when and who accepted the order. He signed the return on the back of the writ and returned it to the Clerk of court. The writ and its return were then filed with the suit as part of the permanent record.

The court could issue a *capias or* capias *ad respondendum*, which could also begin a civil action. These writs ordered the sheriff to take the party named in the writ into custody and produce him in court to *respond* to the plaintiff. It served to notify the defendant of the suit and secured his arrest until he could provide security for the plaintiff's claim.

Step 2. **The Plaintiff filed a statement of claim, a complaint, a declaration, "narratio" or petition.** The declaration or "narratio" explained clearly the plaintiff's reason for taking legal action. The jacket of the suit may abbreviate declaration with "Decl" and narratio with "Narr". The court used both terms interchangeably. The declaration was the common law equivalent of an equity "*bill*", and a civil action, "*petition*". The purpose of the declaration was to explain clearly the plaintiff's reasons for taking action so that the defendant knew the nature of the claim. The defendant was then served *notice* that the declaration has been filed. The defendant or his attorney would also receive a copy of the declaration.

Step 3. **The Defendant countered with an answer** in the form of a sworn statement either admitting or denying the various claims in the plaintiff's declaration. He could also present new information bearing on his defense. The clerk filed the answer, serving a copy on the plaintiff or his attorney.

Step 4. **If the defendant failed to file an answer within the time specified by law,** then the plaintiff was entitled, upon motion of the court, to enter judgment by default. The clerk entered the judgment in the court records and the court provided for its enforcement.

Step 5. **When the declaration and answer have been filed, if the suit has not been judged before, then it was said to be "at issue".** This meant the suit was ready for trial before a judge and jury. Parties could waive a jury trial and choose to have their case heard by the judge alone. *The case is then scheduled on the court's docket.*

Step 6. **The court summoned witnesses by writs called subpoenas to testify for the plaintiff and/or the defendant.** The sheriff or one of his deputies served subpoenas directly on witnesses and submitted a return on the back of the original to the court. If the witness failed to appear, the court issued a bench warrant for his arrest and an officer of the court went out to find him.

Step 7. **The court commissioned representatives to take Depositions** from witnesses who lived outside the court's jurisdiction or who were ill, disabled or unable to attend in person. Sometimes the testimony consisted of written questions called *interrogatories* prepared by the court and forwarded to the local jurisdiction in which the witness resides. Depositions had to be witnessed and signed. The court's representatives then returned the depositions to the local court.

Depositions and interrogatories became part of the permanent record of the case. In early causes, depositions may have been the only written account of what witnesses actually said. These records could be especially valuable in matters of probate and divisions of property.

Step 8. **A jury was selected** by drawing names from a list prepared at the beginning of the court term. If the parties waived a jury trial, then the judge would hear the case directly. If a judge heard the case, the suit took up less time than one heard by a jury.

Step 9. **The parties presented their case to the court and/or jury.** This included statements by the plaintiff and defendant, usually by their attorneys; it could also include testimony from witnesses, introduction of written depositions and the review of documents or other exhibits presented to the court. The attorneys for both sides made a summation of their case concerning their view of the points of law at issue.

Step 10. **The judge or jury retired to consider the case or to arrive at a verdict.** If this is a jury trial, the verdict must be unanimous. If this was a case heard before a judge, it was up to him to rely on his own personal deliberations and knowledge of the law in order to render a decision in the case.

Step 11. **It was the judge's responsibility to render judgment.** The clerk of the court was required by law to record the names of the parties, the judgment, amounts of money recovered if any and the time allowed for meeting the judgment.

Step 12. **Once the Judge has rendered the judgment in the case, the court commands the sheriff or other officer of the court to carry it out.** In cases of debt, imprisonment was often useless since the person in debt had no way of earning money to pay the judgment.

Sometimes the court issued a *capias ad satisfaciendum* (abbreviated as a *casa*), which charged the Sheriff to *take* the party named in the writ and keep him safely so that he appeared in court to *satisfy* the damages or debts. A *casa* deprived the defendant of his liberty until he made satisfaction. A *casa* is awarded to force the losing party to adhere to the judgment of the court.

Step 13. However, **if the defendant owned property, the court could (and did) issue an order for the Sheriff to "attach" the property of the defendant** and sell enough of it to satisfy the creditor's claims. In some instances, the court ordered an attachment *before* judgment was rendered. In this instance, the attached property was treated as security for payment if the defendant failed to pay.

In other instances, the defendant's property could be attached to ensure his appearance in court to answer the declaration. Once the person appears in court, the property was returned to him. This type of action was called "distraint". The defendant was required to bring his personal property to the courthouse; the sheriff or other officer of the court took an inventory of the distrained goods. Sometimes, the plaintiff had to take out a bond for the value of the property to indemnify the officer of the court against unlawful seizure by the defendant.

When real property was seized, it was done so by recording a writ against the title called a *judgment lien*. The plaintiff was required to give notice to the defendant that the land in question was now court property and could not be sold or otherwise disposed of by the defendant.

If the defendant still won't pay the judgment, the court charges the sheriff to condemn the property and sell it by public auction to the highest bidder. The sheriff is required by law to advertise the sale and to post notice of the auction in conspicuous public places. Once the auction has taken place and the land has been "cried off", the proceeds were used to pay the judgment, costs and damages.

Each step in this process created court records. Court Minute Books may contain brief or detailed descriptions of the case. Declarations, court orders, testimony, exhibits, documents, writs, judgments and notices may all appear in the suit papers.

Step 14. **Either party, if dissatisfied with the outcome of the suit, could appeal the judgment to an appellate court.** If the appellate court decided to hear the case, it issued a writ for that purpose. The parties then prepared concise summaries of the facts of the case called *briefs*, along with an account of the errors they believed that the judge committed and the reasons for the appeal.

New trials were granted for a number of reasons. 1) The judge may have erred on the admissibility of evidence; 2) the verdict of the jury may have been contrary to the evidence or contrary to the law; 3) the judge may have erred in his charge to the jury; 4) or new evidence, not part of the trial record, may have become available. When errors occurred, the case was tried only on the legal technicalities involved, not on the evidence. The appellate judges consider the matter individually and collectively, and rendered their opinions accordingly.

If the appellate court granted a new trial, they sent the case back to the local trial court. The case was then retried according to the rules laid down by the appeals court.

3. The Steps in a Criminal Action

Step 1. **A Court summoned a Grand Jury to draw up an Indictment.** The grand jury met and prepared a presentment against the person whom they believed committed a crime. This was the written notice of any criminal offense, from the Grand Jury's own knowledge or observation. It acted as the accusation that lead to drawing up a bill of indictment against the person believed to have broken the law.

Sometimes, Ended Causes will have criminal cases brought to Court "upon information". This meant that the person was accused by a public officer on oath rather than by a grand jury. The purpose of *"an information"* was to *"inform"* the defendant of the nature of the charge so that he could prepare for trial.

Step 2. **The Court ordered the offender to be summoned by a "warrant" or a "writ of capias"** A writ of *capias* gave the Sheriff or other officer of the court the power to *take* the defendant into custody and produce the accused before the court for a hearing. The court, at the hearing, could recommit the accused to jail or release him on bail to await trial.

*Step 3. **The accused could post an "appearance bail"*** – that is, he could take out a bond in a set amount of money to insure his appearance in Court. If the court does not allow bail, he was re-committed to jail to await trial.

*Step 4. **A magistrate held a preliminary hearing*** to determine whether there was sufficient evidence against the accused to justify holding him for trial. Witnesses may be called. The magistrate did not determine guilt or innocence; just whether there was enough evidence to warrant a further trial.

The magistrate then prepared copies of the hearing, within a set period, and sent them to the court where the trial was to take place. The copy of the hearing contained the name of the defendant, the nature of the charge, the names of the prosecutor and the witnesses, the information upon which the arrest was made and the bail bond. It became part of the permanent record of the suit.

If this was a murder case, the coroner held an inquest before a coroner's jury, which heard evidence and rendered a verdict concerning the cause of death. The coroner then provided a return to the court based on his and the jury's findings. The report was usually presented at the preliminary hearing and became a part of the court record at that point.

*Step 5. **If there is enough evidence to justify a trial, the Court brought the prisoner before the bar and arraigned him.*** This meant that the accused appeared in court and pleaded either "guilty" or "not guilty". If he pleaded "guilty the judge sentenced him immediately without further trial; if he pleaded "not guilty" he was bound over for trial.

*Step 6. **Subpoenas were issued for witnesses to testify in the case***. At this point in the proceedings, the procedures for the trial of a criminal proceeding are the same as that for a civil trial. (See Steps 6-11 in Steps in A Civil Action)

[Author's Note: For further information on Civil and Criminal Proceedings found in Dead Papers, Ended Causes and Judgments, see Arlene Eakle & Johni Cerny's *The Source: A Guidebook of American Genealogy*, pp. 151-157; Val Greenwood, *The Researcher's Guide to American Genealogy 1973 edition*, pp. 337-339 and 352-353; for definitions of legal terminology in these actions, see *Black's Law Dictionary, 6th Edition* and *Random House Webster's College Dictionary*.]

4. A Glossary of selected terms found in Ended Causes

- *Action on the Case* – sometimes called *Trespass on the Case* or *in case*. These are civil law suits brought to recover monetary damages for an injury to the plaintiff by some kind of wrongful act not accompanied by force. A common *trespass on the case* was a suit involving libel or slander.

- *Alias execution* – An alias execution is a writ of execution, a formal, written order of the court to the sheriff to execute, carry out or enforce a court judgment. An *alias pluries capias* are subsequent writs of execution that are issued by a Court to enforce a judgment that has not yet been satisfied.

- *Arraignment* – A defendant is brought before the Court to plead "guilty" or "not guilty" or "nolo contendere (literally, "I will not contest") to a criminal indictment from a grand jury or upon an information. Arraignment is conducted in open Court.

- *Assault* – A type of civil or criminal lawsuit brought by someone who has been the object of violent physical or verbal attack. Assault may also refer to an unlawful threat or an unsuccessful attempt to harm another person physically to such an extent that they fear for their life.

- *Assault and Battery* – A type of civil or criminal lawsuit brought by a plaintiff who has suffered an intentional or unlawful beating.

- *Assumpsit* – An *assumpsit* is a civil suit to recover damages when one party breaks a contract or agreement.

- *Bonds* – A bond is a written obligation to pay money for goods or for the non-0erformance of an obligation.
    - *Bail Bond* – Someone who insures that the defendant will appear at court at the specified time takes out a bail bond.

    - *Delivery Bond*— A defendant whose property has been seized by an attachment takes out a delivery bond. There are two conditions to a delivery bond. First, the defendant has his attached property *delivered* or returned to him until the suit has been decided. Second, the defendant promises that he will *deliver* the property or its value in satisfaction if he loses the case. A delivery bond is the same as a *Forthcoming Bond*.

    - *Peace Bond*—This is an obligation to keep the peace by someone who has threatened to break it or has already done so in the past.

    - *Penal bond* – This is a promise to pay a monetary penalty for the non-performance of an obligation. The bond is conditioned so that if the performance of the obligation takes place, the bond is void.

- *Covenant* – A covenant is a signed and sealed written agreement or a promise by two or more parties. The Agreement concerns the performance of a specified task. A *breach of covenant* occurs when any part of the written agreement is not completed or when something is done that is not in the agreement. A *breach of contract* occurs when there is a failure by one of the parties to perform the promises cited in the agreement.

- *Demurrer* – A demurrer occurs when a defendant does not dispute the truth of the plaintiff's claim but believes that there is not a sufficient basis to warrant legal action. A *demurrer to an interrogatory* occurs most often when depositions are taken in a pending suit. The deponent (the person giving the deposition) objects to a question and states his reasons for the objection and subsequent refusal to answer.

- *Detinue*—An action of *Detinue* is brought by a plaintiff for the recovery of personal property wrongfully or unlawfully detained by a defendant. The plaintiff has only to prove that he owns the property and that the goods are now in the possession of the defendant.

- *Distrain* – Distrained goods are ones that are seized by an officer of the Court in order to obtain satisfaction on a claim for damages.

- *Petition*—In a judicial sense, a petition is a formal written application to a court requesting legal action.

- *Plea*—A plea is an allegation made on behalf of a party in a lawsuit in defense of his or her claim or defense. It may also be the defendant's answer to a plaintiff's complaint.

- *Replevin* – This is a lawsuit for the recovery of goods or chattels wrongfully taken or detained by an officer of the court.

- *Rules* – Rules are formal orders made by a law court, especially for governing court procedures.

- *Subpoena duces tecum* – This subpoena compels an individual to bring specific records or other relevant materials with him when he comes to court.

5. Finding your way around Dead Papers, Ended Causes & Judgments
Series Title: Ended Causes
Color Code: **White Dots on Boxes**

Series Dates: **1759-001 to 1858-001. Includes 3 boxes of "Sundries"**
Series Extent: *261 Boxes. 108.75 linear feet*
Series Arrangements: *Filed by Year and Court Session.*

Series Finding Aid: *No Inventory. No Index. No Cross Index.*

Types of Ended Causes include
- **a. Judgments** – Judgment papers include
    1) Bill of Complaint, Declaration, Narrations, Pleas
    2) Detinues (Unjust Detainers)
    3) Subpoenas, Summons, Warrants, Recognizances
    4) Errors
    5) Attachments
    6) Bonds – Delivery and Forthcoming Bonds, Replevin Bonds, Appeal Bonds
    7) Orders and Writs
    8) Depositions and Affidavits
- **b. Office Judgments (reached in the Clerk's office by the parties; suits did not go to trial)**
- **c. Rules**
- **d. Commonwealth/King Causes**
    1) Grand Jury Presentments/Indictments
    2) Types of Records
        - Slander
        - Trespass, Assault and Battery (TAB), Trespass, Assault
        - Murder
        - Burglary and Theft
        - Rape
        - Adultery
        - Poisoning
        - Breaking and Entering
        - Property Damage
    3) Breach of Contract and Covenants Broken (*included to maintain intellectual control*)

Plates 16-19 on pages 41-44 illustrate examples of records found in Dead Papers, Ended Causes and Judgments. A list of 1798 presentments given by the Grand Jury is shown on page 41. The 1786-016 folder contains an interesting suit between William Stuart and Joseph Minter. Scanned images of the bond and part of the receipt found in this Ended Cause are found on page 42. Page 43 and 44 contain scanned images of a suit found in the 1786-013 folder, a suit between Thomas Lee and Thomas Blackwell. Scanned images of the Declaration, capias and an account exhibited with the suit papers are shown here.

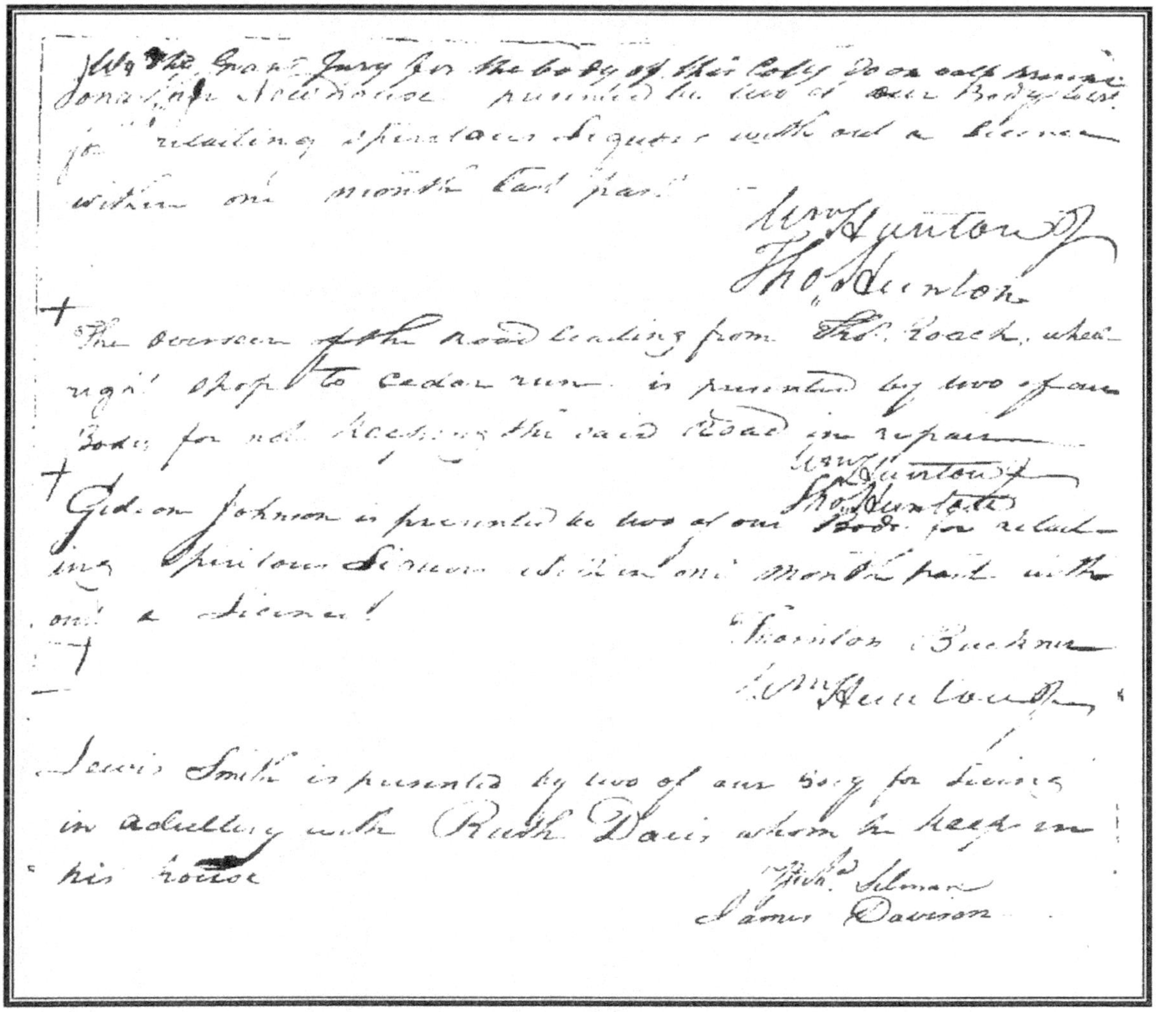
We the Grand Jury for the body of this County do on oath present Jonathan Newhouse presented by two of our Body for retailing spiritous liquors without a license within one month last past

Geo. Hunton
Tho. Hunton

The overseer of the road leading from Thos. Roach, wheelwright shop to Cedar run is presented by two of our Body for not keeping the said Road in repair

Geo. Hunton
Tho. Hunton

Gideon Johnson is presented by two of our Body for retailing Spiritous Liquors within one month past without a license

Thornton Buckner
Wm. Hunton

Lewis Smith is presented by two of our Body for living in adultery with Ruth Davis whom he keeps in his house

Richd. Silman
James Davison

Plate 16. Scanned Image of Grand Jury Presentments from 1798 Box of Commonwealth Causes

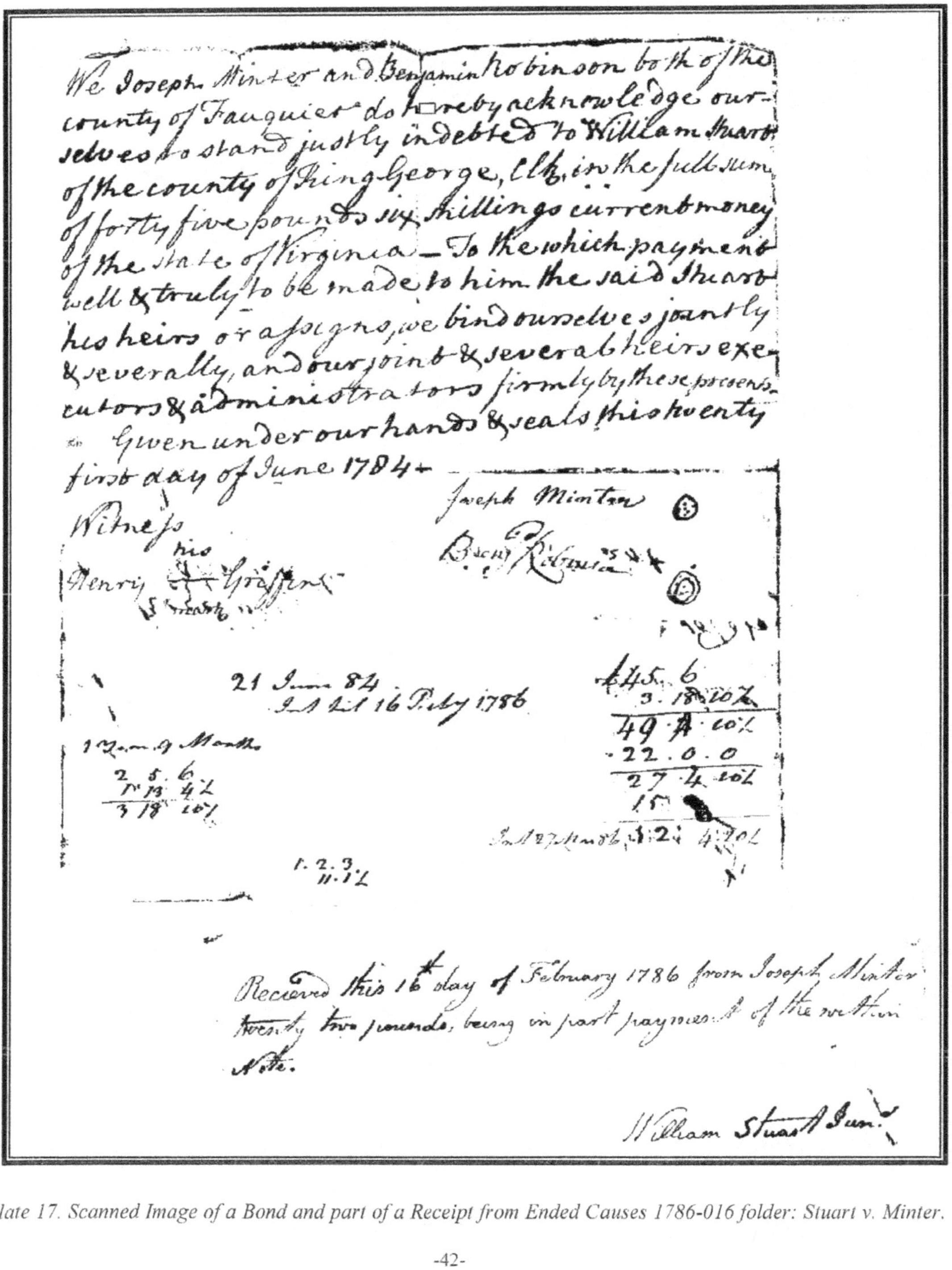

> We Joseph Minter and Benjamin Robinson both of the county of Fauquier do hereby acknowledge ourselves to stand justly indebted to William Stuart of the county of King George, Clk, in the full sum of forty five pounds six shillings current money of the state of Virginia — To the which payment well & truly to be made to him the said Stuart his heirs or assigns, we bind ourselves jointly & severally, and our joint & several heirs executors & administrators firmly by these presents. Given under our hands & seals this twenty first day of June 1784.
>
> Witness   Joseph Minter (Seal)
>   his
> Henry X Griffin   Benj. Robinson (Seal)
>
> Received this 16th day of February 1786 from Joseph Minter twenty two pounds, being in part payment of the within Note.
>
> William Stuart Junr.

Plate 17. Scanned Image of a Bond and part of a Receipt from Ended Causes 1786-016 folder: Stuart v. Minter.

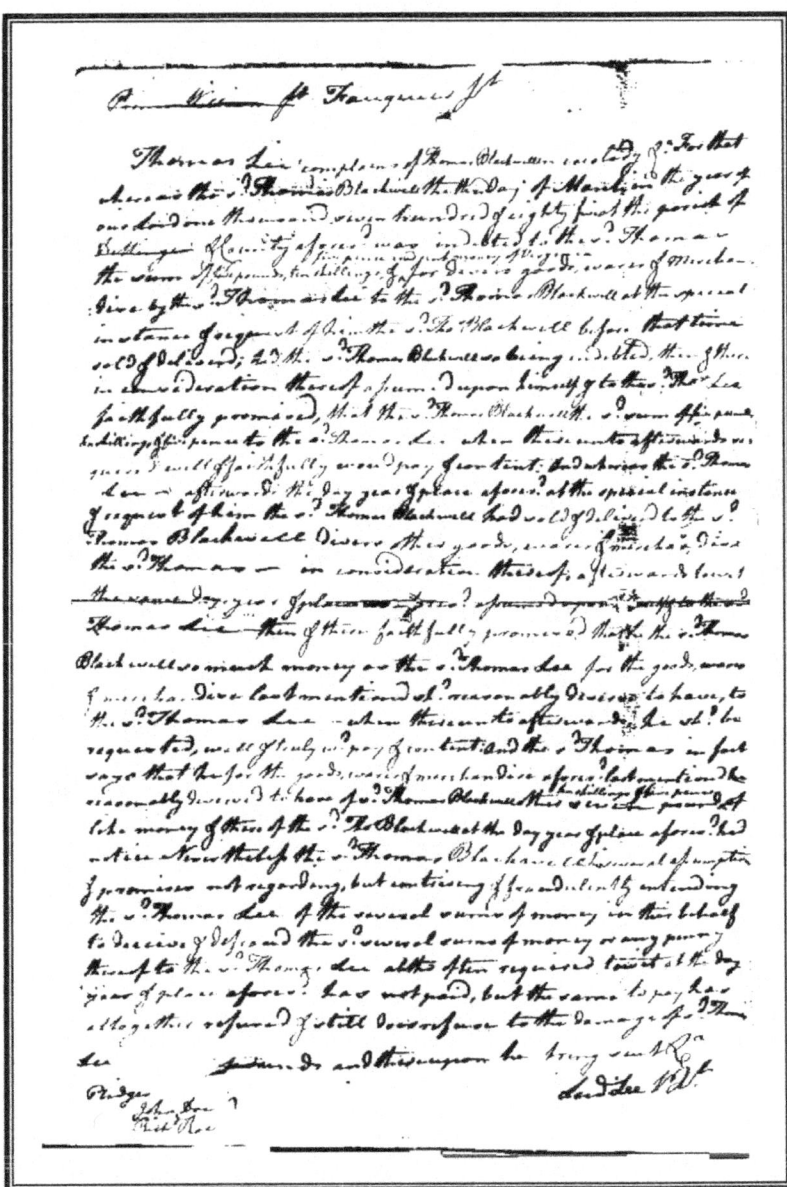

Plate 18. Scanned Image of a Declaration in Ended Causes 1786-013 Folder: Lee v. Blackwell. Trespass on the Case

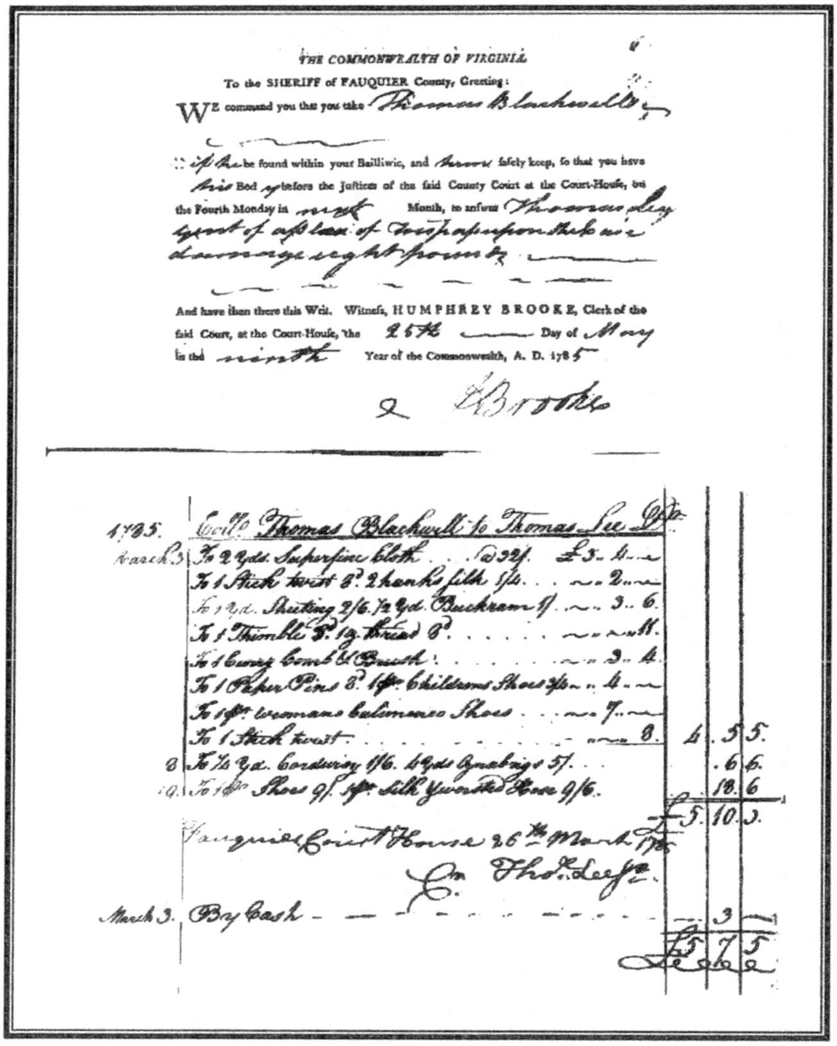

THE COMMONWEALTH OF VIRGINIA

To the SHERIFF of FAUQUIER County, Greeting:

WE command you that you take Thomas Blackwell

if he be found within your Bailliwic, and him safely keep, so that you have his Body before the Justices of the said County Court at the Court-House, on the Fourth Monday in next Month, to answer Thomas Lee gent of a plea of trespass upon the case damage eight pounds

And have then there this Writ. Witness, HUMPHREY BROOKE, Clerk of the said Court, at the Court-House, the 25th Day of May in the ninth Year of the Commonwealth, A. D. 1785

H Brooke

1785. Captn Thomas Blackwell to Thomas Lee Dr.

March 3	To 2 Yds. Superfine cloth . . @ 32/. £3.. 4.. –				
	To 1 Stick twist 8d. 2 hanks silk 1/4 . . . – .. 2.. –				
	To 1 Yd. Sheeting 2/6. ½ Yd. Buckram 1/ . – .. 3.. 6.				
	To 1 Thimble 3d. 1 lb. thread 8d. . . . . . – .. – .. 11.				
	To 1 Curry Comb & Brush . . . . – .. 3.. 4.				
	To 1 Paper Pins 8d. 1 pr. Childrens Shoes 3/4 .. 4.. –				
	To 1 pr. womans calimanco Shoes . . . – .. 7.. –				
	To 1 Stick twist . . . . – .. – .. 8.	4	5	5.
8	To ½ Yd. Corduroy 1/6. 4 Yds Ognabrigs 5/. . .		6	6.
10	To 1 pr. Shoes 9/. 1 pr. Silk Worsted Hose 9/6.		18	6
		£5.	10.	5.

Fauquier Court House 26th March 1786

Errors Excepted Thos. Lee Jr.

March 3.	By Cash – – – – – – – –		3	
		£5	7	5

Plate 19. Scanned Image of a Capias and an Account from Ended Causes 1786-013 Folder: Lee v. Blackwell. Trespass on the Case.

Fauquier County, Virginia's Clerks Loose Papers: A Guide to the Records 1759-1919

CHAPTER 6
FREE NEGRO & SLAVE RECORDS (AFTER 1865: NEGRO RECORDS)

1. Overview

Free Negro & Slave records consists of original documents or their copies taken from these record series in the Clerk's Loose Papers: Chancery, Ended Causes, Land Records and Disputes, Miscellaneous, Military, Overseer of the Poor, Probate and Tax and Fiscal records. The series has two headings to reflect the transition from slavery to free people of color after 1865.

Copies of records are taken from Chancery, Land Records and Disputes, Miscellaneous records, Military and Probate. The originals of these records are found in the above record series. The copies may refer to listings of slaves found in Chancery causes, a Deed of Gift in Land Records and Disputes, a service record from Military records or a division or sale of slaves found in the Probate records of the Clerk's Loose Papers.

Other records are original ones, taken from Ended Causes, Overseer of the Poor records and Tax and Fiscal records. The vast majority of the original records come from Ended Causes and related to the Detinue (Unjust detainer) of Negro slaves. They concern suits to recover money owed due to the hiring of slaves. There are also numerous Commonwealth Causes, both before and after 1865, which refer to people of color, free and slave.

Records relating to Free Negroes are diverse documents like Emancipations, Petitions to recover freedom, Certificates of freedom, Presentments for Unlawful Assembly and Petitions by free Negroes to remain in the Commonwealth. In many instances, these records act as a mirror for eighteenth and nineteenth century Black Codes.

There is a whole box of Free Negro and Negro Apprenticeships. The Overseers of the Poor bound out children of color if the families were too poor to support them. The Overseer of the Poor records contains a great deal of information about the names (and sometimes ages) of the working poor of the community, whether of African descent or Caucasian. The tax and fiscal records referring to African-Americans may ultimately prove to be one of the most useful records in the Clerk's Loose Papers relating to Free Negro/Negro & Slave families.

2. Types of records in the Free Negro/Slave and Negro Record series

This record series is the most diverse and draws from the largest number of other record series in the Clerks Loose Papers. A listing and brief explanation about the records appear in random order here.

- *Attachments, Forthcoming and Delivery Bonds* – These documents are part of the civil process primarily involving slaves. An *attachment* is an order issued by a law court to seize property of the defendant to secure a debt. If the defendant owned slaves, *attachments* were issued to the sheriff, giving him the authority to come to the defendant's home and take away a slave or slaves, depending on the amount of the debt. If the debt was not paid, the sheriff sold the slave. The proceeds from this sale then went to pay off the debt.

  Forthcoming or delivery bonds are bonds that promise to deliver seized property back to the defendant, if so determined by a court of law. If a defendant has had property seized by an *attachment*, then the delivery bond acts as a guarantee that the defendant will surrender the property or its equivalent value to the court if he loses the suit. There are many forthcoming or delivery bonds in this record series involving slaves. Creditors often went to court to recover debts and looked around for any property the defendant might own in order to do so.

The *forthcoming bond* guaranteed that the property, in this instance a slave or slaves, would be *forthcoming* or *delivered* up to repay the debt. It was a very effective way to insure prompt payment of debts since slaves were considered valuable property and showed the defendant that the creditor and the court meant business. If the debt were not repaid, the slave, through no fault of his own, would then be sold away from his family to a different owner.

Both attachments and the forthcoming bonds and delivery bonds are part of the record series known as Ended Causes. These documents make only one part of the legal steps taken by creditors in the process to recover what is owed them. The jacket of the actual suit papers themselves would give information concerning the final disposition of the suit – i.e. whether the debt was repaid or the property was sold to repay it. In many instances, however, the attachment or bond is all that is left of that process, so the final disposition of the suit remains unknown. In that instance, Court Minute books should be consulted to see if there is information there regarding the outcome of the suit.

- *Detinue* or *Unlawful detainer of slaves*—*Detinue* is another type of civil action brought by a plaintiff for the recovery of personal property either wrongfully or illegally held by a defendant. The plaintiff has only to prove he owns the property and that the defendant is in possession of it.

In this instance, a plaintiff may have hired out a slave to someone else for a certain amount of time. When the term of hiring is up, if the person refuses to deliver the slave back to his owner, the owner will go to court to force his return. The law suit that results is a suit *in Detinue*. The other term for this is *unlawful detainer*.

The value of these suits is two-fold: 1) The suit names the slave and his owner and 2) names the person to whom the slave has been hired out. Understanding the hiring-out process is helpful in establishing neighborhood linkages, social interactions and patterns of travel between the white infrastructure and local farmers.

- *Recovery of Debt involving hiring out of slaves*— There was often a contract involved in the hiring out of slaves. The owner and the person to whom the slave was hired were the two parties in the contract. The person hiring the slave agreed to pay a sum of money or part of a crop as the price for hiring the slave. If the sum agreed to was not paid, then the owner went to court to recover it. These suits are found throughout the Free Negro/Slave Record series.

- *Ill-treatment suits involving hiring out of slaves* – Within the contract signed by the owner and the person hiring the slave were clauses regarding the humane treatment of the slave along with provisions for his clothing and attire. If these clauses were not followed to the letter, owners would go into court to force the return of the slave and to ask for damages for the ill treatment of his property. Suits for improper treatment of slaves are also found throughout this record series.

- *Suits brought against owners for letting their slaves hire themselves out* – The Commonwealth could, and did, sue owners for letting their slaves hire themselves out. As the level of trust developed between a slave and his or her owner, slaves were often allowed to hire themselves and their skills out to others. In the third and fourth decade of the nineteenth century, there were quite a few suits against owners because of this practice

- *Commonwealth Causes* – The Commonwealth brought suits against both slaves and free Negroes for a number of reasons. Criminal suits against slaves could be brought for poisoning, theft, murder, arson and other actions that were contrary to the Black Codes of the nineteenth century. At the same time free Negroes could be brought into court for a variety of reasons. If free Negroes could not produce their register on demand, they could be jailed. If they had been freed after 1809, they were not allowed to remain in Virginia unless they petitioned for that right.

Fauquier County, Virginia's Clerks Loose Papers: A Guide to the Records 1759-1919

People of color were not allowed to carry weapons. They were discouraged from associating with slaves. It was a crime to assemble with other slaves or free Negroes, especially in a large group.

Enforcement of the Black Codes was left to local jurisdictions and varied widely throughout the state. When the fear of slave rebellion was high, laws were strictly enforced and free people of color were brought in to register again as free Negroes. *Patrollers*, usually young white men of military age, were put together in a quasi-military company and assigned to "patrol" the countryside to make sure that slaves and free Negroes were home after dark and not out and about planning mischief against the white population.

- *Petitions to sue for Freedom* – If a slave believed that he or she was being held illegally in slavery, they could sue the County Court and their owner for their freedom. There are several of these suits in this record series. If the court was of the opinion that the slaves were entitled to their freedom, they could grant it. The decisions could be appealed so freedom could be delayed or negated altogether depending on the higher court's judgment.

- *Registers of Free Negroes and Certificates of Freedom*

    When white owners emancipated their slaves, the ex-slaves were required to come into the County Court register as free men or women of color. They were to renew their register every three years. If their register was lost or misplaced, the free person of color was required to come into court immediately to replace it.

    These registers contained their name, age and description, including any identifying marks or scars. Their status was also recorded. If they were born free, that was in the register. If they had been emancipated, that also was supposed to go into the register, with the name of the person who freed them and whether they were freed by deed or by will.

    The County Court was required to record all of this information into a book of Registers or Certificates of Freedom. Every county had books to identify their free people of color. Fauquier's book is now in the possession of the Virginia Historical Society. If a search for either the book or an ancestor's register proves fruitless, the County Court Minute Books may have the information.

    The court minute books may contain a summary of the information in the register or it may only note that the free person of color came in to register according to law. However, in the absence of the register itself or the court's copy, the minute books are often the only route remaining to prove free ancestry.

- *Coroner's Inquests* – When someone died under suspicious circumstances, an inquest was held to determine the probable cause of death. There are coroner inquests in this record series relating to deaths of slaves – adults, males, females, children, toddlers and infants.

- *Overseers of the Poor Apprenticeships* – If a poor family were likely to become the responsibility of the County to care for, the Overseers of the Poor (and their predecessor, the Churchwardens of the Parish) would step in and *bind out* the children to an adult to learn a skill. As a result, free families of color who were too poor to maintain themselves, were eligible for their children to become apprentices to white adults.

Free children of color were bound out to learn a trade or a skill – the boys until they were 21 and the girls until they were 18. Boys could learn to be farmers, blacksmiths, shoemakers or other skilled trades. Girls were taught spinning and weaving and tasks associated with being paid servants in white households.

Box #1 of this Record Series deals exclusively with these Apprenticeships. The information in these papers is invaluable in establishing ancestry. The children's names and ages along with the names of their parents are often included. The apprentice often lived right in the household of the person to whom they were hired. Within the contract made between Overseers of the Poor and the person to whom the child was apprenticed, were clauses ensuring his humane treatment and the money to be paid to the free family of color during the apprenticeship.

If the parents of the apprentice were not satisfied with the treatment accorded their child, they could go to court to rescind the apprenticeship. These suits are also found in the Free Negro/Slave and Negro record series.

- Copies of *Insolvent Lists* from Tax & Fiscal. The names of people who did not pay their taxes are found on these lists. The list included free men of color. Free Negroes were to be hired out to whites at a rate set according to law, until the taxes were paid.

- Copies of *Wills, Inventories, Sales* and *Divisions of Slaves* from Probate.

- Copies of *Bills* and *Exhibits naming slaves* from Chancery.

- Copies of *Deeds of Gifts, Bills of Sale, Emancipations and Manumissions, Trusts, Certificates of Importation or Non-Importation* from Land Records and Disputes.

- Copies of *Military Pensions* for identified free Negroes and *World War 1 Service Records* from Military Records of the Clerks Loose Papers.

As you can see from the foregoing list, there is a wealth of information in this record series. These records may help a researcher identify unknown ancestor, supply clues for the research of other records in related series and provide insight into an ancestor's place in eighteenth and nineteenth century social and economic structure.

3. The value of these records for African-Americans

This record series is a little different from the other series in the Clerk's Loose Papers. Part of the records found here has been taken from other record categories – Chancery or Probate, for example. Thus, in one sense, this is a *created* record series. Copies of pertinent records were added to this series in order to differentiate and call attention to the wealth of free Negro/ Negro and Slave records found in the Clerk's Loose Papers. There are Commonwealth Causes, Tax and Fiscal records and Overseer of the Poor records that contain a wealth of information about people of color, whether free or slave, before and after 1865.

This series, for the first time, attempts to combine a wealth of information for African-Americans researching their family's roots in Fauquier County. The tax and fiscal records may offer hints to those seeking an elusive slave owner or provide evidence concerning the earliest notice of an ancestor's reputed freedom. A register may present a hitherto unknown description of an ancestor. Inventories, Divisions and Sale Lists from the Clerks Loose Papers may prove that obscure connection from an ancestor to a progenitor.

Records from another series in the Clerks Loose Papers may also provide hitherto unknown family names and ancestry. These are records associated with the Overseer of the Poor record series and should be examined carefully for the accounts there may have unidentified family hidden within them. The records in this record series, along with records from the Overseers of the Poor are among the ones of utmost importance to African-American family researchers.

Many of the former slaves, for example, found themselves destitute after the Civil War, without the ability to feed or clothe themselves. White families, accustomed to slave labor to cultivate their land, now did not have the wherewithal to pay their Negro tenants to farm the land. Confederate bonds, now worthless, were in generous supply; U.S. currency and gold were not.

This, in turn, placed a crushing burden on the county to care for its own, regardless of color, while it was still faced with the consequences of a devastating war. Warrenton, its county seat, had been recently occupied by Union troops; Mosby had had free rein in the northern end of the county; so much so that it was known as Mosby's Confederacy to federal and confederates alike. Both the Orange and Alexandria and Manassas Gap railroads, needed to transport agricultural goods to markets, had been destroyed.

Added to this were the Congressional acts passed forbidding anyone who had served as an officer in the Confederacy from holding an elective office in the county. This swept away the county infrastructure in one fell swoop. A dispossessed labor force, a defeated elite and a disenfranchised electorate all added to the confusion after the war.

The Overseers of the Poor, charged with the responsibility of caring for the county's poor, struggled to find white and Negro families for the children of former slaves and free people of color. Their accounts well illustrate the problems inherent in dealing with an attempt to bring about stability in an increasingly chaotic situation.

African-American family historians may well find the documents contained in Free Negro & Slave and Negro Records to be the most valuable of any of the records in the Clerk's Loose Papers. An examination of this important record base, along with other record series in the Clerks Loose Papers, quickly brings about a realization of utmost significance: There is an absolute treasure trove of *family* information in these records. Even more importantly, the documents themselves may offer hints, clues and evidence of antecedents, heritage, and ancestry for African-Americans researching their roots in this county.

4. The Law, Slavery and the Free Negro

When researching slave or free ancestry, it is essential to understand the law and how the people of color, whether enslaved or free, "fit" into the system. A thorough understanding of the Black Codes and their relationship to those in bondage as well as to free people of color will provide greater insight into the workings of eighteenth and nineteenth century life.

The Black codes made clear the degree of control the white infrastructure thought it needed in order to maintain their lifestyle -- that is, their customs, habits, daily routines, their way of life. The white infrastructure viewed the black codes as a way to maintain the status quo.

There are still copies of the Black codes around today. One such copy, by June Guild, can be ordered from the Afro-American Historical Association of Fauquier County.

Fauquier County, Virginia's Clerks Loose Papers: A Guide to the Records 1759-1919

5. Finding Your Way Around Free Negro/Slave (before 1865) and Negro Records (after 1865)

Series Title: **Free Negro/Slave and Negro Records**
Color Code: Green dots on Boxes

Series Dates: 1759-001 to 1920-044. Includes No Date 001 to 007.
Series Extent: 31 Boxes. *15.5 linear feet.*
Series include:
1 Box	*Free Negro/ Negro Apprenticeships 1765-1892.*
16 Boxes	*Free Negro/Slave Records 1759-1832*
14 Boxes	*Free Negro/Slave and Negro records from County Court Records 1832-1920*

Series Arrangement: Filed by Index number.

Series Finding Aids: Free Negro & Slave Index sorted by Record series. There are **four** *Name Indices* associated with this series: **1.)** Apprenticeship Index 1765-1892. **2.)** African-American Transactions and Conveyances from the Clerks Loose Papers 1759-1832. **3.)** African-American Suits and Accounts from the Clerks Loose Papers 1759-1832. **4.)** African Americans in the County Court Records 1832-1920.

6. Contents of the Free Negro-Slave and County Court Record Series

Box 1 contains Free Negro and Negro Apprenticeships (1765-001 to 1892-001).

Box 2-31 (1759-001 to 1920-044) include
  a. Records naming slaves and free people of color from Ended Causes
      1) Commonwealth Causes
      2) Detinues (for slaves)
      3) Judgments involving the recovery of debts associated with hiring slaves out
      4) Patroller claims and returns
      5) Overseer of Poor Claims
      6) Petitions for Freedom
      7) Freedom Suits
      8) Certificates of Freedom and Registers of Free Negroes
      9) Testimony regarding births, deaths, free or slave status
      10) Coroner Inquests
      11) Various bonds that give names of slaves
  b. Selected records from the Probate record series
      1) Wills—for distribution of slaves to heirs or for emancipation from slavery
      2) Inventories
      3) Divisions of Slaves
      4) Sales Accounts
  c. Selected records from the Chancery record series
      1) Copies of the Bill naming slaves
      2) Copies of exhibits from Chancery that name slaves – like Deeds of Trusts, and Wills and Inventories
      3) Copies of Commissioner's Reports that name slaves
  d. Selected Records from the Land Disputes and Records series
      1) Deeds of Gift
      2) Bills of Sale
      3) Emancipations and Manumissions
      4) Deeds of Trust
      5) Certificate of Importation or Non-Importation of Slaves

Fauquier County, Virginia's Clerks Loose Papers: A Guide to the Records 1759-1919

    e. Selected Records from the Military Record series
        1) French and Indian and Revolutionary War Public Service Claims that related to slaves or free people of color
        2) Civil War records – proceedings of slaves requisitioned for public service
        3) Pensions
        4) World War 1 Selective Service Records
        5) World War 2 Records

7. A Preview of the Name Indexes for African-American Records from the Clerks Loose Papers 1759-1832

Figures 11 and 12 illustrate the kinds of information found in African-American Transactions and Conveyances from the Clerks Loose Papers and African American Suits and Accounts. Each index is a name index.

Surname	Given Name	FN-S Index #	Found in Instrument	From Record Group In CLP
	Abby	1818-006	Inventory of Charles Duncan	Probate Record Series
Beane	Joseph (Free Negro)	1817-024	Free Register of Joseph Beane, age ca. 53, former slave of Baker & Roe	FN/S Record Series
	Robert	1828-002	Trust from Joseph Weaver to Samuel Weaver	Land Records & Disputes Record Series

Figure 11. Selected examples of records found in the African-American Transactions &c. Index.

8. A Preview of the Name Index for African-American Suits and Accounts and other Records from the Clerk's Loose Papers.

Surname	Given Name	FN-S Index #	Found In	For	From Record Group in CLP
	Aaron	1822-014	Ended Causes Suit styled Dade v. Saunders	Hire of Negro slave Aaron	FN/S
Blue	Cupid (Free Negro)	1822-039	Ended Causes Suit styled Taliaferro v. Blue	Recovery of Debt	FN/S
Duncan	Olivia (Free Negro)	1820-003	Como. v. Olivia Duncan, &c.	Remaining in Virginia contrary to law	FN/S

Figure 12. Selected examples of records found in the African-American Suits &c. Index

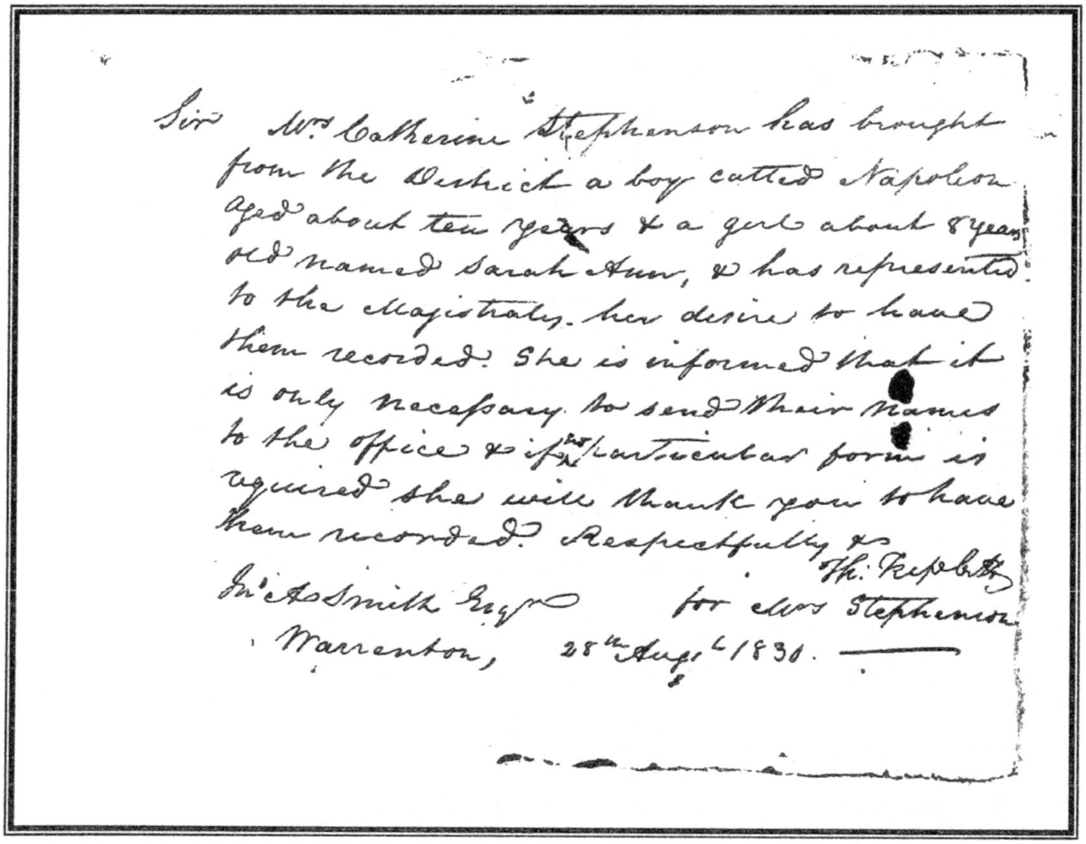

> Sir Mrs Catherine Stephenson has brought from the District a boy called Napoleon aged about ten years & a girl about 8 years old named Sarah Ann, & has represented to the Magistrate her desire to have them recorded. She is informed that it is only necessary to send their names to the office & if any particular form is required she will thank you to have them recorded. Respectfully &c
>
> Th. Riplets
> for Mrs Stephenson
>
> Mr As Smith Esqr
> Warrenton, 28th Augt 1831.

Plate 20. Scanned image of Free Negro/Slave 1838-008 Catherine Stephenson's Certificate of Importation of Slaves

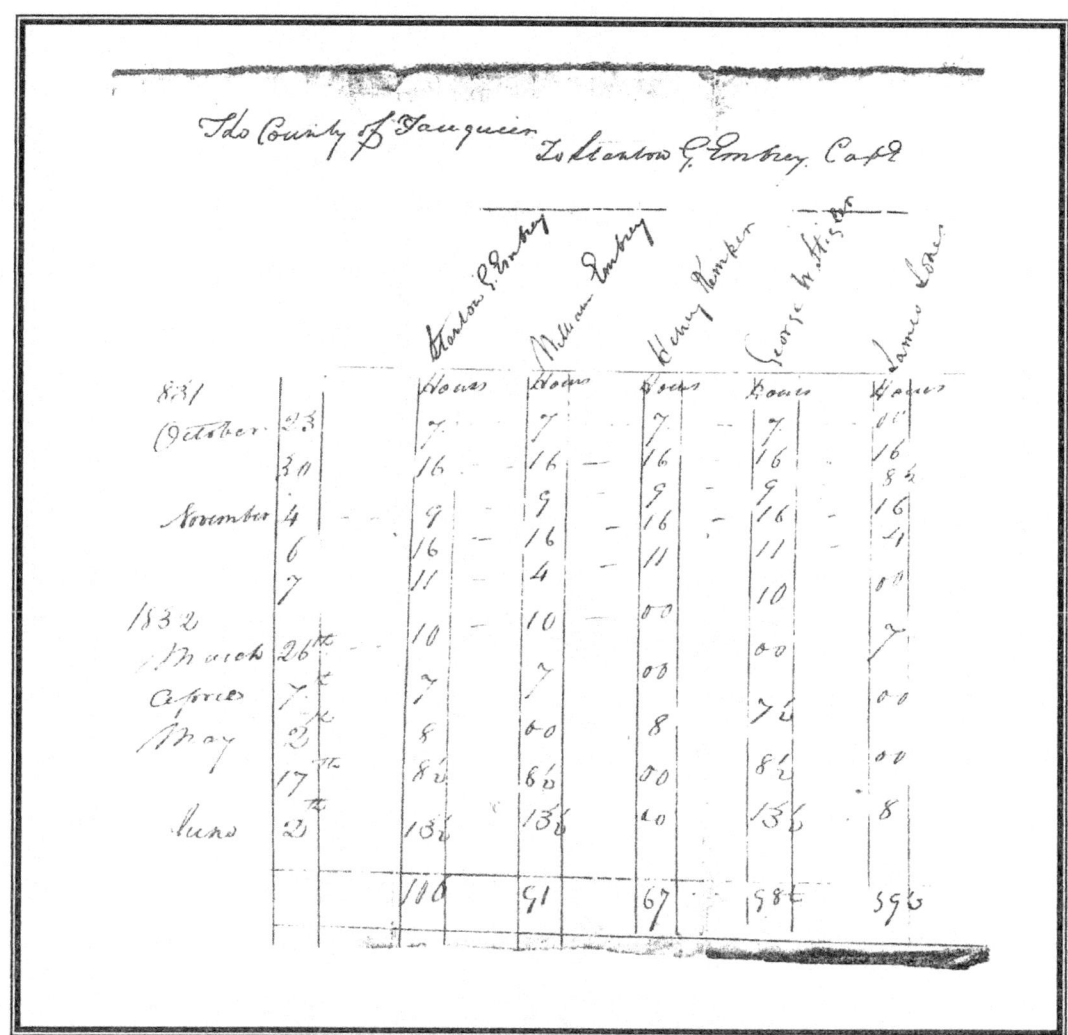

Plate 21 Scanned Imaged of Free Negro/Slave 1832-021 Patroller Account from County Claims

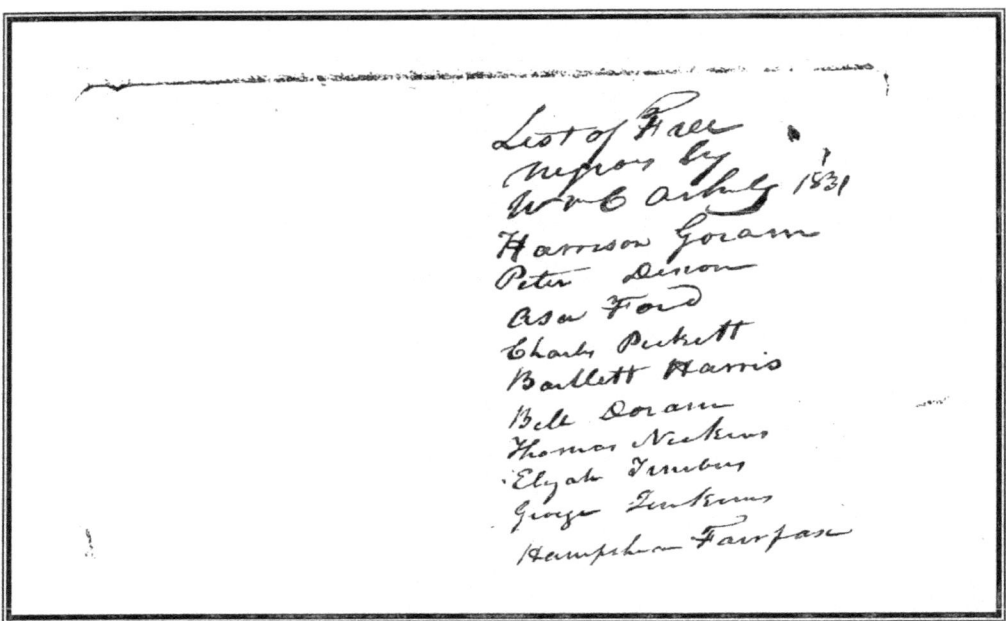

Plate 22. Free Negro/Slave 1832-037. Wm. C. Ashby's List of Free Negroes who were delinquent for 1831 taxes. In June 1832, the Court ordered these free men of color to be hired out until their taxes were paid.

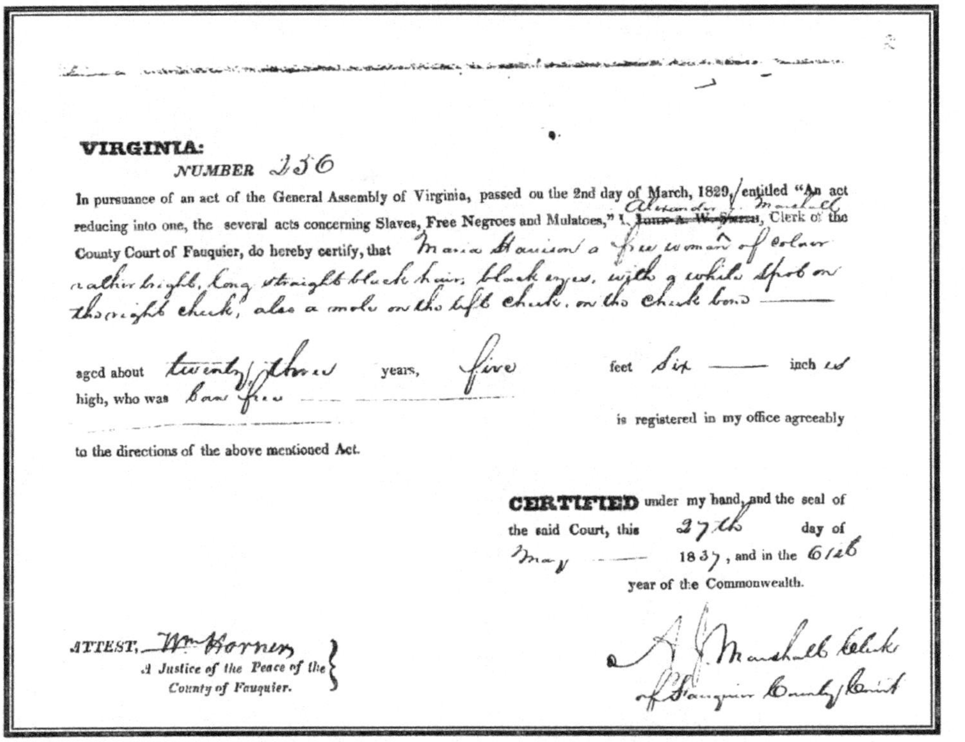

> **VIRGINIA:**
> NUMBER 256
>
> In pursuance of an act of the General Assembly of Virginia, passed on the 2nd day of March, 1829, entitled "An act reducing into one, the several acts concerning Slaves, Free Negroes and Mulatoes," I, Alexander J. Marshall, Clerk of the County Court of Fauquier, do hereby certify, that Maria Harrison a free woman of colour rather bright, long straight black hair, black eyes, with a white spot on the right cheek, also a mole on the left cheek, on the cheek bone
>
> aged about twenty three years, five feet six inches high, who was born free is registered in my office agreeably to the directions of the above mentioned Act.
>
> **CERTIFIED** under my hand, and the seal of the said Court, this 27th day of May 1837, and in the 61st year of the Commonwealth.
>
> ATTEST, Wm Horner
> A Justice of the Peace of the County of Fauquier.
>
> A. J. Marshall Clerk
> of Fauquier County Court

Plate 23. Free Negro/Slave 1837-001. Maria Harrison's May 5, 1837 Free Register.

Fauquier County, Virginia's Clerks Loose Papers: A Guide to the Records 1759-1919

> **NOTE.** This Questionnaire should be completed so far as possible with such information as [...] and returned with photographs and additional notes or letters, if available, to *Secretary, Virg[inia] [...] mission, State Capitol, Richmond, Va.*
>
> # WAR HISTORY COMMISSION
> ## State of Virginia
> ### MILITARY SERVICE RECORD
>
> Compiled by the Virginia War History Commission for a permanent record in the State Library, where it will be filed, as a memorial of the deeds of Virginia soldiers and sailors in the service of the federal, state and allied governments during American participation in the World War.
>
> Name in full: **Oliver** (family name) **William** (first name) **Frederick** (middle name)
> Date of birth: **December** (month) **8th** (day) **1894** (year)
> Place of birth: **Midland** (town) **Fauquier** (county) **Va.** (state) **U.S.A.** (country)
> Name of father: **William Frederick Oliver** Birthplace **U.S.A.** (country)
> Maiden name of mother: **Bettie Whitney** Birthplace **U.S.A.** (country)
> Are you White, Colored, Indian or Mongolian: **Colored**
>
> Citizen **Yes** (yes or no) Voter **Yes** (yes or no) Church _____ (denomination)
> Married **No** , 1____ at _____
> To _____ (maiden name) Born 1____ at _____
> Children _____ (name) Born 1____ at _____
> _____ Born 1____ at _____
> _____ Born 1____ at _____
>
> Fraternal Orders _____
> College Fraternities _____
> Previous military service or training _____
>
> Education (Preparatory) _____ (College) _____
> (University) _____ (Degrees) _____
> Occupation before entry into the service: **Rigger**
> ; employer **Bethlehem Steel Co.**
> Residence before entry into the service: **819 J St.** (street number) **Sparrows point** (town) **Baltimore** (county)
> Present home address: **1005 N. Chapel St.** (street number) **Baltimore** (town) _____ (county) **Maryland** (state)

Plate 24. 1920-025. Scanned Image of page 1 of William Frederick Oliver's World War 1 Military Service Record including attached photograph.

Fauquier County, Virginia's Clerks Loose Papers: A Guide to the Records 1759-1919
CHAPTER 7
LAND RECORDS AND DISPUTES

1. Overview

The Land records in the Clerks Loose Papers include the traditional deeds, leases, assignments, agreements, divisions, trusts, bargains and sale, lease and releases, and bills of sales you find elsewhere in the court records.

These records also contain a large variety of land disputes – trespass, ejectments, writs of Replevin, breach of covenants, arrear in rent suits and unlawful detainer of land. Many of these disputes have names of historically significant persons as parties to the suits and important genealogical information within their papers.

2. Types of Records dealing with Land in Land Records

The list that follows explains representative examples of conveyances from this records series that relate to property or land.

- *Memorandum of Agreement* – An agreement is an arrangement that is accepted by all parties in the transaction. It can range from a mutual understanding to a binding obligation. Two or more persons *agree* or consent to the transmission of some property, right, or benefit, with the view of contracting an obligation or a mutual obligation. The term is often synonymous with a "contract".

  There are many Agreements found in the Clerks Loose Papers. Some deal with the purchase and sale of land. Others deal with services to be provided by skilled artisans – for example, an agreement between a carpenter and a house owner for work to be done on the house.

- *Conveyances and Deeds* – A conveyance is the actual transfer of the title to property from one person to another by an instrument in writing that is signed and sealed by the grantor. Conveyances of title include deeds of gift, grants, assignments of leases, leases, bills of sale, mortgages and trusts.

  Deeds are written, signed and seal instruments that convey land, personal or heritable property and/or dwellings from one person to another. These types of conveyances are found in the Land Records of the Clerks Loose Papers:

  - *Bargain and Sale* -- This is a term associated with Deeds. It is abbreviated "B & S". It is simply the conveyance of property to someone in exchange for money, or its equivalent.

  - *Bill of Sale* – A Bill of Sale is a written agreement whereby one person transfers his rights and interest in goods, and /or personal property to someone else. It is done under seal. It is often abbreviated as "B of S".

  - *Deed of Gift* – These were conveyances given for "natural love and affection" toward a family member and usually dealt with personal property like slaves or with part of a landed estate.

  - *Deed of Lease and Release*—This eighteenth century practice transferred a lease into a straight deed or indenture. The lease usually contained a nominal rent (like a peppercorn) and was immediately followed by a second conveyance, the Deed of Release. The Deed of Release contains the phrase "for transferring uses into possession".

  - *Deed of Release* – A deed of release releases property from a trust or a mortgage. It serves to divest the trustee or mortgagor of the title and to return it to the original owner.

- - Deed of Trust – A deed of trust is similar to a mortgage since it places the title of the property in the hands of trustees until the grantor has fulfilled the conditions of the trust. Property may be placed in a trustee's hands to secure the payment of a debt, for example. If the debt is not paid according to the trust, the conditions of the trust may allow the trustee to sell the property and use the proceeds to pay the debt.
  - Leases for Lives – A lease for 3 lives is the usual lease found in the Land Records of the Clerks Loose papers. Richard Henry Lee, Thomas Lord Fairfax, George Washington and other notable Virginians leased their lands in Fauquier to tenants in exchange for rent.
- Covenants – A covenant is an agreement between two or more persons to do or not do something. If the agreement is a formal one and is signed and sealed, it has legal validity. If the terms within the agreement are not met or if something else is done entirely, the injured party may sue the offending party in a court of law for Breach of Covenant.
- Proprietary Grants or Deeds – There are quite a few proprietary grants and proprietary deeds from Thomas Lord Fairfax or his agents to early settlers of Fauquier County. The Clerks Loose Papers even contain a 1716/17 proprietary grant from Catharine, Lady Culpeper. This is our earliest land record in the Clerks Loose Papers.

This list explains examples of the types of **suits** or **disputes** involving land or property:

- Breaches – A *Breach* occurs when someone *breaks* or violates a law, obligation, engagement or duty. It exists when a party fails to carry out the terms, promises or conditions of a contract.
  - Breach of the Close/ Trespass of the Close – This is an unlawful entry on someone's soil, land or enclosed area called a close. A close was originally an enclosed area around a cathedral or the narrow passageway from a street to a court and the houses therein.
    - In a legal sense, in the eighteenth and nineteenth century, a close was a portion of land enclosed by a hedge, fence or other physical enclosure. A close could be limited by an invisible or imaginary enclosed boundary delineated by a plaintiff's metes and bounds in his deed.
    - A *breach* or "invasion" of the close could bring about a law action by the landowner, who would sue, asking for damages for unlawful entry by the defendant. There are Trespass and Breach of the Close suits through out the Land causes.
  - Breach of Contract – A breach of Contract occurs when one of the parties in the contract fails to perform one or any of the duties specified in the agreement. The land causes contain suits over breaches in contracts.
  - Breach of Covenant – A *covenant* is any agreement or contract. *Breach of Covenant* is the non-performance of any arrangement agreed upon in the contract. It could also refer to doing something in the covenant that has **not** been agreed upon.
- Action or Declaration in Ejectment – Ejectment was a law action to regain possession of land; the complainant could also sue for damages against the person who unlawfully detained its possession. Most of the suits in the Land Disputes of the Clerks Loose Papers appear to involve two people claiming title to the same piece of land. Ejectments could also be filed by leasors seeking to evict tenants for non-payment of rent. John and James Marshall continually attempted to evict tenants in the Manor of Leeds who were in arrears of their rent or who had moved away and assigned their lease to another party.

- The suits normally involved fictitious names for both parties, especially if the real names could not be ascertained. There were many fictitious names used to denote the complainant and defendant in these actions. *Aminadab Seekright*, as the complainant, was the most common name used as the fictional lessee in a supposed lease. If or when the real person's name was discovered, Aminadab's name was replaced by that person as the complainant. *Ferdinand Dreadnought* was the fictitious name most often used as the defendant. He served as the fabricated representative for the other "owner" of the land in question.

  - An Ejectment occurred when Aminadab Seekright, as the lessee, in a lease for a term of years or lives from the person claiming title was *ejected*, or driven off the lease by another lessor, represented by Ferdinando Dreadnought.

  - The plaintiff must first establish a right to possession in himself and then must show that the defendant was in wrongful possession. Thus, the rightful title to the land had to be established in order to settle the suit, if recovery of the land was to be made. So establishing the title, though nominally incidental to the recovery of the land, in reality, became the object of the action. Hence, an action of ejectment became the usual method for trying the title to land.

  - Other fictitious names used as parties that identify these suits as Actions in Ejectment are "Sampson Holdfast," "Timothy Cleartitle," " Roger Basetitle," " Timothy Trespass," " Symon Wronghead," " Timothy Turnout," " Thomas Thrustout," " Timothy Dreadnought," "John Turff," " Timothy Twigg," and "Peter Goodtitle"

- *Fairfax and Marshall suits for back rent* – Back rent suits by Thomas Lord Fairfax and his successors in the Manor of Leeds fill the Land Disputes in the Clerks Loose Papers. George Washington and Martha Washington also attempted to collect their rents on lands in Fauquier leased by them either for a term of years or for lives.

    John Marshall and James Marshall, when they became the owners of the Manor of Leeds, first attempted to collect the back rents. When those attempts failed, James Marshall moved on to instituting actions of ejectments against the offending lessees. There is a one complete box dedicated to the Marshall Ejectment causes in the Clerks Loose Papers.

- *Replevin* – Replevin is an action at law to recover goods or property wrongfully taken or detained.

  - *A Writ of Replevin* is the legal instrument issued by a court of law to recover the goods or property. Suits In Replevin are found through out the Land Records and Disputes..

- *Unlawful Detainer of land* – Landowners often sued tenants, especially if the tenant owed back rent, for the recovery of the land "unlawfully detained" by the occupant. "Unlawful detainer" differs from an Ejectment in that the landowner did not evict the tenant before the suit is brought. He waited for the decision of the court before taking action.

- *Writs of Right* – A writ of right was issued by the court to a party seeking to recover land that he owned which was in the actual possession of someone else. These writs were often the result, in favor of a plaintiff, of a suit for unlawful detainer.

- *Plats & Surveys* – Plats and Surveys were found in suits where two parties contested the ownership of the same piece of land. They could also be found as exhibits in Trespass, Breach of the Close and Ejectment cases. The Plat and Survey of Augustine Washington's Deep Run tract was found in just such a case in 1799 – the Land 1799-011 Joseph Hickerson v. Samuel Blackwell Trespass suit.

Fauquier County, Virginia's Clerks Loose Papers: A Guide to the Records 1759-1919

3. Finding your way around Land Records and Disputes

Series Title: Land Records and Disputes
Color Code: Royal Blue Dots on Boxes

Series Dates: 1723-001 to 1873-001
Series Extent: 21 Boxes. *8 linear feet.*
   Series includes
      12 Boxes - Land Records and Disputes
      5 Boxes - Clerks Copies of Deeds
      3 Boxes - Processioner Lists
      1 Box - Marshall Ejectment Suits from the Superior Court Papers
Series Arrangement: Filed by Year.
Series Finding Aids:
   Land Disputes: Plaintiff and Defendant Indices. No Cross Index.
   Land Records and Clerk's Copies: Grantor and Grantee Indices.
   Processioner Lists: An inventory.

Boxes 1-12 contain Land Disputes, Deeds, Grants and Leases in the Clerks Loose Papers. Included in these records are copies of 33 Fairfax Leases found in a drawer marked "Recorded Deeds". The originals are found in Oversize Records.

Boxes 13-15 are Processioner Books, Returns and Lists from the Clerks Loose Papers. **NOTE:** At the time of indexing the land records, Box 13, with the county's earliest Processioner lists, was discovered to be missing from the collection .

Boxes 16-20 are Clerk's Copies of Deeds, Leases and other conveyances found in Drawers labeled "Unrecorded Deeds"

Box 21 contains the Marshall Ejectment Suits found in the Superior Court papers.

4. The Marshall Ejectment Suits

Included in the Land Records and Disputes series is a box of ejectment suits filed by John and James Marshall and their successors over the title of leases in the Manor of Leeds, which John and his brother and others purchased from Lord Fairfax.

While these ejectments were part of the Circuit Superior Records in the vault and not, strictly speaking, in the Clerks Loose Papers, they are included here for continuity and for historical interest.

Fauquier County, Virginia's Clerks Loose Papers: A Guide to the Records 1759-1919

5. The Folders for Land Records (Deeds, Leases, Trusts, etc.)

The Deeds, Leases and Trusts in this record series are all found in white folders in the boxes labeled Land Records. Each white folder will look something like this.

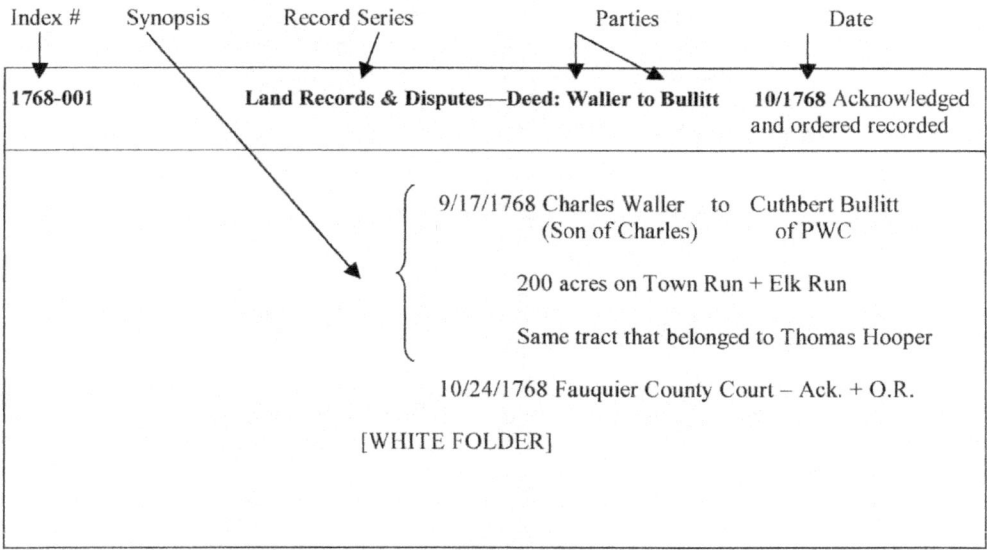

6. The folders for Land Disputes: Small Suits

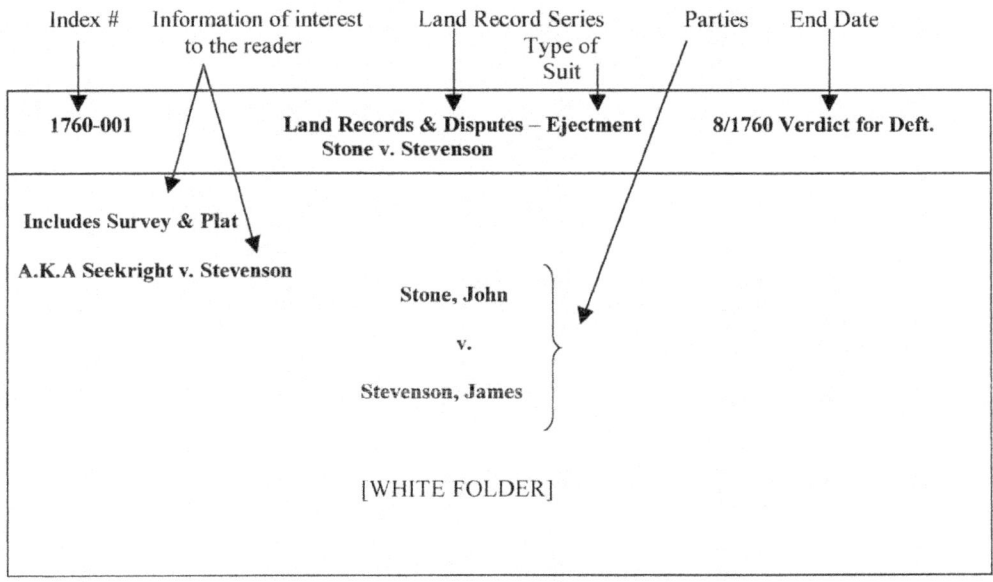

Small suits (those that have only a few records) are filed in white folders and look like the folder shown on page 61. The suits are arranged by their index number.

The suits in these folders are **always** arranged inside the folder in the following manner:
1) The Bill of Complaint, if present is **always** the first record in the suit papers.
2) The response of the defendant, if present, will **always** be the next record in the papers.
3) Summons, subpoenas, bonds and the like are filed next. These are part of the Court "process" – records designed to get the defendant and/or witnesses into court.
4) Any exhibit filed with the suit papers will come next – Deeds, Leases, Wills, Plats & Surveys.
5) Finally, depositions, if present, will close out the suit papers.

Many of the disputes in these records concern rent suits by Lord Fairfax or his executors. These suits may only contain one or two records, like a summons or a bond.

7. The Folders in Land Disputes: Large Suits

Larger suits are filed in white folders within brown folders. The brown foldered suits are arranged just like the small suit folders. There is *a definite order to the way these records are found.*

The first folder will **always** contain the Bill of Complaint, if present. In the sample below, containing the 1767-003 Trespass suit of Wm. Duling as the Plaintiff v. Edward Ball and others as the Defendants, the first folder contained the court process because the bill of complaint was no longer extant. The exhibits then followed, each in their own separate white folder. There were no depositions in this suit.

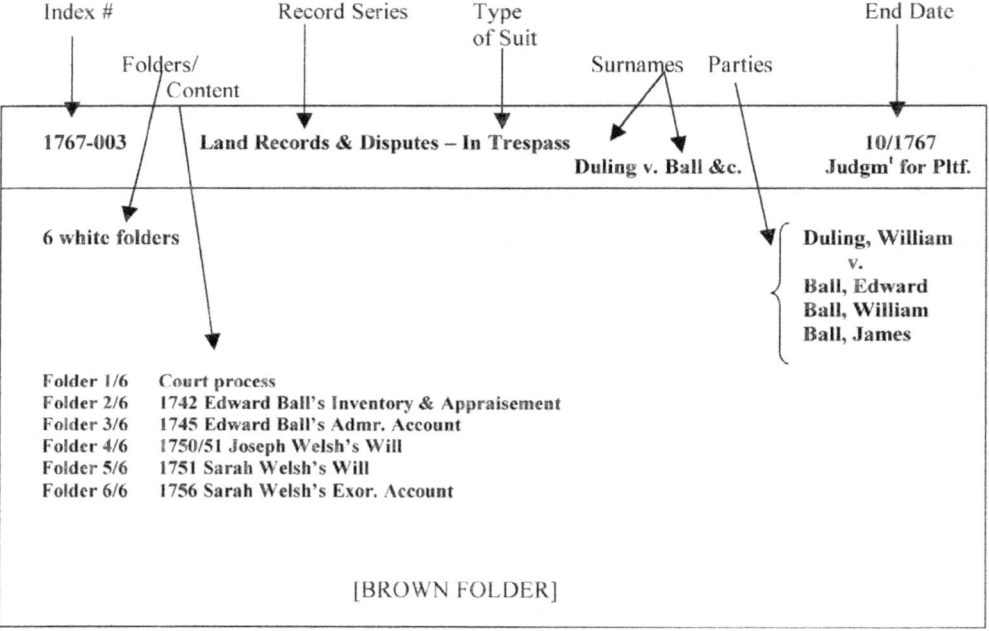

If you have further questions about the arrangement of these suits, see Chapter 4 Chancery, section 4. Land disputes are set up the same way as the chancery suits.

7. The Land Disputes Indices

The records in these boxes contain disputes and deeds, leases, trusts and other conveyances. There are three separate indices associated with these records. There is a Land Disputes index, for plaintiffs and defendants; a Land Record Index and a Clerk's Copies of Deeds Index for grantors and grantees.

8. The Land Records Index – Grantor and Grantee Index

There are two indices associated with Deeds: One index has to do with conveyances found in this record series. The other indexes Clerks Copies of any conveyance that was needed in other suits. These records included any conveyance or transfer of land or property from one party to another. In both indices, the computerized Grantor Index resembles the sample index found in Figure 13 below, all taken from the Land Records (indicated by "LR" in sample below). The Index for Clerks Copies is identical to the index for Recorded Deeds. The printed version of the Land Records index illustrated below may differ slightly due to page size and space considerations.

Index #	Grantor	to	Grantee	Instrument	Date	Synopsis
LR 1830-007	Adams, Sarah	to	Adams, Thompson	B&S	11/1830	for 60 acres of SW Quarter, Section #1, Township #3, Range #10 in Licking Co. OH
LR 1804-007	Arnold, Humphrey	to	Hitch, Nathan	B&S	1804	tract in Leeds Manor. Part of the tract that was conveyed by Isaac Arnold to Humphrey Arnold and held by lease under Denny Fairfax.
LR 1796-004	Catlett, Peter	to	Rust, Samuel	Lease Assignment	1797	Lease assignment for terms in the original Lease from Peter Glascock for lives of Peter and Susan Catlett. Tract is in in Fauquier Co. near Ashby's Gap.
LR1810-016	Elliott, Elisabeth	to	Dawson, Benjamin	Trust	1810	for hire of Peter Knight until $237.00 is raised. After money is obtained, Dawson is to emancipate Knight from slavery forever.

Figure 13. Some examples of names and conveyances found in the Grantor Index to Deeds in Land Records & Disputes, in the Clerks Loose Papers.

Fauquier County, Virginia's Clerks Loose Papers: A Guide to the Records 1759-1919

The computerized Grantee Index for Deeds in this records series is similar to the sample index in Figure 14 below. The printed version of the Grantee Index may vary slightly due to page size and space considerations.

Index #	Grantee	from	Grantor	Instrument	Date	Synopsis
LR 1725-001	Chambers, Joseph	from	Fairfax, Lord Thomas	Proprietary Grant	1735	424 acre tract in King George Co. on the Upper Great Run.
LR 1796-002	Edmonds, Elias	from	Buckner, Richard & wife Judith of Caroline Co, VA.	B&S	1796	for 600 acres in Fauquier Co. This is the same tract devised by Simon Miller to Judith Buckner, wife of Richard Buckner.
LR 1752-001	Hay, Thomas	from	Judd Isaac	Plat & Survey	Undated	Part of a patent for 1,798 acre Proprietary Grant to Isaac Judd.
LR 1820-018	Marr, Daniel	from	Yeatman, Henry L.	Trust	1820	for lot in town of Warrenton. This is the same lot conveyed to Yeatman in Trust by John Marr to secure debt to Samuel Fisher.
LR 1797-008	Monroe, George	from	Thornberry Samuel Jr.	Lease	1798	lease for 10 years for land beginning at Carter's Mill and the house where the late John Waller dwelt.
1801-008 LR	Rust, Peter C.	from	Catlett, Peter	Lease	1797	Lease for Lot # 40 in Paris and part of Lot #368 behind Paris. The original lease was for the lives of Joseph Glascock, Benjamin Glascock and Joseph Berry, son of Joseph Berry Sr.

Figure 14. Some examples of names and conveyances found in the Grantee Index to Deeds in Land Records & Disputes, in the Clerks Loose Papers.

9. The Land Records Index: Land Disputes

Land disputes included Trespass, Trespass and Breach of the Close, Breach of Covenant, Fairfax, Marshall and Washington suits for back rents, other back rent suits brought by other landowners, Ejectments, Replevin, Unlawful Detainer or Possession of Land and general land disputes where the parties both claimed the same parcel of land.

There is a plaintiff and a defendant index for Land Disputes found in this record series. The suit is indexed under the primary plaintiff if there were more than one.

The plaintiff index to Land Disputes on computer looks like the sample index in Figure 15 on this page. The printed version of this index may differ slightly due to page size and space considerations.

Index #	Plaintiff	v.	Defendant	Type of Suit	Synopsis
1799-002	Baker, Richard	v.	Weedon, George	Land Dispute	Plat & Survey of disputed tract on Rocky Run.
1799-012	Ball, Benjamin	v.	Thomas, James &c.	Trespass	Suit papers contain 7 deeds and 1751 Will of John Dagg of Prince William County.
1814-004	Byrne, Uriah	v.	French, George	Trespass	Suit papers include 3 copies of Plat & Survey of disputed land.
1766-003	Fairfax, Lord Thomas	v.	Duling, William	Back Rent	Suit for rent for year 1766 for a 200 acre lease in Leeds Manor.
1815-010	Henry, George	v.	Brown, Thomas	Ejectment	
1799-011	Hickerson Joseph	v.	Blackwell, Samuel	Trespass 1799 Verd. for Plaintiff	Suit papers contain Deed from George And Martha Washington to their nephew Robert Lewis; a 1726 Plat & Survey of Augustine Washington's Deep Run Tract; A copy of Augustine Washington's Will.

Figure 15. Examples of names found in the Plaintiff Index of Land Disputes in the Clerks Loose Papers.

As you can see from this small "sampling" of plaintiffs, there were a wide variety of suits over land and property in this records series.

The defendants in these Land Disputes found themselves hauled in to court for holding land unlawfully, for back rent, for ejectments, for trespass and for other disputes where they were in occupation but not ownership of the disputed land.

While the computerized version of this index looks like the sample index in Figure 16, the printed version may differ slightly due to page size and space considerations.

Index #	Defendant	Plaintiff	Type of Suit	Synopsis
1822-008	Arell, Richard	Taylor, Evan	Breach of Covenant	Breach of Covenant over Agreement for lot in Alexandria
1810-005	Bowen, James	Blackwell, Joseph	Land Dispute	Suit over Treasury Warrant #2439 for Tract of ungranted Land in Fauquier County
1824-010	Chichester, Richard McCarty	Kemper, John	Land Dispute - Trespass and Breach of the Close	
1809-010	Crump, Travis &c.	Allen, Joseph	Land Dispute - Ejectment and Trespass	
1766-002	Fairfax, Lord Thomas	Hume, Andrew	Suit for Back Rent	
1815-001	Fairfax, Denny's Exors.	Payne, Francis &c.	Suit for Back Rent	
1827-003	Grigsby, Nathaniel &c.	Chilton, Joseph	Land Dispute	Dispute over 210 acres and mill
1813-007	Lomax, John	Crump, John	Suit over use and occupation of tenement	
1811-006	Michael, Daniel	Carter, Moore F.	Writ of Right Suit	
1813-003	Price, Nalls &c.	Marshall, James M. &c.	Suit for Back Rent	
1827-007	Walden, John	Thompson, Elizabeth's Bailiff	Replevin	

Figure 16. Examples of names found in the Defendant Index of Land Disputes in the Clerks Loose Papers.

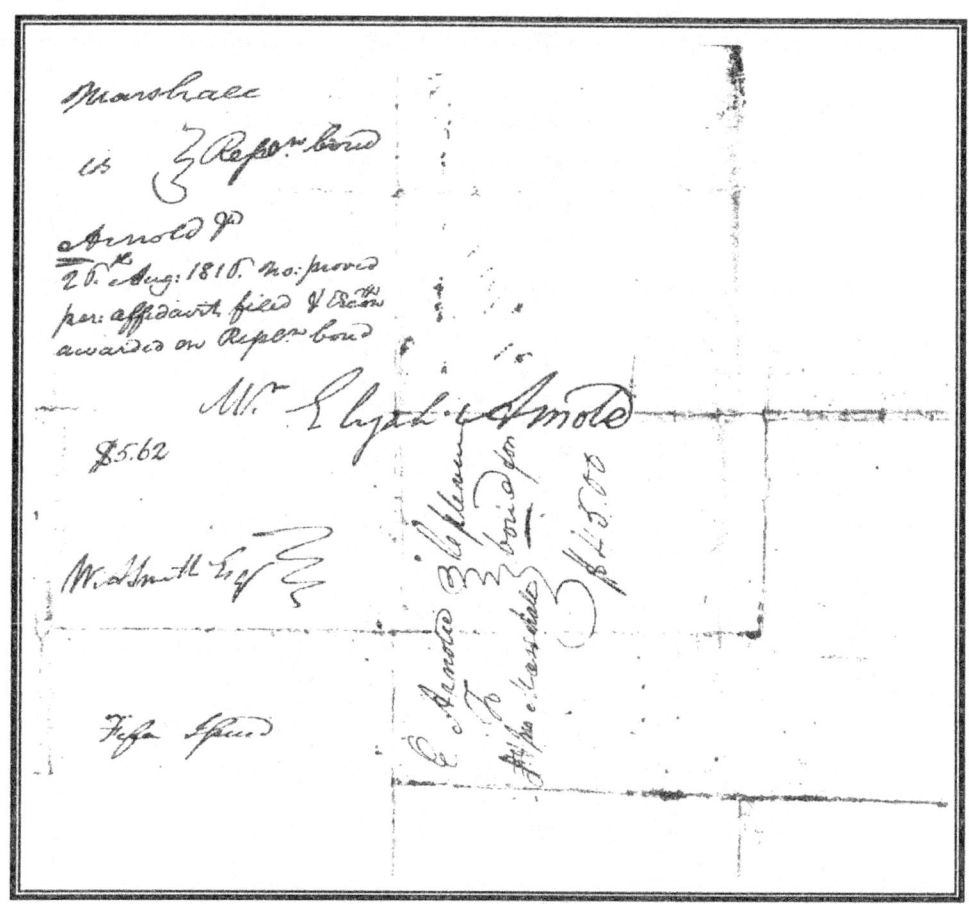

Plate 25. Scanned image of Land 1815-005 suit papers in Marshall v. Arnold, a suit to collect back rent.

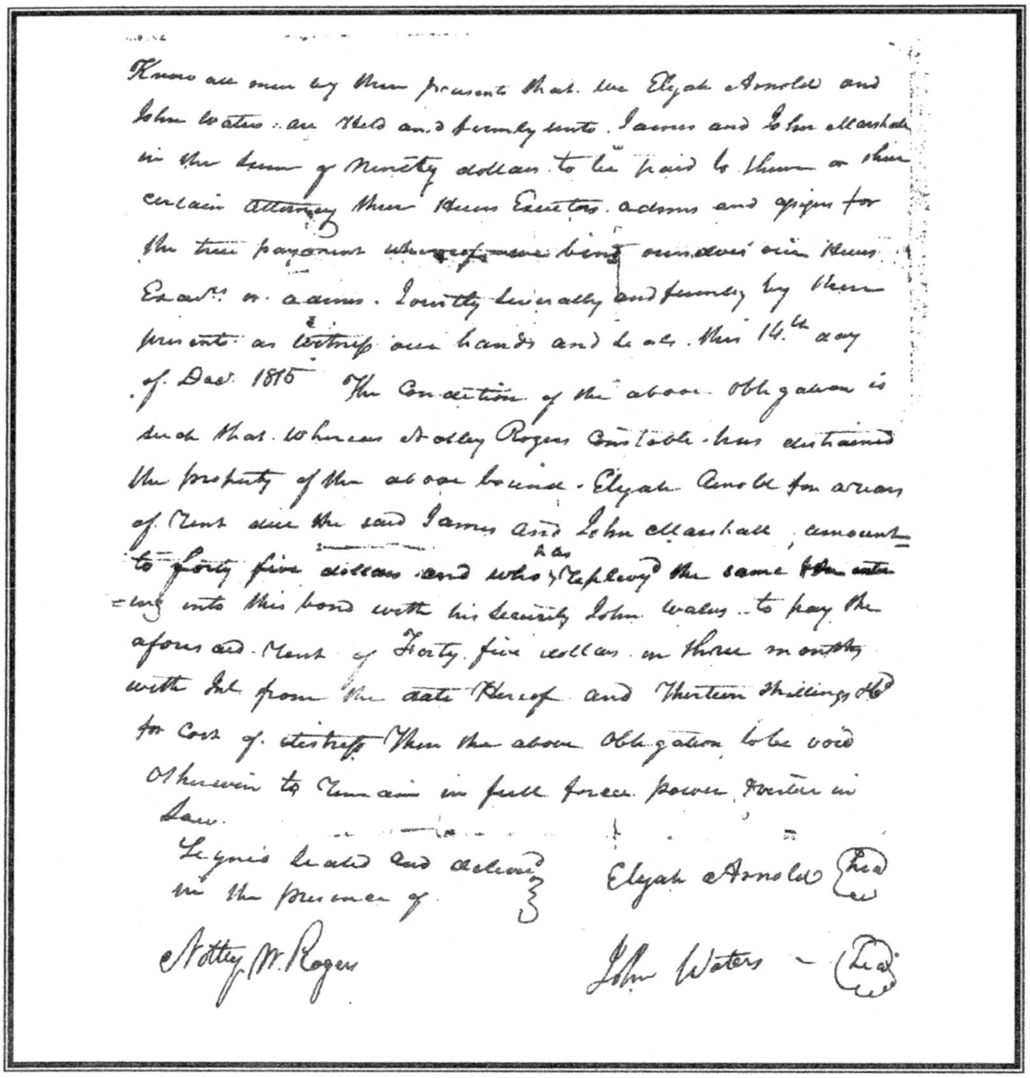

Know all men by these presents that we Elijah Arnold and
John Waters are held and firmly unto James and John Marshall
in the sum of Ninety dollars to be paid to them or their
certain attorney their Heirs Executors admrs and assigns for
the true payment whereof we bind ourselves our Heirs
Exors or admrs Jointly severally and firmly by these
presents as witness our hands and seals this 14th day
of Decr 1815 The Condition of the above obligation is
such that whereas Notley Rogers Constable has distrained
the property of the above bound Elijah Arnold for arrears
of Rent due the said James and John Marshall amounting
to forty five dollars and who has replevied the same by entering into this bond with his security John Waters to pay the
aforesaid Rent of Forty five dollars in three months
with Int from the date hereof and Thirteen shillings 6d
for Cost of distress Then the above obligation to be void
Otherwise to remain in full force power & virtue in
Law.

Signed sealed and delivered
in the presence of

Notley W. Rogers

Elijah Arnold (Seal)

John Waters (Seal)

Plate 26. Scanned image of Replevin Bond in Land 1815-005 suit papers in Marshall v. Arnold, a suit to collect back rent

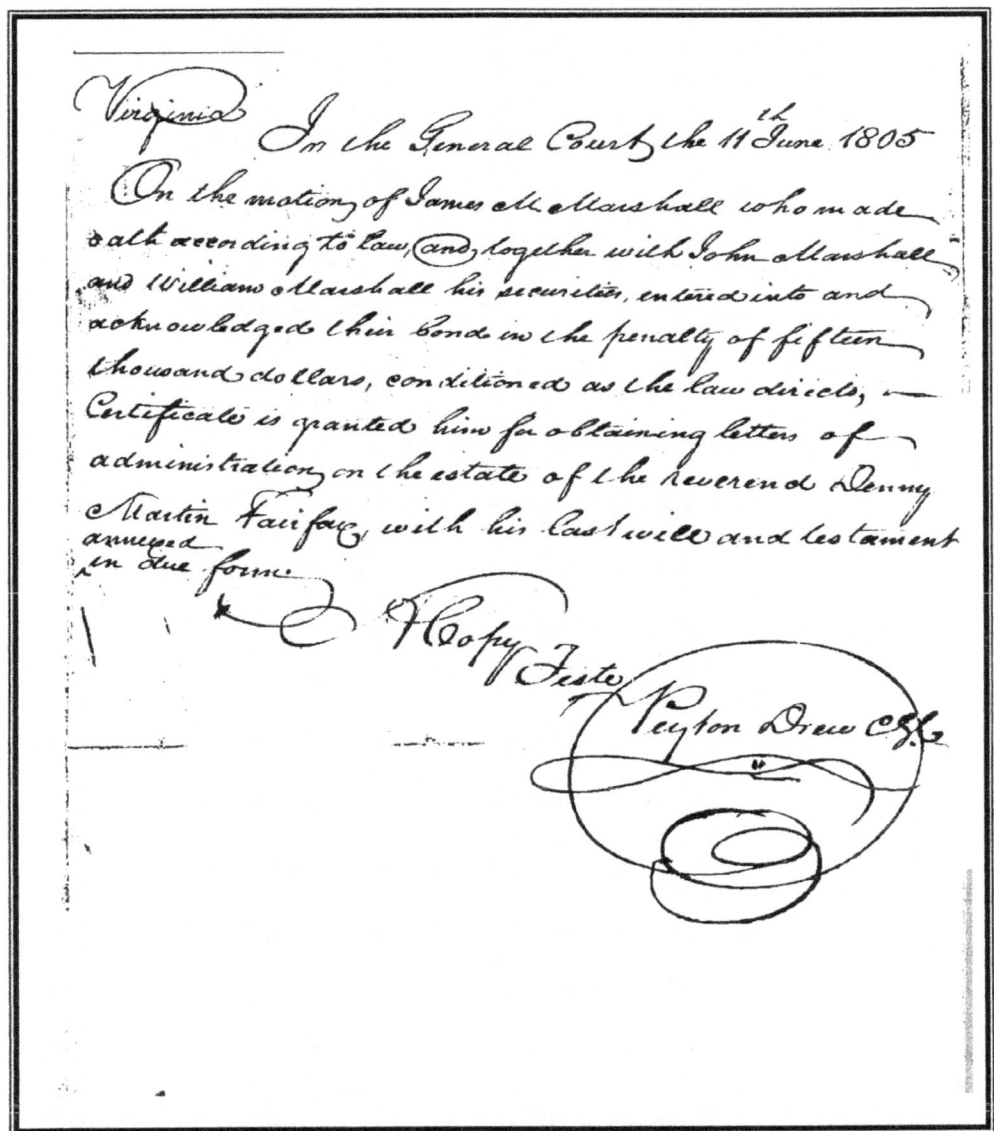

Plate 27. Scanned image of suit papers from Land 1815-001 Denny Fairfax Admrs. v. Francis Payne &c. This motion to grant Letters of Administration on Denny Fairfax's estate to James M. Marshall is found in this suit.

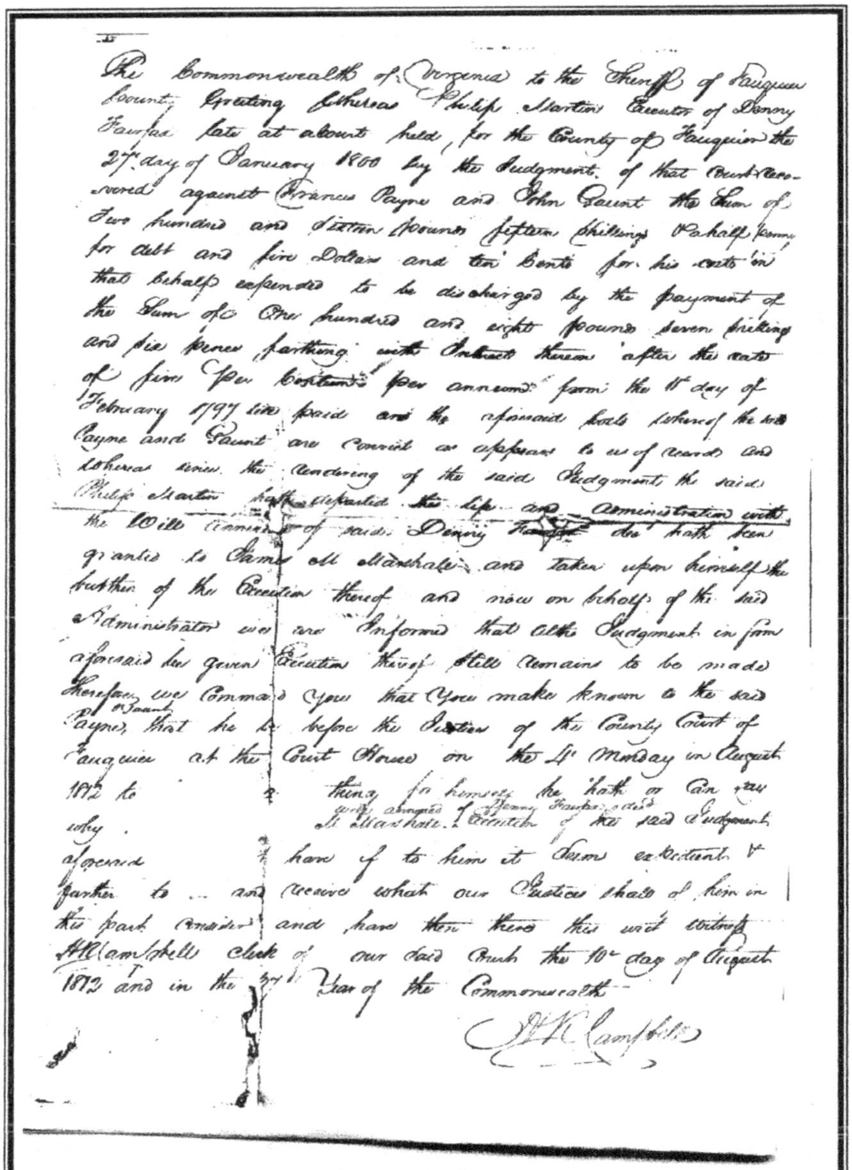
The Commonwealth of Virginia to the Sheriff of Fauquier County Greeting Whereas Philip Martin Executor of Denny Fairfax late at a Court held for the County of Fauquier the 27th day of January 1800 by the Judgment of that Court recovered against Francis Payne and John Blount the Sum of Two hundred and Sixteen pounds fifteen Shillings & a half penny for debt and five Dollars and ten Cents for his costs in that behalf expended to be discharged by the payment of the Sum of One hundred and eight pounds seven shilling and six pence farthing with Interest thereon after the rate of five per centum per annum from the 1st day of February 1797 till paid and the aforesaid costs whereof the said Payne and Blount are convict as appears to us of record and whereas since the rendering of the said Judgment the said Philip Martin hath departed this life and administration with the Will annexed of said Denny Fairfax dec'd hath been granted to James M Marshall and taken upon himself the burthen of the Execution thereof and now on behalf of the said administrator we are Informed that altho Judgment in form aforesaid be given Execution thereof still remains to be made Therefore we Command you that you make known to the said Payne & Blount that he be before the Justices of the County Court of Fauquier at the Court House on the 4th Monday in August 1812 to [illegible] thing for himself he hath or can say why [illegible] J. M. Marshall Executor of the said Judgment aforesaid [illegible] have of to him it seems expedient & further to [illegible] and receive what our Justices shall [illegible] him in this part consider and have then there this writ Witness H. Campbell clerk of our said Court the 10th day of August 1812 and in the 37th Year of the Commonwealth

H Campbell

Plate 28. Scanned Image of the Court's opinion, dated 8/10/1812, in Land Records & Disputes 1815-001, Denny Fairfax's Exor. v. Francis Payne &c.

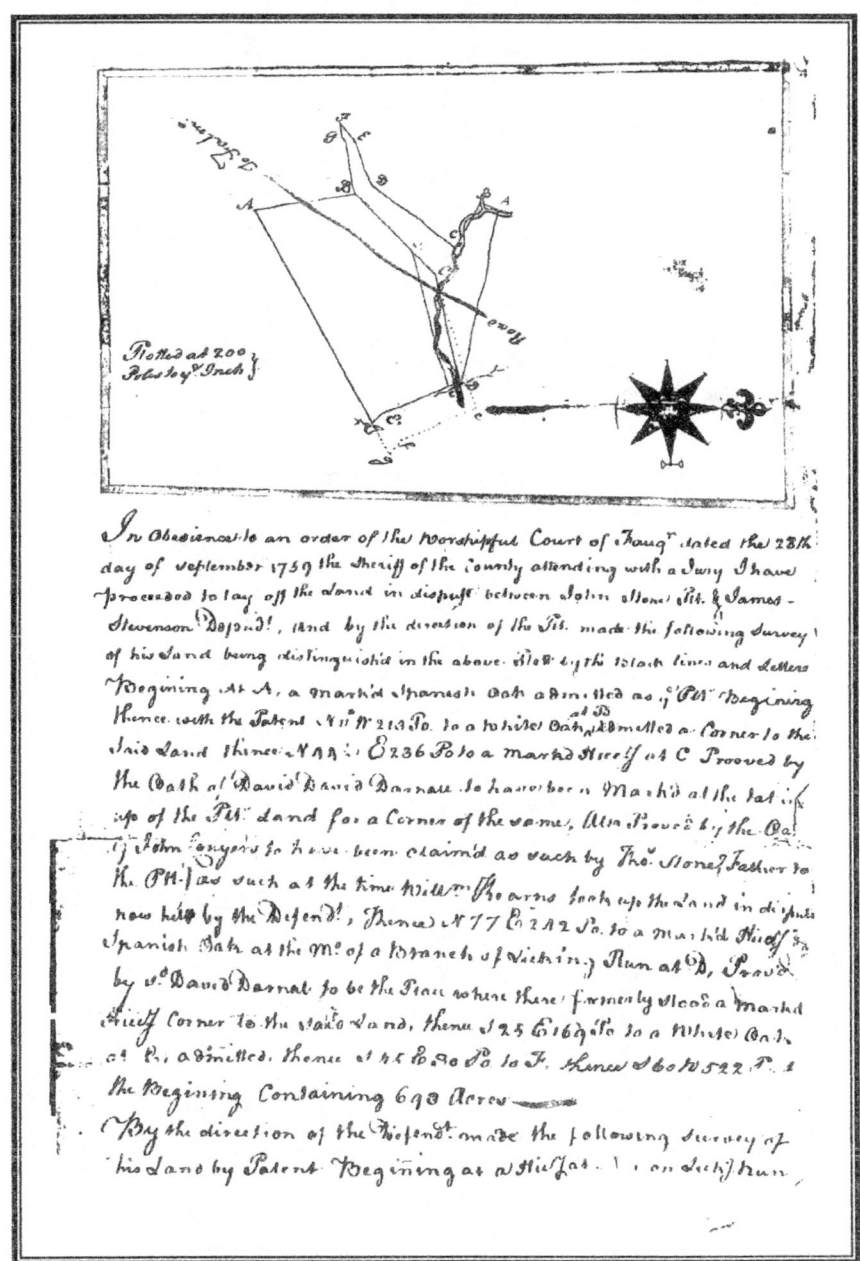

Plate 29. Scanned Image of Plat and page 1 of the Survey of Land Dispute 1760-001 John Stone v. James Stevenson. In Ejectment.

> ## Instructions for serving the ejectment
>
> THE sheriff or any other person may serve it. He ought to deliver a copy of the declaration and notice to the defendant, if possible on the land itself. He ought to inform the defendant of the purport of it at the same time, according to what he is to swear to before the magistrate. This being done, let the person who delivered the copy of the declaration and notice to the defendant, go before some justice of the peace for his county, and make oath according to the affidavit annexed thereto. Let the magistrate fill up the blanks and return it to the plaintiff. Then let the plaintiff send this very paper to me or the clerk of the general court by some safe hand without delay.
>
> EDMUND RANDOLPH.

Plate 30. Instructions for "Serving the Ejectment."
From Land Records and Disputes 1790-007 Withers v. Jett. In Ejectment.

Plate 31. Scanned Image from Land Records 1801-007.
Henry Hooe's Request for record search for land devised in a forged Will.

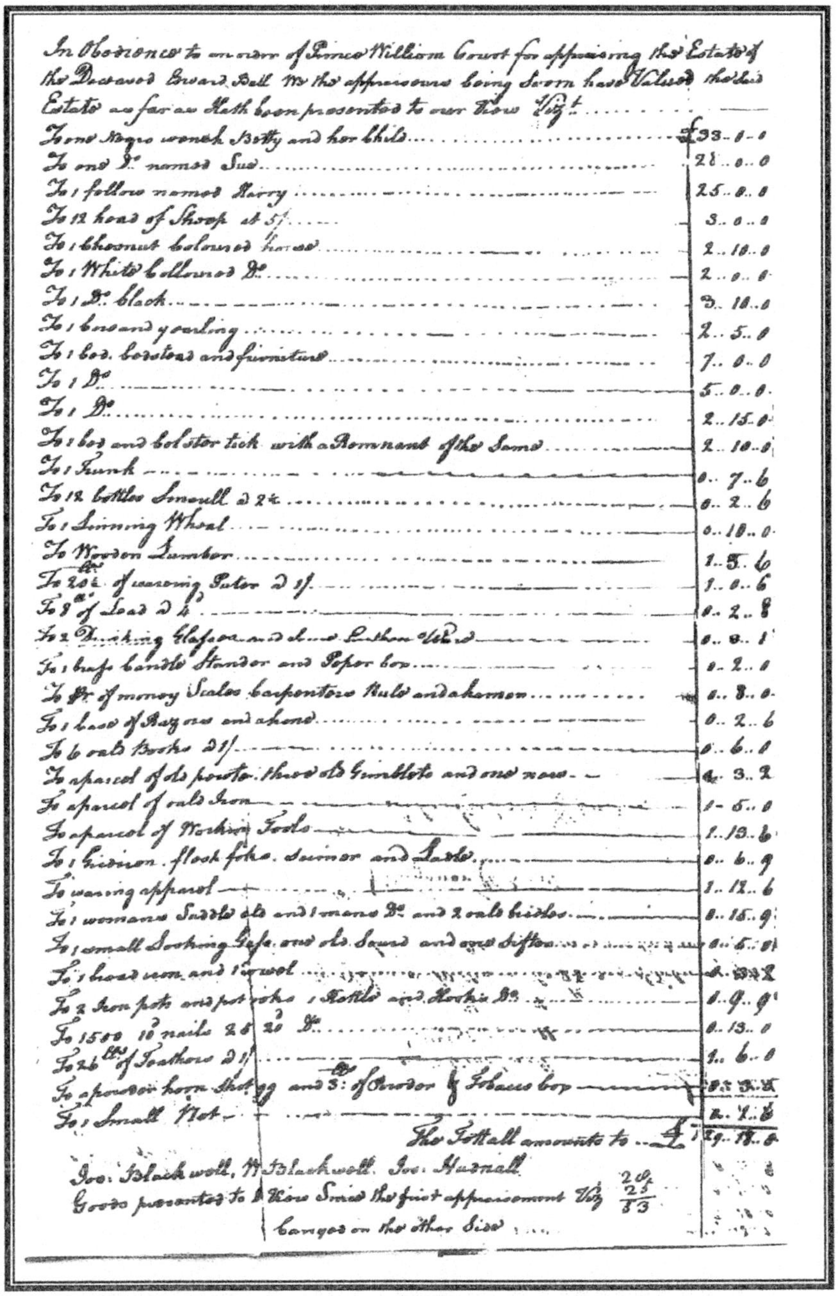

In Obedience to an order of Prince William Court for appraising the Estate of the Deceased Edward Ball We the appraisers being Sworn have Valued the said Estate as far as Hath been presented to our View Viz^t.

To one Negro wench Betty and her Child	£33..0..0
To one D^o named Sue	28..0..0
To 1 fellow named Harry	25..0..0
To 12 head of Sheep at 5/	3..0..0
To 1 Chesnut Coloured horse	2..10..0
To 1 White Collored D^o	2..0..0
To 1 D^o Black	3..10..0
To 1 Cow and yearling	2..5..0
To 1 bed. bedstead and furniture	7..0..0
To 1 D^o	5..0..0
To 1 D^o	2..15..0
To 1 bed and bolster tick with a Remnant of the Same	2..10..0
To 1 Trunk	0..7..6
To 12 bottles Snuff @ 2^d	0..2..6
To 1 Spinning Wheel	0..10..0
To Wooden Lumber	1..5..6
To 20^lb of wearing Pewter @ 1/	1..0..6
To 8^lb of Lead @ 4^d	0..2..8
To 2 Drinking Glasses and [illegible]	0..3..1
To 1 brass Candle Stander and Pepper box	0..2..0
To P^r of money Scales Carpenters Rule and a hammer	0..8..0
To 1 Case of Razors and a hone	0..2..6
To 6 old Books @ 1/	0..6..0
To a parcel of old pewter. three old Gimblets and one new	4..3..2
To a parcel of old Iron	1..5..0
To a parcel of Working Tools	1..13..6
To 1 Gridiron. flesh forks. skimmer and Ladle	0..6..9
To wearing apparel	1..12..6
To 1 womans Saddle old and 1 mans D^o and 2 old bridles	0..15..9
To 1 small Looking Glass. one old Sound and one Sifter	0..5..0
To 1 bread [illegible] and 1 trowel	[illegible]
To 2 Iron pots and pot racks 1 Kettle and Hooks D^o	1..9..9
To 1500 10^d nails 25 20^d D^o	0..13..0
To 26^lbs of Feathers @ 1/	1..6..0
To a powder horn shot bag and 3^lb of Powder & Tobacco box	[illegible]
To 1 Small Pot	[illegible]
The Tottall amounts to £	1[illegible]9..18..0

Jos: Blackwell, W. Blackwell. Jos. Hudnall

Goods presented to the Since the first appraisement Viz 20 / 25 / 53

Carryed on the other Side

Plate 32. Land Records & Disputes 1767-003 Duling v. Ball &c. Trespass. Scanned image of Inventory & Appraisement of Edward Ball in suit papers.

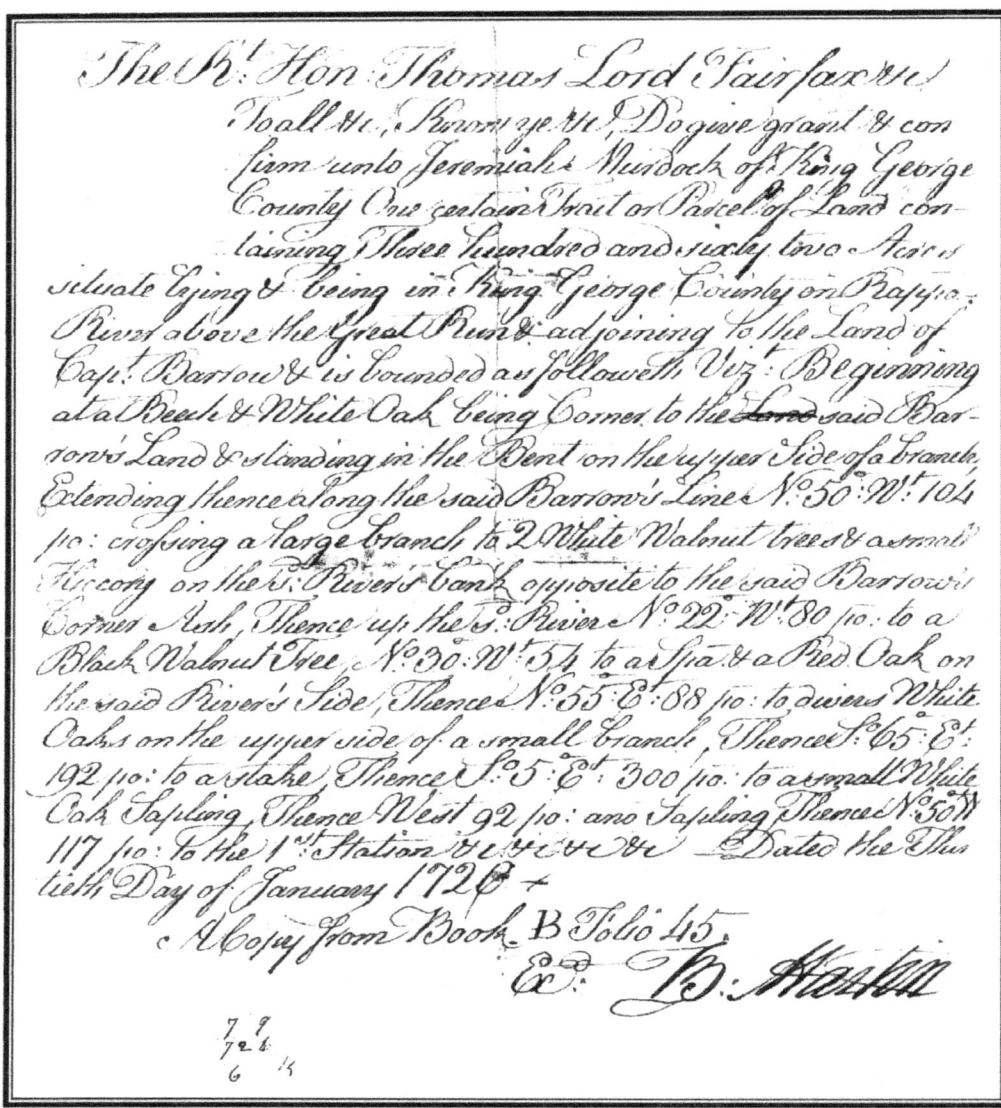

Plate 33. Land Records & Disputes 1790-007 Withers v. Jett Ejectment suit.
Scanned image of a copy of a 1726 Northern Neck Proprietary Deed from Thomas, Lord Fairfax to Jeremiah Murdock for 362 acres in King George above Great Run on the Rappahannock River.

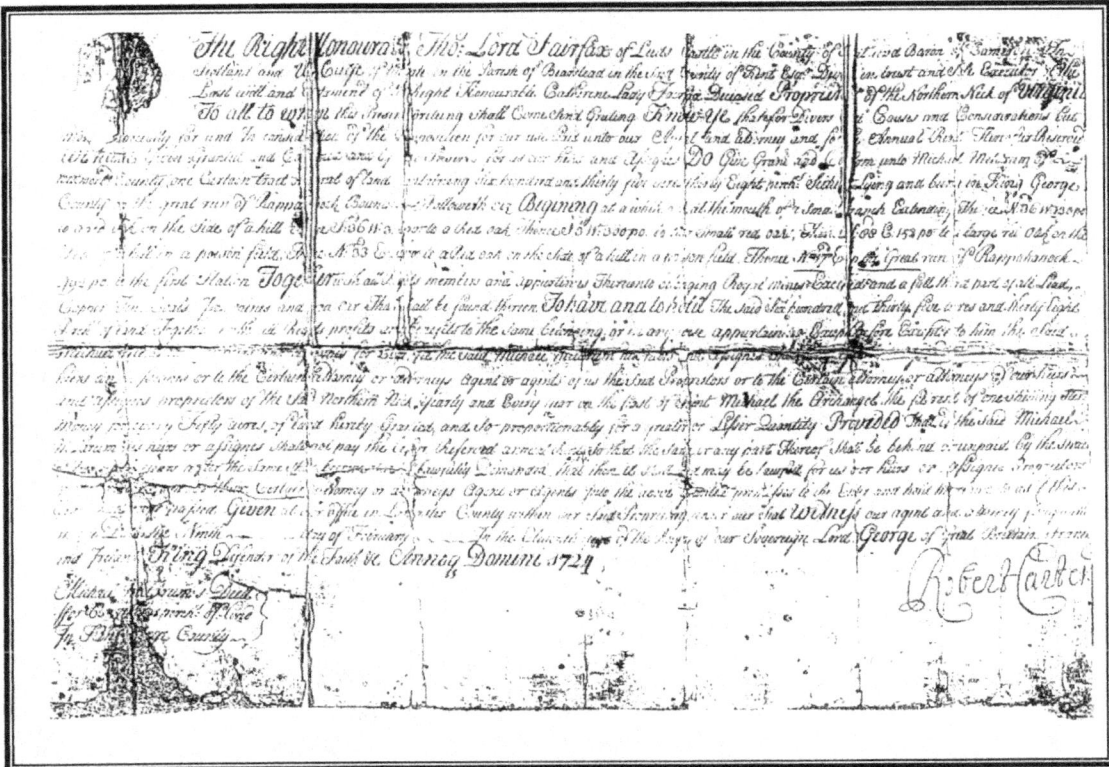

Plate 34. Land Records 1724-001. Scanned image of a Northern Neck Proprietary Grant from Robert Carter as agent for Thomas, Lord Fairfax, to Michael Meldrum for 635 acres 38 perches in King George County on the Great Run of the Rappahannock.

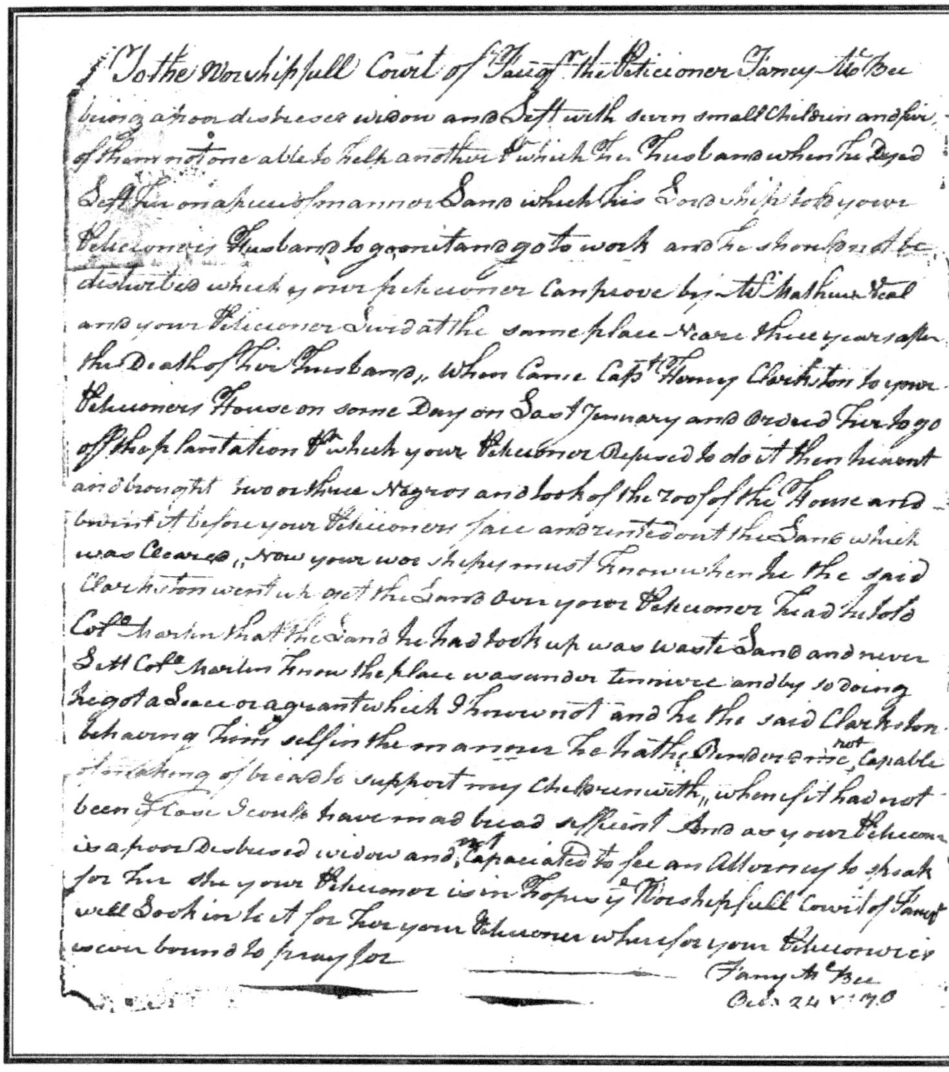

Plate 35. From Land Records & Disputes 1809-001. Fanny McBee v. Captain Henry Clarkson. Scanned image of the Declaration of Fanny McBee, "a poor distresed [sic] widow ... Left with seven small children..."

CHAPTER 8
MEDICAL RECORDS

1. Overview

This series contains Physician's Accounts, Coroner Inquests, suits involving medical accounts for Fauquier's families and Lunacy papers. These records concerned Fauquier's eighteenth and nineteenth century medical community as it related to the judicial system. Information from these records may help researchers to find previously unknown family members.

Coroner Inquests were judicial inquiries into deaths in Fauquier. Lunacy papers included petitions for commitment, discharge papers from institutions and papers relating to the estate of people adjudged by the court to be insane. These papers also dealt with people with disabilities who could not care for themselves.

Doctor's accounts, whether in arrears, for families or for the poor make for some of the most interesting reading in this record base. Oftentimes, these accounts give the family researcher a real "feel" for the times and culture of an elusive ancestor. The accounts may also give the researcher a sense of the state of medical advancements in relation to the eighteenth and nineteenth century family.

2. Finding your way around Medical Records

Series Title: Medical Records
Color Code: Black and Orange Dots on Boxes

Series Dates: 1759 to 1917
Series Extent: *3 Boxes. 312 Records. 1.25 linear feet.*
Series Arrangement: *Filed by Year*

Series Finding Aid: *An Inventory. These records have not been indexed.*

Types of Records include
   a. **Lunacy Papers**
   b. **Coroner Inquests**
   c. **Doctor's Medical Accounts**

3. A Preview of the Inventory for Medical Records
Box #1 of Medical Records contains these records extending from 1759-1833-001

Index #s	In Box #	Types of Records	Number of Folders
1759-001 to 1798-002	1	Accounts, Inquests, Suits, Lunacy	9 folders
1800-001 to 1809-004	1	Accounts, Inquests, Suits, Lunacy	17 folders
1810-001 to 1819-006	1	Accounts, Inquests, Suits, Lunacy	30 folders
1820-001 to 1826-006	1	Accounts, Inquests, Suits, Lunacy	27 folders
1826-001 to 1833-001	1	Accounts, Inquests, Suits, Lunacy	25 folders

Figure 16. Inventory of Medical Records from Box # 1: 1759-1833.

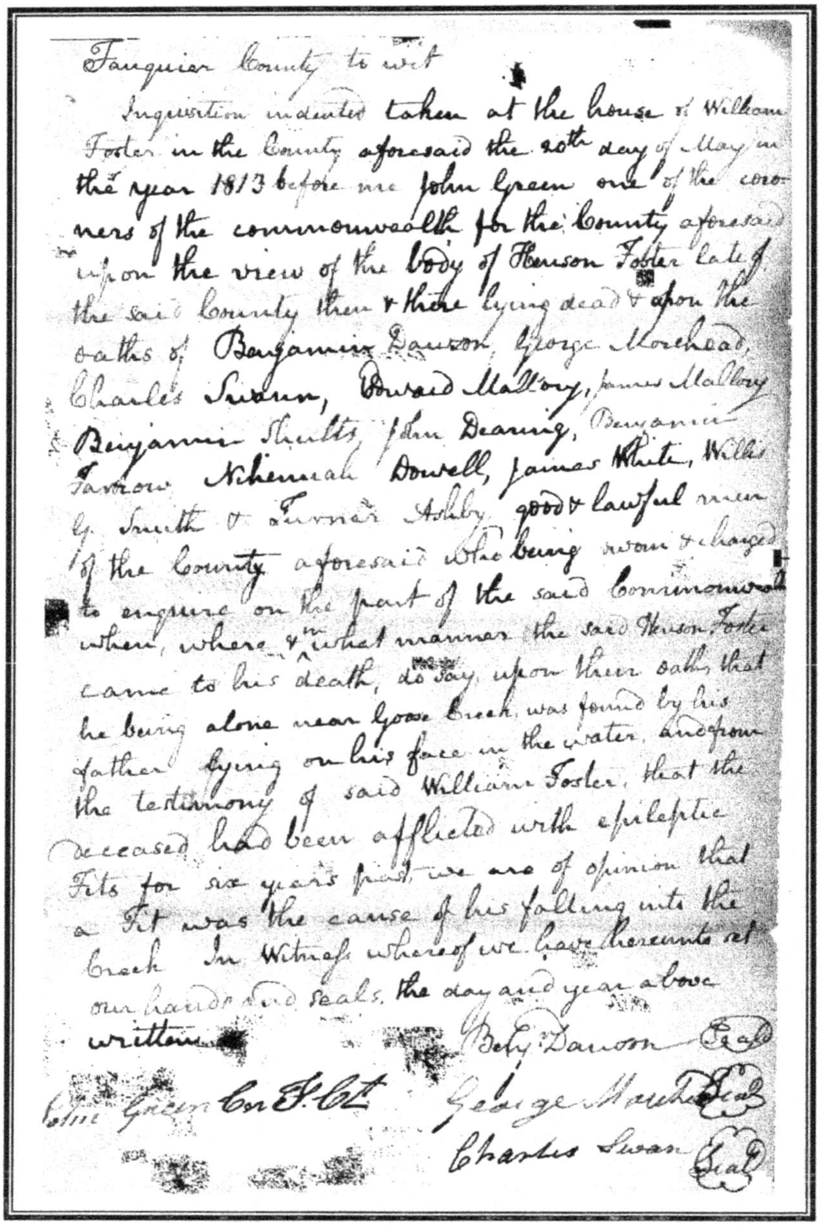

Fauquier County to wit

Inquisition indented taken at the house of William Foster in the County aforesaid the 20th day of May in the year 1813 before me John Green one of the coroners of the commonwealth for the County aforesaid upon the view of the body of Henson Foster late of the said County then & there lying dead & upon the oaths of Benjamin Dawson, George Morehead, Charles Swann, Edward Mallory, James Mallory, Benjamin Shults, John Dearing, Benjamin Farrow, Nehemiah Dowell, James White, Willis G. Smith & Turner Ashby, good & lawful men of the County aforesaid who being sworn & charged to enquire on the part of the said Commonwealth when, where, & in what manner the said Henson Foster came to his death, do say upon their oaths that he being alone near Goose Creek, was found by his father lying on his face in the water, and from the testimony of said William Foster, that the deceased had been afflicted with epileptic Fits for six years past, we are of opinion that a Fit was the cause of his falling into the Creek. In Witness whereof we have hereunto set our hands and seals, the day and year above written.

John Green Cor.F.Ct.

Benj. Dawson (Seal)
George Morehead (Seal)
Charles Swan (Seal)

Plate 36. From Medical Records 1813-004.
Scanned Image of Coroner's Inquest on Henson Foster.

CHAPTER 9
MILITARY RECORDS

1. **Overview**

   There are several different kinds of records in this series. The first two boxes contain military service records and pension declarations for the Revolutionary War and the War of 1812 as well as some public service claims and a number of militia appointments and commissions. There are even records relating to two Court Martials of local regimental officers.

   Box 3 and 4 of this series contain records relating to World War 1 and World War 2.

   In addition to these four boxes are three more boxes of Military records found in the County Court Loose Papers. These boxes contain a wealth of military information, dealing with the Revolutionary War, the War of 1812, the Civil War and World War 2. Records include Revolutionary War Pension Declarations and Heirs at Law, some War of 1812 Pension Declarations and Heirs at Law and sixty-two Confederate Veteran Pension Declaration or Disability Claims.

   Other Civil War records include ones dealing with salt agents and with County Bonds put together by an 1871 Military Committee. There are booklets of Virginia Confederate Rosters from 1909-1934; there are Confederate Pension Lists between 1913-1936 and a 1921 typescript copy of Mosby's Command Roster.

   There are Militia Muster Rolls between 1843 and 1861 and information on the World War 2 Warrenton Rifle unit.

   Many of these records were too large to fit in an Archival Box. These military records make up Box 4 of the Oversize Record series. There are 11 folders in this box which include a 1781 photostatic copy of Lord Cornwallis's parole to General Washington, 1782 Revolutionary War Militia, George W. Henson and A. J. Jones Confederate Pension Application, some 1920 Local Nominations for the World War 1 Honor Roll found in a local newspaper, and seven folders of Fauquier Registrants for World War 2.

2. **Finding your way around Military Records**
   Series Title: Military Records
   Color Code: Red and Blue Dots on Boxes

   Series Dates: 1761-001 to 1952-001
   Series Extent: 7 Boxes. *1.75 linear feet.*
   Series includes:
   4 boxes of Military Records from the Clerks Loose Papers
   3 boxes of Military Records from the County Court Loose Papers
   Series Arrangement: *Filed by Year.*

   Series Finding Aid: *Military Records Index 1761-1840. Sorted by primary party.*
   Military Records Inventory 1761-1952.

3. A Preview of the Military Records Series Index, sorted by primary party.

Index #	Name (Parties)	Type of Record	Synopsis	Family Information
1827-002	Bailey, William	Pension Declaration	Pension Declaration of Wm. Bailey, age 74; enlisted in 1777 for 3 years in Lt. Simon Morgan's Company.	wife and son, age ca. 40.
1800-001	Booker, Sarah	Pensioner List	There are 2 lists of Pensioners for 1800; Names included Fauquier County Residents.	
1822-001	Bray, Timothy	Petition for Disability	Petition to Congress for disability while in service during last war when he enlisted in Artillery. He was wounded in forearm by explosion on Independence Day. He is on Pension Rolls.	Wife (unnamed) and 2 unnamed children, under 7 years of age.
1786-001	Cunningham, Elizabeth	Petition for aid	Husband died in service; widow seeks aid for herself and children.	
1783-002	Garner, Charles	Petition for Tax Relief	Petitioner was soldier for 3 years and unable to make a living	
1807-003	Gillison, John (as Major)	Militia Officer Oath	Gillison's oath as Major in Militia – 85th Rgt., 5th Brigade, 2nd Division	
1786-022	Jenkins, Josiah	Certification of Service in 3rd Va.	Joshua Jenkins enlisted in February 1776 in Captain John Ashby's Co. for 2 years; He died in Phila. December 1776.	
1787-002	Jenkins, Ann (widow of Josiah)	Petition for aid.	Warrant from widow to County for allowance due her as widow of deceased soldier.	

Figure 17. Representative examples from the Name Index for the Military Record Series.

3. A Preview of the Military Records Series Index, sorted by primary party. (Cont.)

Index #	Name (Parties)	Type of Record	Synopsis	Family Information
1809-001	Jenkins, Joshua	Heirs	John Barker swore oath that Thomas Jenkins was heir at law	Thomas Jenkins was heir at law.
1824-001	Kemper, John	Court Martial	Court Martial	
1812-001	Kernes, Mary (widow of Jeremiah)	War of 1812 Pension Papers	Widow's Pension for War of 1812.	Jeremiah Kernes was decd. husband.
1818-005	Powell, John	Pension Declaration and Property Schedule	Pension Declaration of John Powell, age 62	
1822-004	Purcell, George	War of 1812 Pension Papers	George Purcell, age 53 served in US Army under Lt. John W. Kincaid for 5 years. He saw service in Canada and was wounded there.	
1821-001	Rector, John	Militia Officer's Oath	Oath for Lt. In Va. Militia.	
1821-005	Rookwood, Hiram	Militia Officer's Oath	Oath for Lt. In Va. Militia	
1793-003	Wheeler, John	Pension Warrant	Pension warrant for Disability	

Figure 17. Representative examples from the Name Index for the Military Record Series. (Cont.)

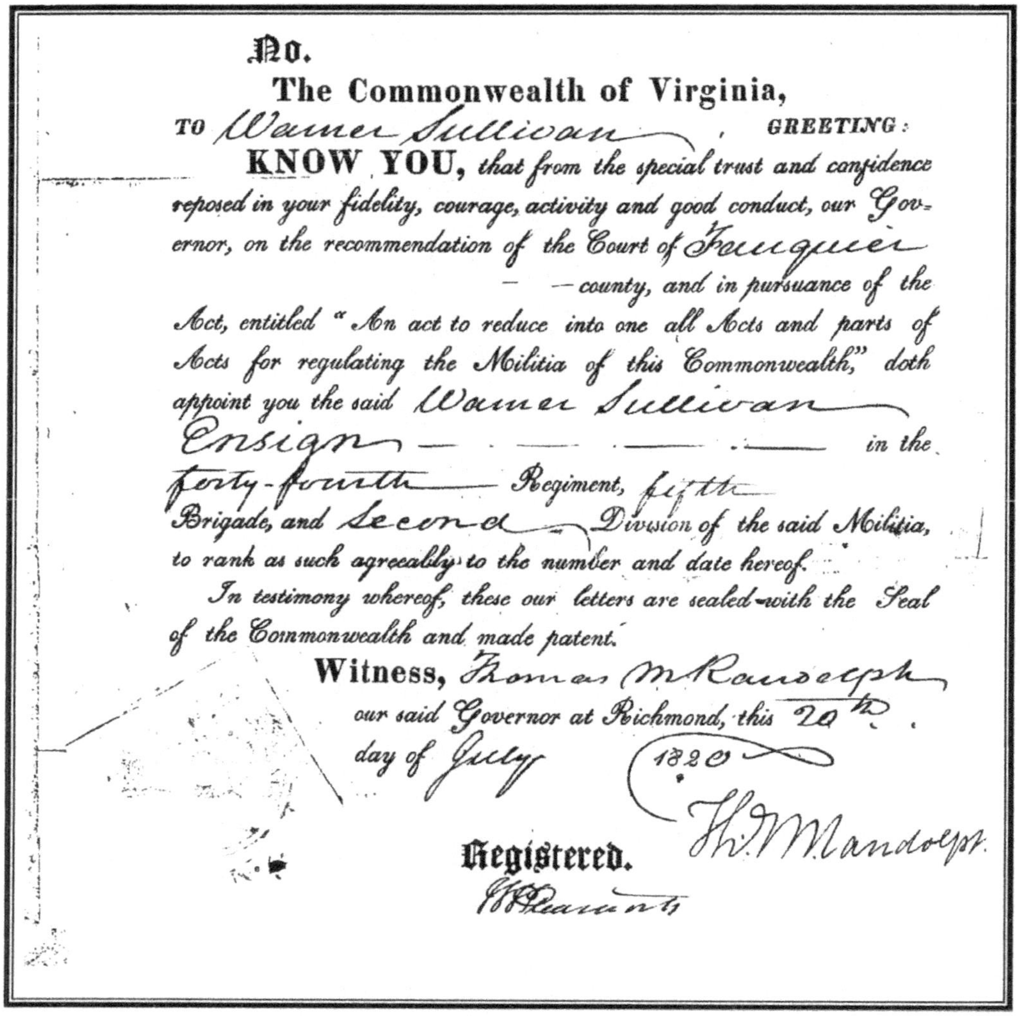

No.

The Commonwealth of Virginia,

TO Warner Sullivan, GREETING:

KNOW YOU, that from the special trust and confidence reposed in your fidelity, courage, activity and good conduct, our Governor, on the recommendation of the Court of Fauquier county, and in pursuance of the Act, entitled "An act to reduce into one all Acts and parts of Acts for regulating the Militia of this Commonwealth," doth appoint you the said Warner Sullivan Ensign in the forty-fourth Regiment, fifth Brigade, and second Division of the said Militia, to rank as such agreeably to the number and date hereof.

In testimony whereof, these our letters are sealed with the Seal of the Commonwealth and made patent.

Witness, Thomas M Randolph our said Governor at Richmond, this 20th day of July 1820

Th M Randolph

Registered.

W Pleasants

Plate 37. Military Records. Scanned Image of MR 1821-006. Warner Sullivan's Military Commission as Ensign, 44th Regiment, 5th Brigade, 2nd Division of Militia.

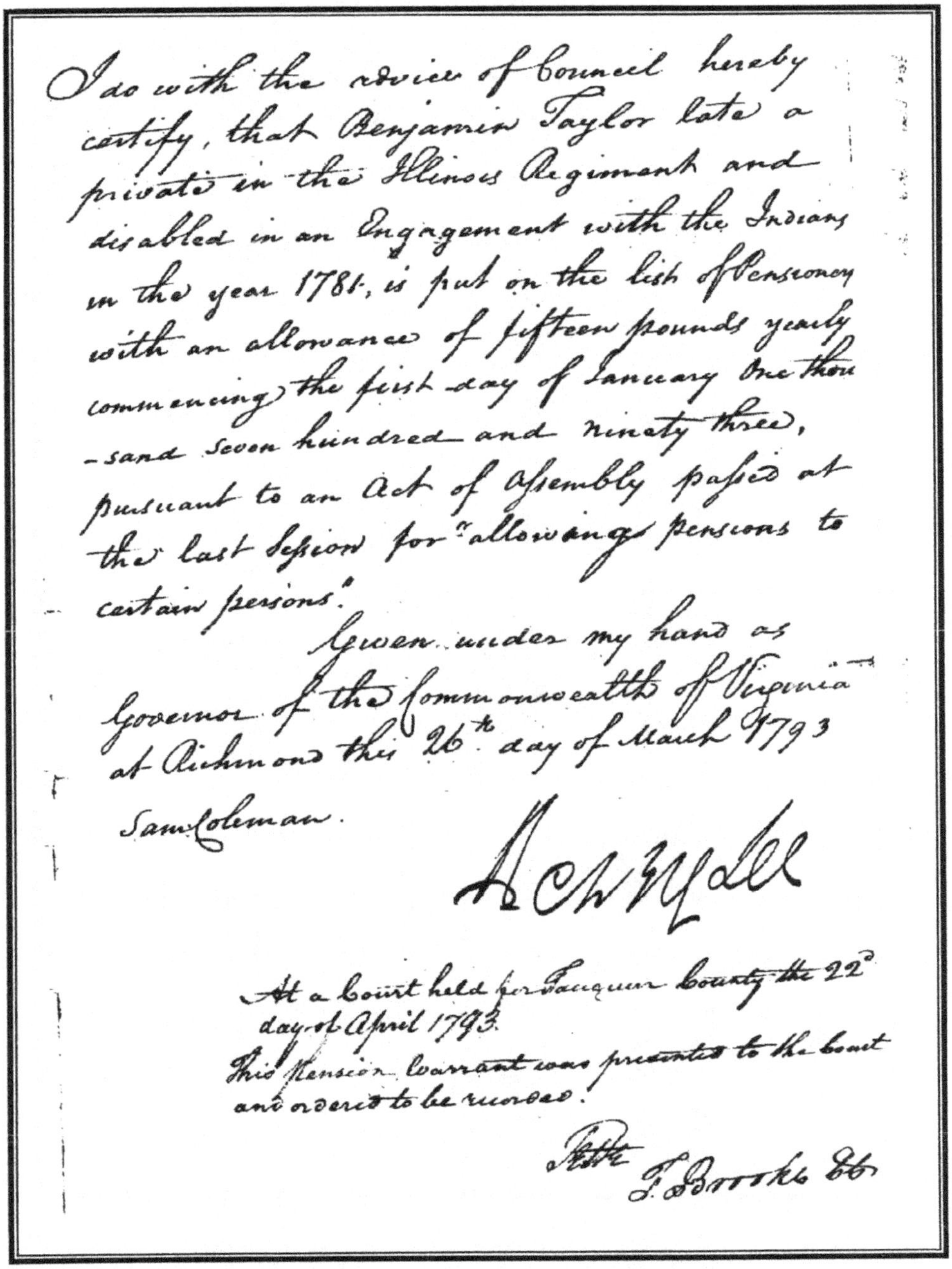

> I do with the advice of Council hereby certify, that Benjamin Taylor late a private in the Illinois Regiment and disabled in an Engagement with the Indians in the year 1781, is put on the list of Pensioners with an allowance of fifteen pounds yearly commencing the first day of January One thousand seven hundred and ninety three, pursuant to an Act of Assembly passed at the last Session for "allowing pensions to certain persons."
>
> Given under my hand as Governor of the Commonwealth of Virginia at Richmond this 26th day of March 1793
>
> Sam Coleman.
>
> H. Lee
>
> At a Court held for Fauquier County the 22d day of April 1793.
> This Pension Warrant was presented to the Court and ordered to be recorded.
>
> Test. T. Brooke CC

Plate 38. Military Records. Scanned Image of MR1793-002 Benjamin Taylor's Pension Warrant.

A List of PENSIONERS, continued by the Honorable the Executive, for the year 1802—to be paid out of the Revenue for that year.

NAMES.	ALLOWANCE PER ANN.	
Bradfton Wm.	£. 12	
Booker Sarah,	8	
Cullins Jno.	12	
Clements Charles,	12	
Cornhill Mary,	12	
Courtney Wm.	12	
Cunningham Elifh.	12	
Cook Mary	12	
Dillard Mary	12	
Davis Ann	12	
Furgufon Robert	12	
Fofter Frederick	12	
Goulding Wm.	12	
Gordien Albion	22	
Hodges Jof.	12	
Hyland Fergufon	10	
Howell Jemima	10	
Hargrove Ann	6	
Leonard Robert	12	
M'Clintick Alice	12	
Hayes James	8	
M'Carty Mary	9	
Shepherd Jno.	12	
Scrurry Jno.	8	
Stuart Alexander	8	
Shepherd Wm.	7	10
Shepherd Ann	18	
Tucker Wm.	12	
Tanner Dorothy	8	
Thatcher Hanna	8	
Toomey Elifh.	12	
Willfon Willis	40	
Windham Mary	8	

Auditor's Office, 27th January, 1803.

S. SHEPARD. Auditor.

Plate 39. Military Records. Scanned Image of MR 1803-002.
List of 1802 Revolutionary Pensioners for Virginia

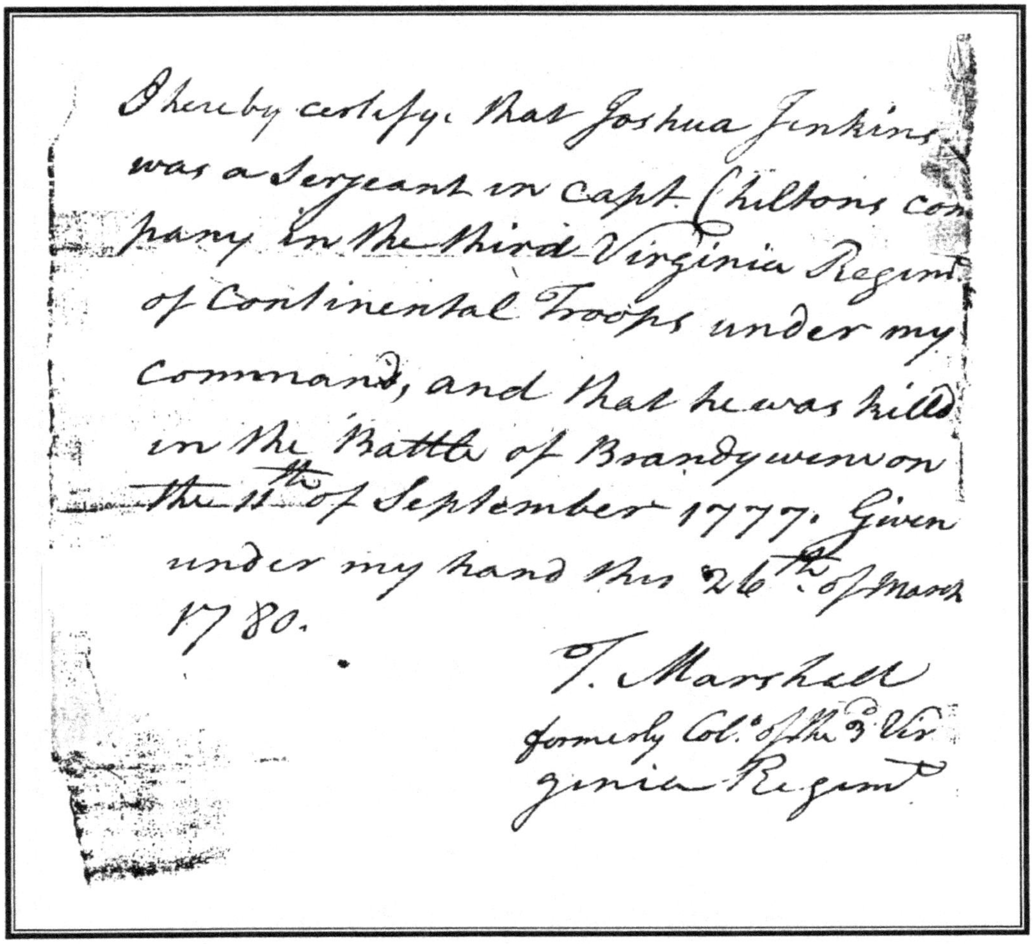

> I hereby certify, That Joshua Jenkins was a Sergeant in Capt. Chiltons company in the Third Virginia Regiment of Continental Troops under my command, and that he was killed in the Battle of Brandywine on the 11th of September 1777. Given under my hand this 26th of March 1780.
>
> T. Marshall
> formerly Col.º of the 3d Virginia Regiment

Plate 40. Military Records. Scanned Image of MR 1809-001.
Heirs at Law of Joshua Jenkins

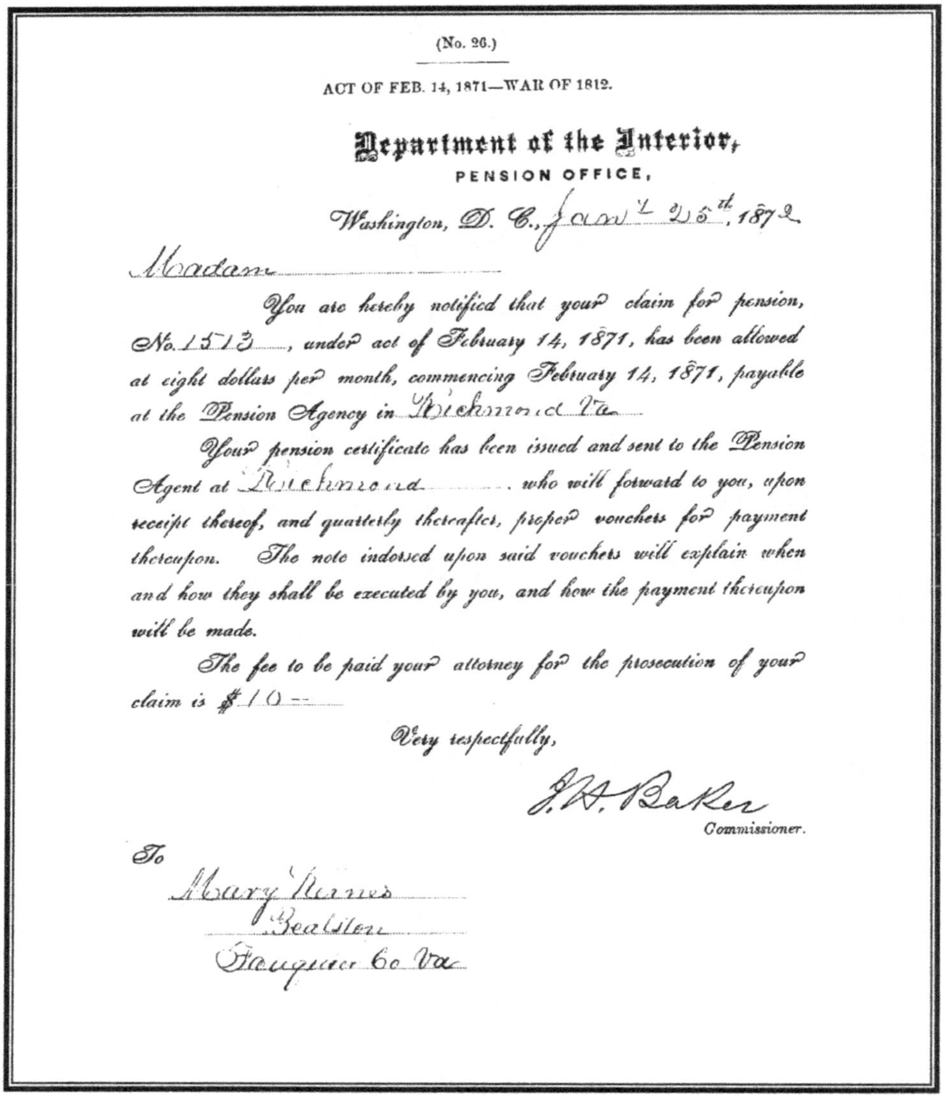

(No. 26.)

ACT OF FEB. 14, 1871—WAR OF 1812.

Department of the Interior,
PENSION OFFICE,

Washington, D. C., *Jan'y 25th, 1872*

Madam

You are hereby notified that your claim for pension, No. 1513, under act of February 14, 1871, has been allowed at eight dollars per month, commencing February 14, 1871, payable at the Pension Agency in *Richmond Va.*

Your pension certificate has been issued and sent to the Pension Agent at *Richmond* who will forward to you, upon receipt thereof, and quarterly thereafter, proper vouchers for payment thereupon. The note indorsed upon said vouchers will explain when and how they shall be executed by you, and how the payment thereupon will be made.

The fee to be paid your attorney for the prosecution of your claim is $10 --

Very respectfully,

J. H. Baker
Commissioner.

To
Mary Kerns
Bealiton
Fauquier Co Va

Plate 41. Military Records. Scanned Image of MR 1812-001
Mary Kerns' War of 1812 Pension Certificate from her War of 1812 Pension Papers.

OFFICIAL FORM.

Application for Aid to Citizens of Virginia Wounded and Maimed during the late War.

Virginia:

In the _____ County _____ Court of _____ Fauquier _____ County,

July 26 188_

Upon the application of _____ J. M. Moore _____ for aid under an act of the General Assembly, approved February 25, 1884, entitled "An act to give aid to the citizens of Virginia wounded and maimed during the late war, while serving as Soldiers or Marines."

The Court having carefully considered the written application of the said _____ J. M. Moore _____ verified by his oath, and the evidence adduced in support of said application, is of opinion that the said _____ J. M. Moore _____ is entitled to aid under said act, and directs the said application and all the evidence in the case to be certified to the Auditor of Public Accounts.

[Here insert the application and evidence.]

Virginia – Fauquier County, to wit: I, J. M. Moore do solemnly swear that I am now a citizen of the State of Virginia, and that during the late war and while a citizen of this State I was engaged as a private in Company K, 31st Regiment Va Volunteers, Early's Brigade, Ewell's Corps, Jackson's Division – and while in said service on the 22nd day of Aug't 1862 at Harrisonburg near Freeman's Ford in Culpeper Co. in a fight there, I was wounded by the explosion of a shell, a piece of which entered my right side below the ribs making a hole as large as my fist, cutting some of my ribs and exposing the entrails — another piece struck just under right shoulder blade, tearing skin and flesh away, the other piece struck my back, inflicting severe wounds. I believe that a ball penetrated my body and still remains in my left lung – causing severe pain + prostration — and permanently disabling me from manual labor. Since said time I have remained in the State of Virginia and am now a citizen thereof – that I have not at any time received an artificial limb or eye or commutation money or pension from this State or any other State or the United States – that he is dependent on physical labor for subsistence.   J. M. Moore

Sworn to before me this 21st day of July 1887 – A. R. Bartenstein J.P.

Virginia – Fauquier County, to wit: I, J. M. McDonald a citizen of this Commonwealth do solemnly swear that I belonged to Co. D 4th Virginia Cavalry during the war and saw J. M. Moore a few days after he was shot. I saw the wound dressed – saw them take the pus out of a hole in his side above the eye of my fist and wash and dress it – he had other wounds. I have known him intimately since – working with me on same farm he was always unable to do hard labor. I gave him the lightest work on the farm. He is now utterly prostrated and believes that a ball has dislodged itself and is moving from the lungs.   M. M. McDonald

Sworn to before me this 13th day of July 1887
A. R. Bartenstein J.P.

Virginia Fauquier County to wit:

I, George S. Hamilton a practicing Physician have examined J. M. Moore – a Confederate Soldier and find the scars of four wounds – two of the scars are large and irregular in outline – both of the large wounds I would infer from the appearance at this date penetrated the cavity – one of the thorax + abdomen + the other the abdomen the ninth tenth and eleventh ribs are evidently fractured. These wounds are frequently the seat of severe neuralgic pains and after any exertion involving the bending of his body the soreness is so great as to require him to leave off work. This has been the case with him recently + he has been + is still under treatment for great soreness in the chest with considerable difficulty in respiration. Given under my hand this 19th day of July 1887 –

Sworn to before me
A R Bartenstein J.P.   George S. Hamilton M.D.

Full name of applicant.   J. M. Moore
Residence,   Fauquier County
Post Office address,   Rappahannock Station, Fauquier County Virginia

A copy—Teste: R. H. Downman _____ Clerk.

AUDITOR'S OFFICE OF VIRGINIA. Received and filed the _____ day of _____ 1886.

Plate 42. Military Records. Scanned Image of MR 1887-001.
J. M. Moore's Confederate Pension Application as member of Company K, 31st Regiment, Virginia Volunteers, Early's Brigade, Ewell's Corp, Jackson's Division.

Confederate Soldiers Claims approved by Pension Board.

NAME.	POST-OFFICE.	DATE.
Anderson, Adeline L.		May 29"1900.
Anderson, E.S.		June 26"1900.
Barber, Mary M.		May 29"1900.
Bragg, Chas. P.	Warrenton	May 29"1900p
Ball, Daniel F.		June 26"1900.
Burgess, M.F.	Auburn	July 23"1900.
Cook, Fannie		June 27"1900.
Conner, Joseph	Mosby	July 23"1900.
Carper, David	Hume	July 28"1900.
Davis, Mrs. Lucy A.		June 26"1900.
Embrey, W.W.		June 27"1900.
Fletcher, B.F.		April 25"1900.
Fletcher, Mrs. Mary Emily.		May 29"1900.
Fields, Charles W.		May 29"1900.
Farmer, Nelson P.		June 26"1900.
Glascock, Nimrod.		May 29"1900.
Gray, Thaddeus.	Ada	July 23"1900.
Groves, Albert.	Upperville	July 28"1900.
Hanback, Silas B.		June 26"1900.
Heflin, James E.		June 26"1900.
Hewitt, Richard.		June 26"1900.
Holtzclaw, C.W.		June 27"1900
James, Edmond T.		May 29"1900.
Johnson, Smith.		May 29"1900.
Kemper, Joshua T.		May 29"1900.
Kemper, John J.		May 29"1900.
Kennard, Lucinda.	The Plains	July 28"1900.
Leach, Wm. M.		May 29"1900.
Miller, G. Allen.		May 29"1900.
Moffett, James H.		June 27"1900

Plate 43. Military Records. Scanned Image of MR 1900-004.
Page 1 of Confederate Soldiers Claims Approved by Fauquier County Pension Board.

Fauquier County, Virginia's Clerks Loose Papers: A Guide to the Records 1759-1919

CHAPTER 10
MILLS, ROADS & BRIDGES

1. Overview

There are mill petitions for the construction of new mills dating back to the formation of the county in 1759. These applications often give the location of the Mill, the location of the run on which the proposed mill is to be located, and any action taken by the court to determine damage caused to adjoining landholders. Ad quod Damnum papers found in the Clerks Loose Papers indicate these damages. As the county grew, so did the roads and mills and the needs for bridges and causeways over runs and rivers.

There are numerous road applications to open, change and close existing roads in Fauquier that also date back to 1759. The Road series contain a variety of papers relating to the petitions and applications for new roads as well as to grand jury actions brought against overseers and surveyor of roads for their lack of maintenance and repair. There are also road, bridge and causeway repair accounts and expense accounts for fixing roads and placing signage at crossroads.

Mills and Roads & Bridges are kept in two different record series to reflect the integrity of the original record bases. They were filed in separate woodruff drawers in the vault. The repair accounts came from County Claims in the Clerks Loose Papers while the Grand Jury Presentments and Indictments came from Ended Causes in the Clerks Loose Papers.

2. Finding your way around Mills, Roads and Bridges

Series Title: Mills
Color Code: Green and Orange Dots on Boxes

Series Dates: 1759-0001 to 1842-001
Series Extent: 2 Boxes. *0.83 linear feet*
Series Arrangement: *Filed by Year, thereunder by Party.*

Series Finding Aid: *Mills Index 1759-1842 (Both Boxes of Mill Records)*

3. A Preview of the Mills Index

Mills are indexed by the name of the person who petitioned or applied for the mill as seen in Figure 18.

Index #	Parties in Papers	Type	Mill Location
1798-003	Anderson, John	Mill Papers	For water grist Mill on Hedgeman River.
1817-002	Boggess, Henley	Mill Papers	For acre of William Rust's land opposite Boggess for dam abutment for water grist Mill on Goose Creek.
1770-001	Churchill, John	Mill Petition	For Mill on Cedar Run
1800-003	Coles, George	Mill Report & Plat	For water grist Mill on Hedgman River PLAT included

Figure 18. Examples of Mills Index, sorted by Parties.

Fauquier County, Virginia's Clerks Loose Papers: A Guide to the Records 1759-1919

Index #	Parties in Papers	Type	Mill Location
1815-001	Cox, Charles	Mill Papers	For Mill on Cabin Branch
1798-004	Dearing, John	Mill Papers	For water grist Mill on Thumb Run
1810-004	Dodd, John	Mill Papers	for Mill on South Run
1764-002	Duncan, Charles	Examination	Intention to build Mill on Summerduck Run
1812-007	Evans, John	Mill Papers	for Mill on Crooked Run
1800-001	Fallis, Thomas	Mill Papers & Plat	for water grist Mill on Wolf Trap Branch. PLAT included.
1827-001	George, Weedon	Mill Papers	for Saw Mill on Marr's Run
1806-004	Mill Seats, Representation of	Map of Seats on Rappahannock River	Map of Mill Seats on Summerduck Run
1768-001	Neavill, George	Mill Papers	for water grist Mill on Cedar Run
1769-001	Neavill, George	Survey	Mill Survey and Plat
1811-003	Peyton, Charles	Mill Papers	for water grist Mill on Broad Run
1808-003	Settle, John &c.	Ad Quod Damnum	for Mill on Barrow's Run
1774-001	Winn, Minor	Mill Petition	to condemn acre of his land on one side of Little River for a water grist Mill

Figure 18. Examples of Mills Index, sorted by Parties. (Cont.)

4. **Finding Your Way around Roads & Bridges**

   Series Title: Roads & Bridges
   Color Code: Green and Orange Dots on Boxes

   Series Dates: 1759-001 to 1900-002
   Series Extent: 10 Boxes. *4.16 linear feet.*
   Series Arrangement: *Filed by Year, thereunder by Party.*

   Series Finding Aids: *Roads & Bridges Index 1759-1799 (**First** Box of Road Records only)*
   Roads Inventory 1759-1890

Fauquier County, Virginia's Clerks Loose Papers: A Guide to the Records 1759-1919

Types of Records found in **Roads & Bridges** include:
  a. Road Application Papers
  b. Grand Jury Presentments for not keeping road in repair or for obstructing the road
  c. Road and Bridge Repair Accounts
     These accounts are found throughout the papers and are filed collectively by year.
  d. Road Reports and Surveys
  e. Overseer and Surveyor of Roads Appointments
  f. Turnpike Suits from Ended Causes

5. Preview of the Road & Bridges Index

A Road & Bridges Index includes records from 1759-1799. Figure 19 shows representative examples from this index.

Index #	Name	Type of Record	Road Location
1796-05	Adams, Charles &c.	Road Petition	for a public Road to Richard Evan's Mill. Proposed course of road to go from Evan's Mill near Rectortown, near the Loudoun Line near Isaac Gibson's.
1786-003	Allason, William	Viewer's Report	for road leaving a turning off from the road from Fauquier Court House to Culpeper Court House.
1775-006	Edwards, John &c.	Road Petition	for way out of Manor Road by Wm Withers into the Great Main Road by Armistead Churchill's, along the old road... for free egress to Market.
1785-004	Field, John &c.	Road Petition	for opening Road from the Manor Road to Rectortown to the most direct way to the Loudoun line and Noland's Ferry.
1784-004	Grigsby, Samuel (as viewer)	Road Report	for most convenient way from the old track from the Loudoun line near Joseph Jackson's into the road now in uses, as petitioned for by Roger Tolle.
1799-009	Hampton, William	Overseer of Road Appointment	as Overseer of Road from Broad Run Meeting House to the Thorofare Mill.
1798-002	Keith, John	Viewer's Report	for road from John Keith's to Manassas road near Butcher's Mill
1775-003	Love, Samuel	Road Petition	for public road to Samuel Love's Mill from the Old Carolina Road.
1765-003	Spiller, Jeremiah &c.	Road Petition	for a Road from Cedar Run to Brentstown.

Figure 19. Representative Examples from the Roads & Bridges Index, sorted by Names.

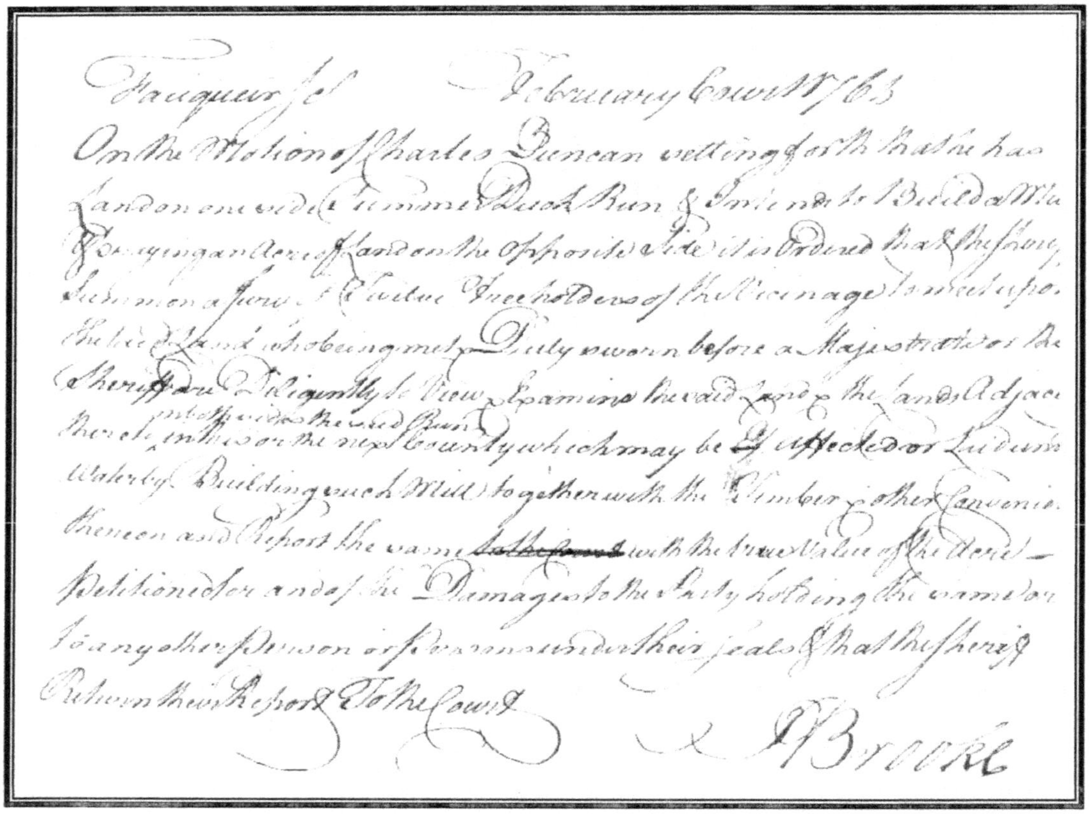
Fauquier Sct February Court 1763
On the Motion of Charles Duncan setting forth that he has
Land on one side Summer Duck Run & Intends to Build a Mill
& praying an Acre of Land on the Opposite Side it is Ordered that the Sheriff
Summon a Jury of Twelve Freeholders of the Vicinage to meet upon
the said Land who being met & Duly sworn before a Magistrate or the
Sheriff are Diligently to View & Examine the said Land & the Lands Adjacent
thereto on both sides the said Run in this or the next County which may be affected or Laid under
Water by Building such Mill together with the Timber & other Convenien-
ces thereon and Report the same with the true Value of the Acre
Petitioned for and of the Damages to the Party holding the same or
To any other Person or Persons under their Seals & that the Sheriff
Return their Report to the Court
P Brooke

Plate 44. Mills. Scanned Image of Mills 1764-003.
Charles Duncan's Mill Petition for Mill on Summerduck Run.

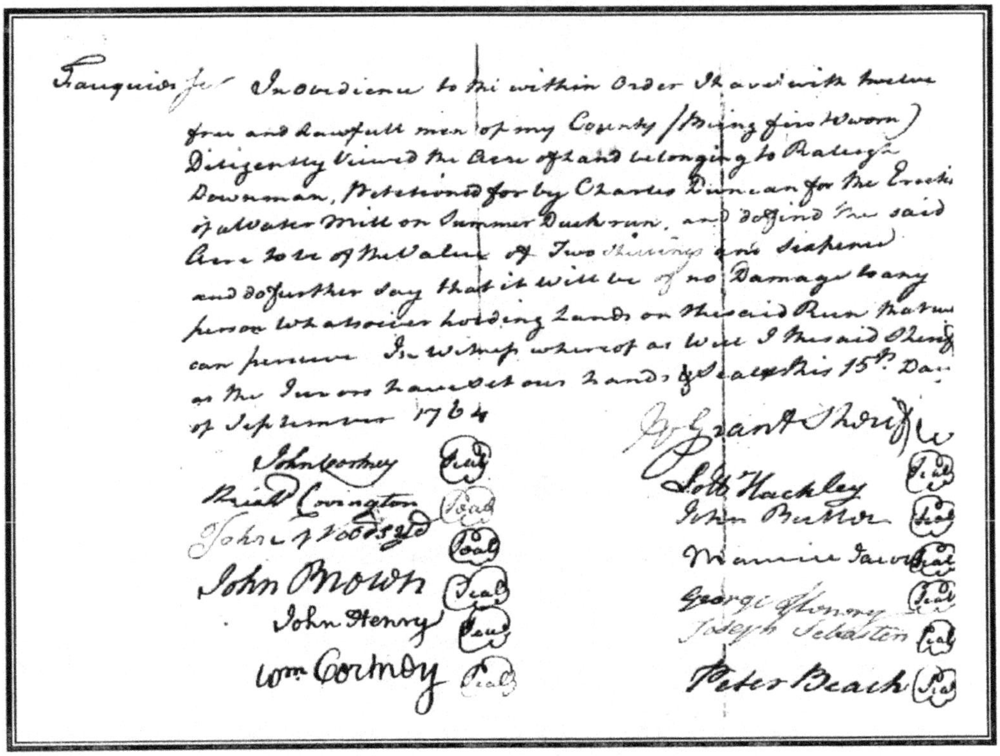

Fauquier Sct In Obedience to the within Order I have with twelve free and lawfull men of my County (being first sworn) Diligently Viewed the Acre of land belonging to Raleigh Downman, Petitioned for by Charles Duncan for the Erectin of a Water Mill on Summer Duck run, and do find the said Acre to be of the Value of Two shillings and sixpence and do further say that it will be of no Damage to any person whatsoever holding Lands on the said Run that we can perceive In witness whereof as well I the said Sheriff as the Jurors have set our hands & Seals this 15th. Day of September 1764

Jn Grant Sheriff

John Cortney (Seal)
Richd Covington (Seal)
John Woods (Seal)
John Brown (Seal)
John Henry (Seal)
Wm Cortney (Seal)

Soth Hackley (Seal)
John Butler (Seal)
Maurice Jacob (Seal)
George Henry (Seal)
Joseph Sebastin (Seal)
Peter Beach (Seal)

Plate 45. Mills. Scanned Image of Mills 1764-003.
Viewer's Report for Mill on Summerduck Run.
From Charles Duncan's Mill Papers

Fauquier County, Virginia's Clerks Loose Papers: A Guide to the Records 1759-1919

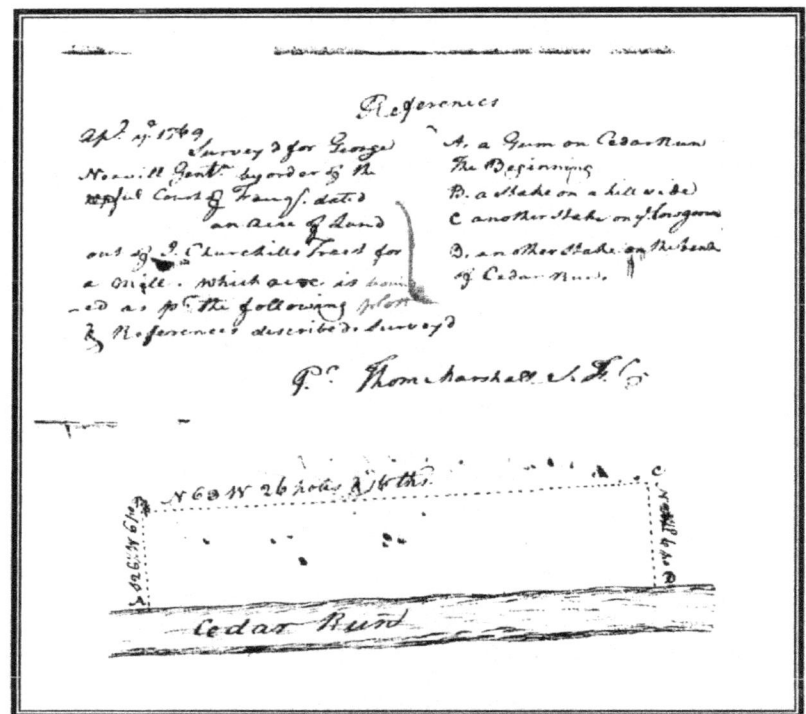

Plate 46. Mills. Scanned Image of Mills 1769-001. George Neville's Mill Survey

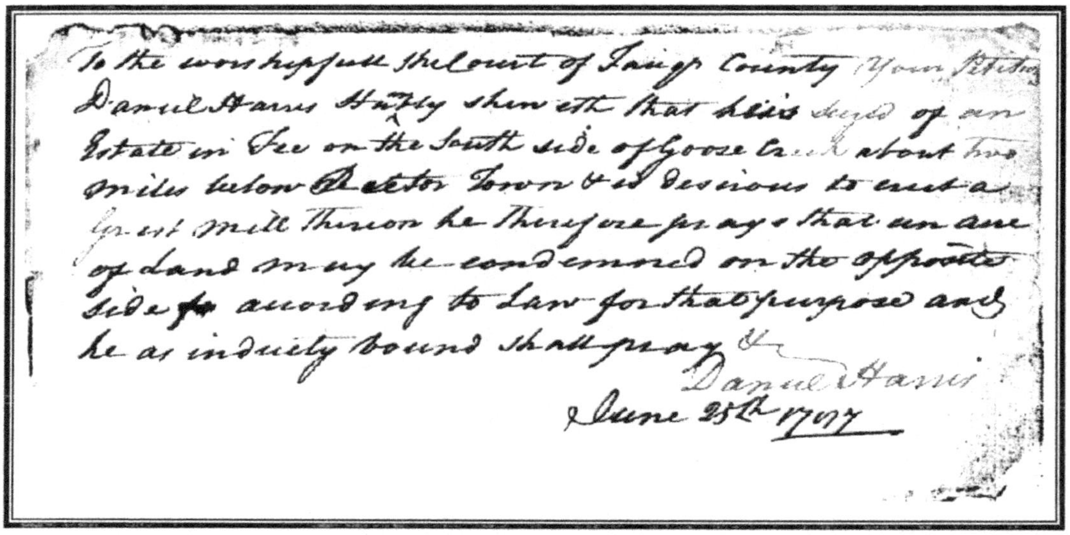

Plate 47. Mills Scanned Image of Mills 1787-001 Daniel Harris' Mill Petition for a Mill on the south side of Goose Creek, around 2 miles from Rectortown.

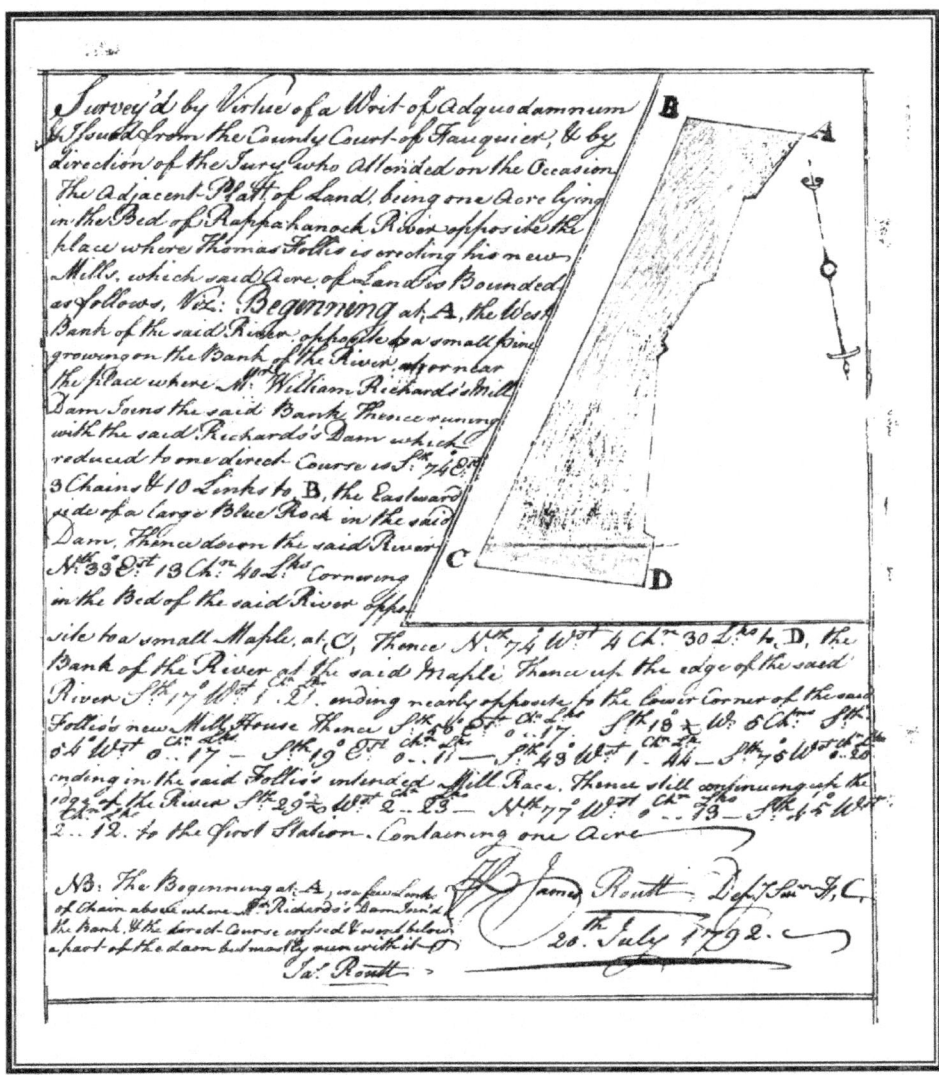

Plate 48. Mills. Scanned Image of Mills 1792-001.
Plat & Survey of an acre in Rappahannock River opposite
Thomas Fallis' site for a new Mill from Thomas Fallis' Mill Application Papers.

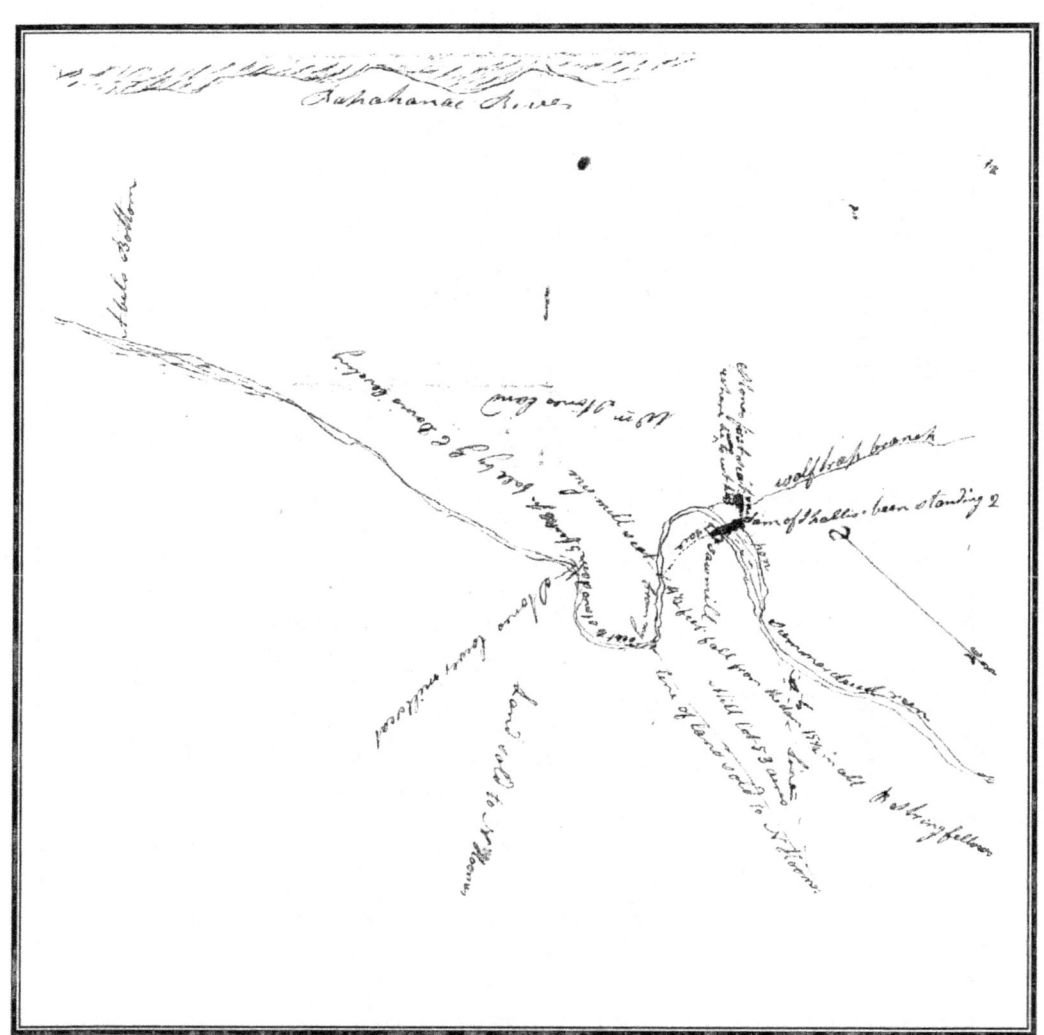

Plate 49. Mills. Scanned Image of Mills 1806-004. "Representation of Mill Seats" On Summerduck Run and Wolf Trap Branch

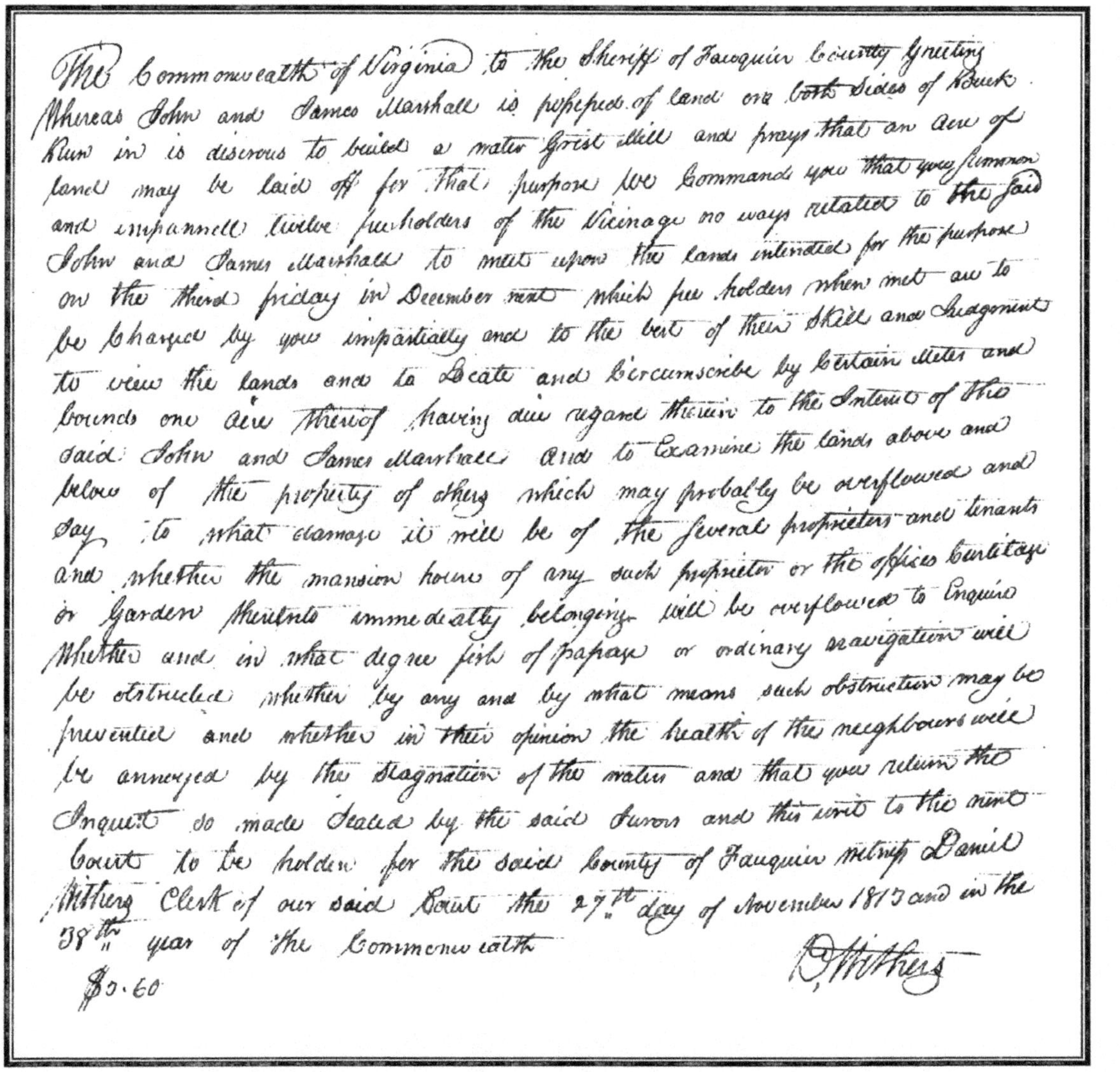

The Commonwealth of Virginia, to the Sheriff of Fauquier County Greeting Whereas John and James Marshall is possessed of land on both sides of Buck Run in is desirous to build a water Grist Mill and prays that an acre of land may be laid off for that purpose We Command you that you summon and impannell twelve freeholders of the Vicinage no ways related to the said John and James Marshall to meet upon the lands intended for the purpose on the third friday in December next which freeholders when met are to be Charged by you impartially and to the best of their skill and Judgment to view the lands and to Locate and Circumscribe by Certain meter and bounds one acre thereof having due regard therein to the Interest of the said John and James Marshall And to Examine the lands above and below of the property of others which may probably be overflowed and say to what damage it will be of the several proprietors and tenants and whether the mansion house of any such proprietor or the offices Curtilage or Garden thereunto immediately belonging will be overflowed to Enquire whether and in what degree fish of passage or ordinary navigation will be obstructed whether by any and by what means such obstruction may be prevented and whether in their opinion the health of the neighbours will be annoyed by the stagnation of the water and that you return the Inquest so made Sealed by the said Jurors and this writ to the next Court to be holden for the said County of Fauquier witness Daniel Withers Clerk of our said Court the 27th day of November 1813 and in the 38th year of the Commonwealth

$0.60

D. Withers

Plate 50. Mills. Scanned image of Mills 1813-004.
John and James Marshall's Petition for Mill on Buck Run.

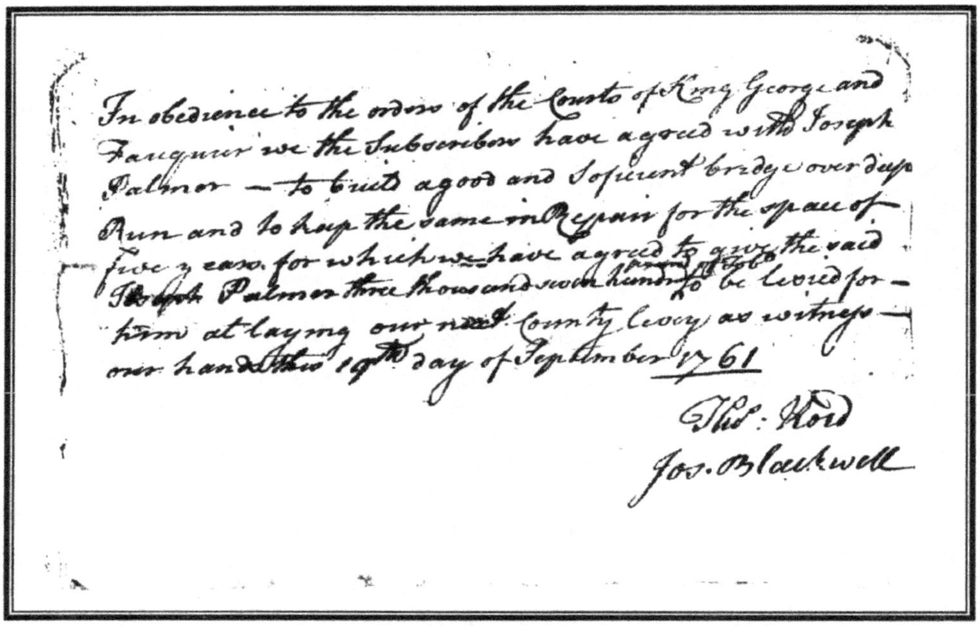

Fauquier County, Virginia's Clerks Loose Papers: A Guide to the Records 1759-1919

> In obedience to the orders of the Courts of King George and Fauquier we the Subscribers have agreed with Joseph Palmer — to build a good and sufficient bridge over deep Run and to keep the same in Repair for the space of five years, for which we have agreed to give the said Joseph Palmer three thousand ~~~ hundred to be levied for him at laying our next County Levy as witness our hands this 19th day of September 1761
>
> Thos: Ford
> Jos. Blackwell

*Plate 51. Roads & Bridges. Scanned Image of R&B 1761-001.
Joseph Palmer's Agreement to build a Bridge over Deep Run.*

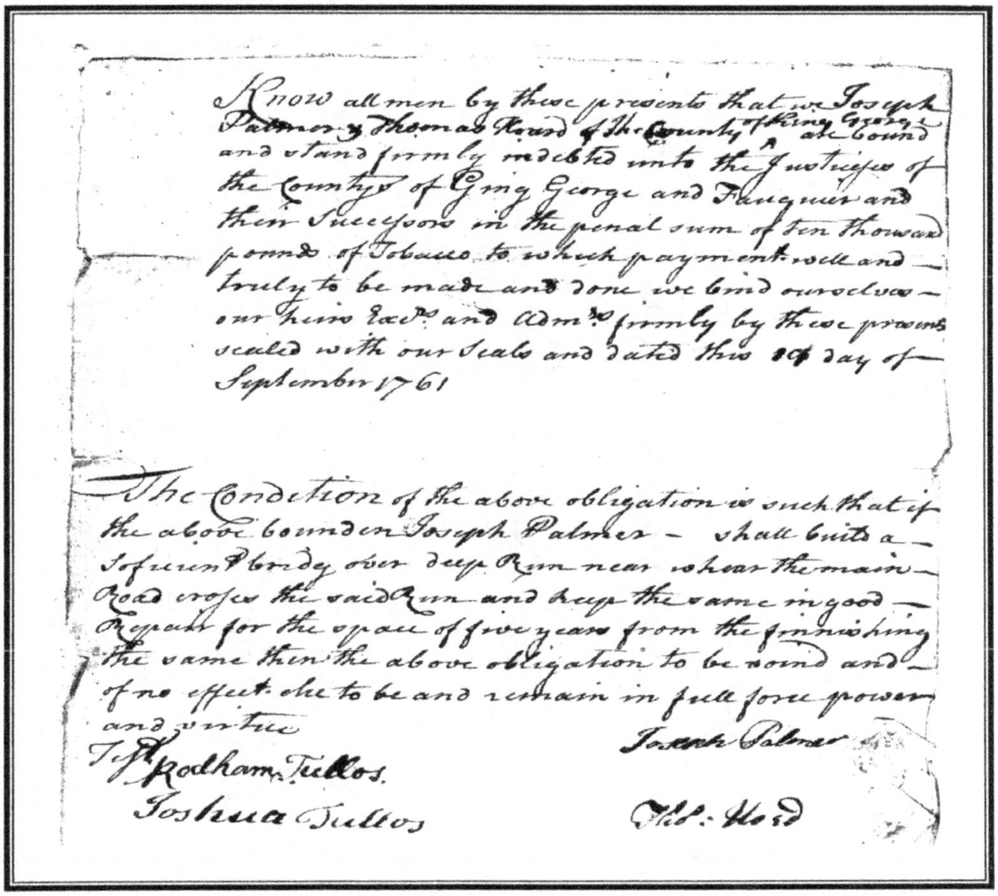

Know all men by these presents that we Joseph Palmer & Thomas Hord of the County of King George are bound and stand firmly indebted unto the Justices of the Countys of King George and Fauquier and their Successors in the penal sum of Ten Thousand pounds of Tobacco to which payment well and truly to be made and done we bind ourselves our heirs Exec.rs and Adm.rs firmly by these presents sealed with our Seals and dated this 1st day of September 1761

The Condition of the above obligation is such that if the above bounden Joseph Palmer shall build a sufficient bridge over deep Run near where the main Road crosses the said Run and keep the same in good Repair for the space of five years from the finishing the same then the above obligation to be void and of no effect else to be and remain in full force power and virtue

Joseph Palmer

Test Rodham Tullos.
Joshua Tullos

Tho.s Hord

Plate 52. Roads & Bridges. Scanned Image of R&B 1761-001
Joseph Palmer's Bond to build Bridge over Deep Run

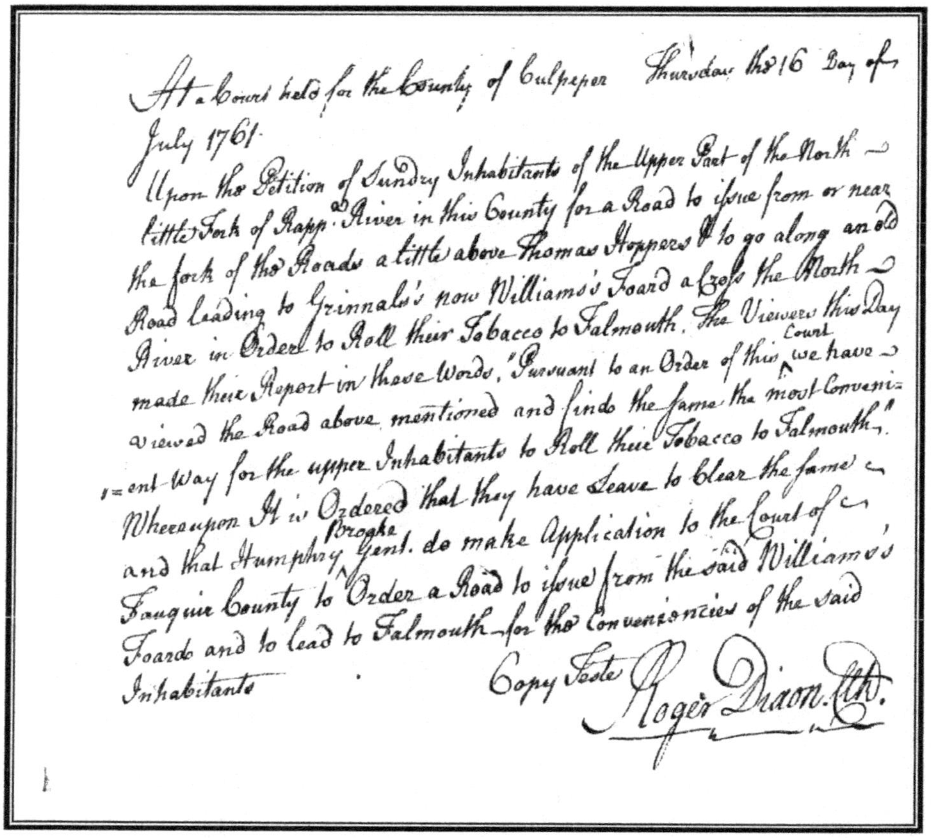

At a Court held for the County of Culpeper Thursday the 16 Day of July 1761.

Upon the Petition of Sundry Inhabitants of the Upper Part of the North Little Fork of Rapp. River in this County for a Road to issue from or near the fork of the Roads a little above Thomas Hoppers & to go along an old Road leading to Grinnali's now Williams's Foard across the Mouth River in Order to Roll their Tobacco to Falmouth. The Viewers this Day made their Report in these Words, "Pursuant to an Order of this Court we have viewed the Road above mentioned and finds the same the most Convenient Way for the upper Inhabitants to Roll their Tobacco to Falmouth." Whereupon It is Ordered that they have Leave to Clear the same and that Humphry Brooke Gent. do make Application to the Court of Fauquir County to Order a Road to issue from the said Williams's Foard and to lead to Falmouth for the Conveniencies of the said Inhabitants

Copy Teste
Roger Dixon, C.C.

*Plate 53. Roads & Bridges. Scanned Image of R&B 1762-002.
Culpeper County Residents' Petition for Road from Williams' Ford to Falmouth*

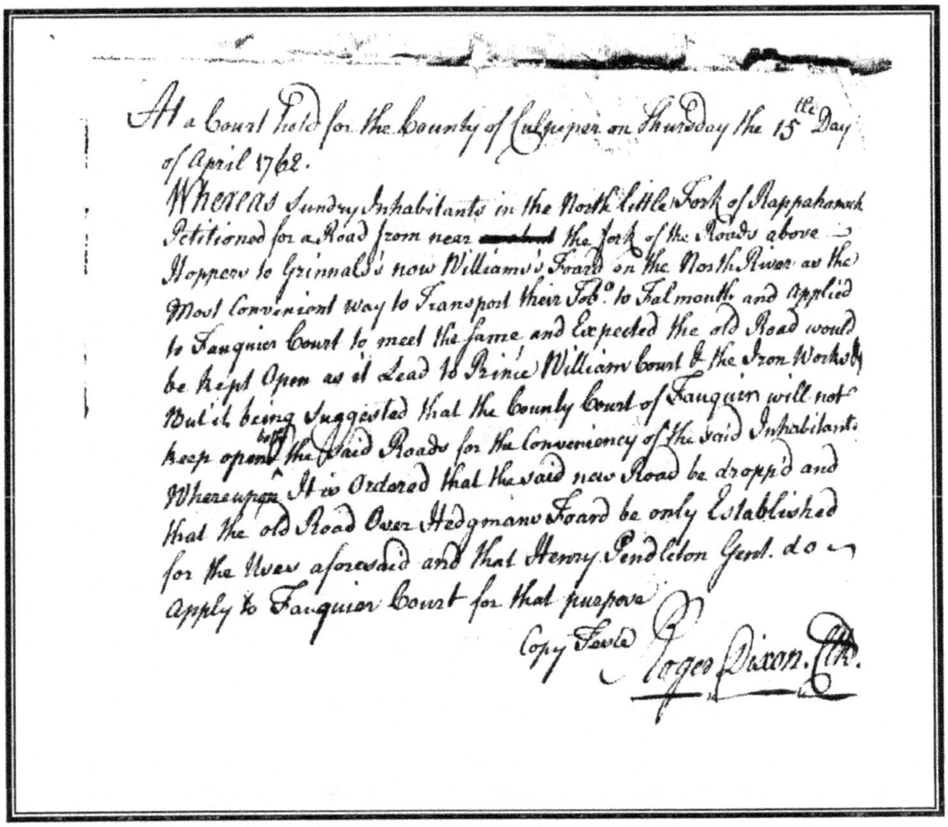

> At a Court held for the County of Culpeper on Thursday the 15the Day of April 1762.
>
> Whereas Sundry Inhabitants in the North little Fork of Rappahanock Petitioned for a Road from near the fork of the Roads above Hoppers to Grinnal's now Williams's Foard on the North River as the Most Convenient way to Transport their Tob°. to Falmouth and applied to Fauquier Court to meet the same and Expected the old Road would be kept Open as it Lead to Prince William Court & the Iron Works But it being Suggested that the County Court of Fauquier will not keep open both the said Roads for the Conveniency of the said Inhabitants Whereupon It is Ordered that the said new Road be dropp'd and that the old Road Over Hedgmans Foard be only Established for the Uses aforesaid and that Henry Pendleton Gent. do apply to Fauquier Court for that puepose
>
> Copy Teste Roger Dixon Clk

Plate 54. Roads & Bridges. Scanned Image of R&B 1762-002. Culpeper County Court Order concerning residents' Petition for Road from Williams' Ford to Falmouth

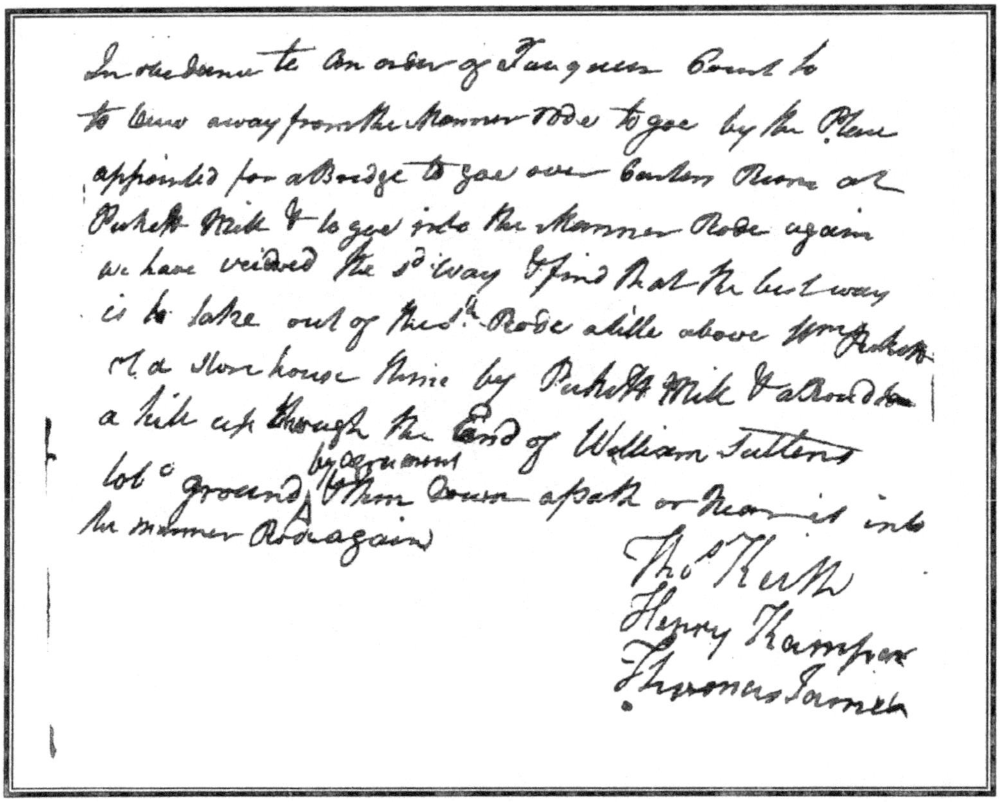

In obedience to an order of Fauquier Court to
to view away from the Mannor Rode to goe by the Place
appointed for a Bridge to goe over Carters Run at
Pickett Mill & to goe into the Mannor Rode again
we have veiwed the sd way & find that the best way
is to take out of the sd Rode a litle above Wm Pickett
old Store house there by Pickett Mill & a Road down
a hill up through the Land of William Suttons
lott ground by agreement & then down a path or near it into
the Mannor Road again

Thos Keith
Henry Kamper
Thomas Garner

Plate 55. Roads & Bridges. Scanned Image of R&B 1773-005.
Viewer's Report for way from the Manor Road by place appointed for Bridge over Carter's Road at Pickett's Mill and back into the Manor Road

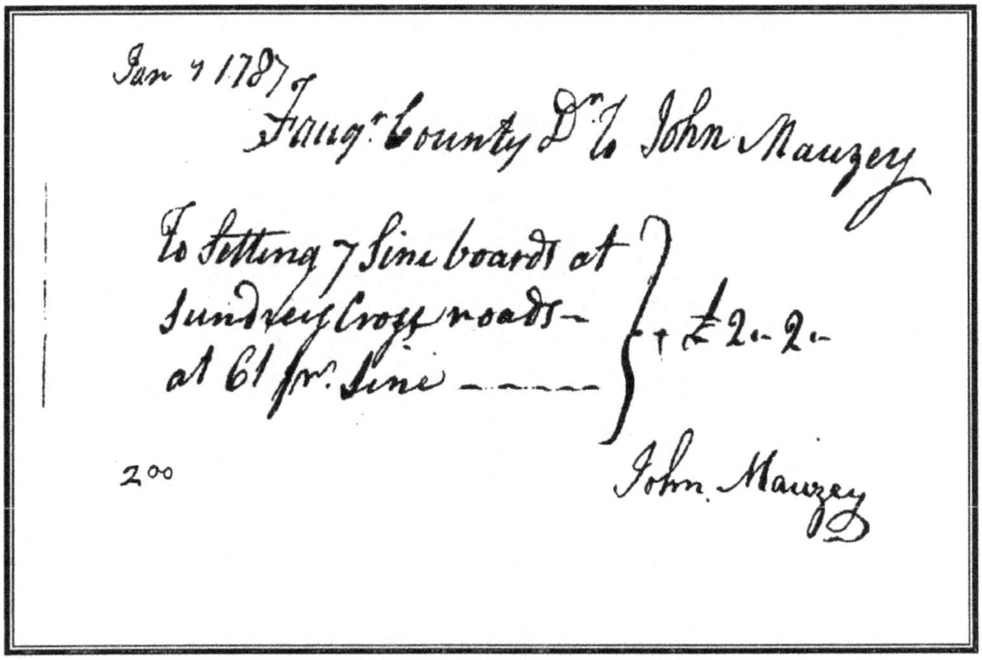

Jan 7 1787

Fauqr County Dr To John Mauzey

To Setting 7 Sine boards at
sundreys Cross roads
at 6/ pr. Sine } £2..2..

200

John Mauzey

Plate 56. Roads & Bridges. Scanned Image of R&B 1786-010.
John Mauzey's Account with Fauquier County for setting 7 sign boards
At sundry Cross Roads in the County

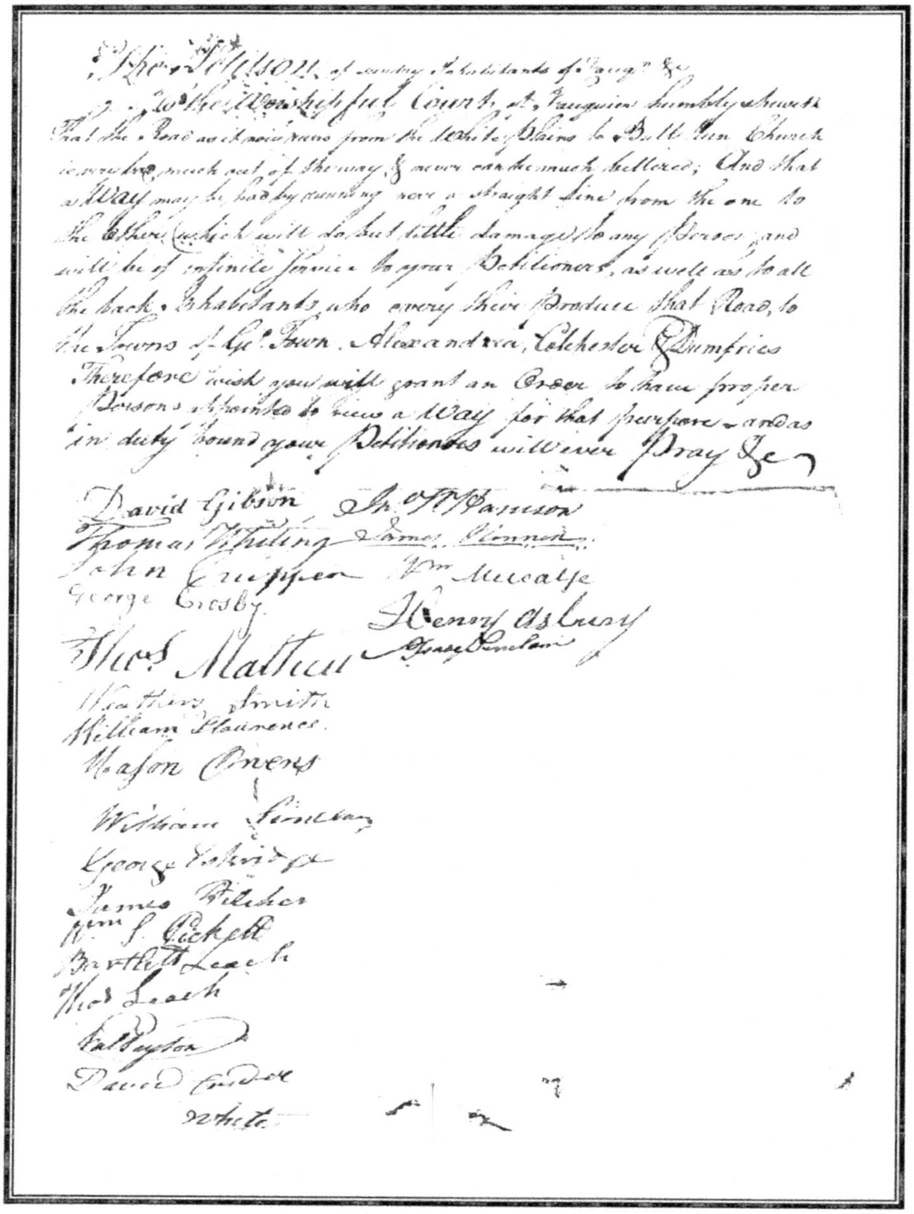
Thos. Wilson of sundry Inhabitants of Fauq.r &c

To the Worshipful Court of Fauquier humbly sheweth That the Road as it now runs from the White Plains to Bull Run Church is very much out of the way & never can be much bettered; And that a Way may be had by running near a straight Line from the one to the other (which will do but little damage to any Person) and will be of infinite service to your Petitioners, as well as to all the back Inhabitants who carry their Produce that Road, to the Towns of Geo. Town, Alexandria, Colchester & Dumfries Therefore wish you will grant an Order to have proper Persons appointed to view a Way for that purpose — and as in duty bound your Petitioners will ever Pray &c

David Gibson
Jn. O. Harrison
Thomas Whiting
James Oconnor
John Crupper
Wm. Metcalfe
George Crosby
Henry Asbury
Thos. Mathew
Isaac Duncan
Weathers Smith
William Lawrence
Mason Owens
William Lindsay
George Eskridge
James Fletcher
Wm. S. Pickett
Bartlett Leach
Thos Leach
Val Peyton
David Crudock
White

Plate 57. Roads & Bridges. Scanned Image of R &B 1794-007
Road Petition for Road from the White Plains to Bull Run Church
For the convenience of travel to Georgetown, Alexandria, Colchester and Dumfries

Fauquier County, Virginia's Clerks Loose Papers: A Guide to the Records 1759-1919

CHAPTER 11
MISCELLANEOUS RECORDS

1. Overview

Miscellaneous Records contain a "hodgepodge" of records: election records, Declaration of Intents and Citizenship papers, Clerks of Court Correspondence, records relating to the Court House and to the Jail. These records were found in both the Clerks Loose Papers (records between 1759-1832) and the County Court papers (the post 1832 papers).

There were also a group of records the preservation team called "Interesting Finds". These were records not easily categorized into any of the other record series; they were records that contained atypical language or were unusual in their content.

In many ways, this record series make up some of the most interesting "local history" records in the Clerks Loose Papers. Many early records talk about the jail and the early development of the courthouse. There are all sorts of accounts and reports and lists of supplies for the County Court, the Superior Court and their respective Clerk's Offices. The records herein allow the local historian to follow the development and construction of both courts and jail through the mid-eighteenth and nineteenth century. The accounts give one a whole new perspective regarding the early development and growth of the county.

The boxes containing the Clerk's correspondence add a new dimension to Fauquier's nineteenth century records. These boxes contain letters from friends, family, business associates and craftsmen to various Clerks of Court, deputy Clerks and local attorneys. These include Thomas P. Knox and William Jennings. There are also accounts that James Murray & Company had with the county.

These papers give one a real sense of nineteenth century history and a feel for the ethics and education of that bygone time. There are even letters written in Latin (!) to Thomas Knox, a local attorney and, for a time, a deputy clerk of the county court. Mr. Knox lived in Fauquier and had family in nearby Loudoun County.

2. Finding your way around Miscellaneous Records

Series Title: Miscellaneous Records
Color Code: Orange and Yellow Dots on Boxes

Series Dates: 1759-1904
Series Extent: 24 boxes. *12 linear feet.*

Miscellaneous Records: Elections (from Clerks Loose Papers)	Box 1	(1819-1832)
Miscellaneous Records: Elections, &c. (from County Court Papers)	Box 24	(1824-1850
Miscellaneous Records: Citizenship Papers (from Clerks Loose Papers)	Box 1	(1819-1831)
Miscellaneous Records: Citizenship Papers (from County Court Papers)	Box 23	(1834-1903)
Miscellaneous Records: Clerk of Court Correspondence (from Clerks Loose Papers)	Boxes 2-8	
Miscellaneous Records: The Jail (from Clerks Loose Papers)	Box 9	(1767-1832)
Miscellaneous Records: The Jail (from County Court Papers)	Box 16	(1824-1892)
Miscellaneous Records: The Courthouse (from Clerks Loose Papers)	Box 10	(1759-1832)
Miscellaneous Records: The Courthouse (from County Court Papers)	Box 18	(1858-1904)
Miscellaneous Records: Haymarket District Court Suits	Box 11	(1800-1812)

Fauquier County, Virginia's Clerks Loose Papers: A Guide to the Records 1759-1919

Series Extent: (Cont.)

Miscellaneous Records: Local History: Interesting Finds	Box 12	(1763-1839)
Miscellaneous Records: Local History (from Clerks Loose Papers)	Box 13-15	(1759-1832)
Miscellaneous Records: Local History (from County Court Papers)	Box 17-22	(1832-1904)
Miscellaneous Records: County Claims &c. (from County Court Papers)	Box 24	(1834-1850)

Series Arrangement: Clerks Loose Papers: *Filed by Year*
County Court Papers: *Filed by Year*

Series Finding Aids:

There are **no** every name or every party indices for records associated with the Clerks Loose Papers. The records in the Clerk's Loose Papers have these **inventories** associated with them:

A Miscellaneous Records Inventory (Overview)
A Miscellaneous Records Inventory for the Jail, Courthouse and Haymarket for Clerk's Loose Papers
A Miscellaneous Records Inventory for the Thomas P. Knox Papers
A Miscellaneous Records Inventory for Interesting Finds

There is a computerized Name Index for Miscellaneous Records (1832-1904) associated with the County Court Papers.

John R. Callow	Name
Isle of Man, and Parish of Maughold	Birth place
Forty five	Age
Great Britain	Nation
King of Great Britain & Ireland	Allegiance
England	Country whence migrated
Fauquier County, State of Virginia	Place of intended settlement

September 16th 1819

John R. Callow

Report of John R. Callow Ex Alien

Plate 58. Miscellaneous Records, Clerks Loose Papers. Scanned Image from Box 1. Citizenship Papers.1819-001. John R. Callow's Alien Report.

Name	Birthplace	Age	Nation	Allegiance	County where migrated	Place of intended settlement
Michael Rusie	Germany on the upper Rhine	24 ayears	Baden	Duke of Baden	Baden	Prince Wm County State of Virginia

Given un my hand this 23d day of April 1821. Michael Rusie

Teste P Ward

Plate 59. Miscellaneous Records, Clerks Loose Papers. Scanned Image from Box 1. Citizenship Papers. 1821-002 Michael Rusie's Alien Report.

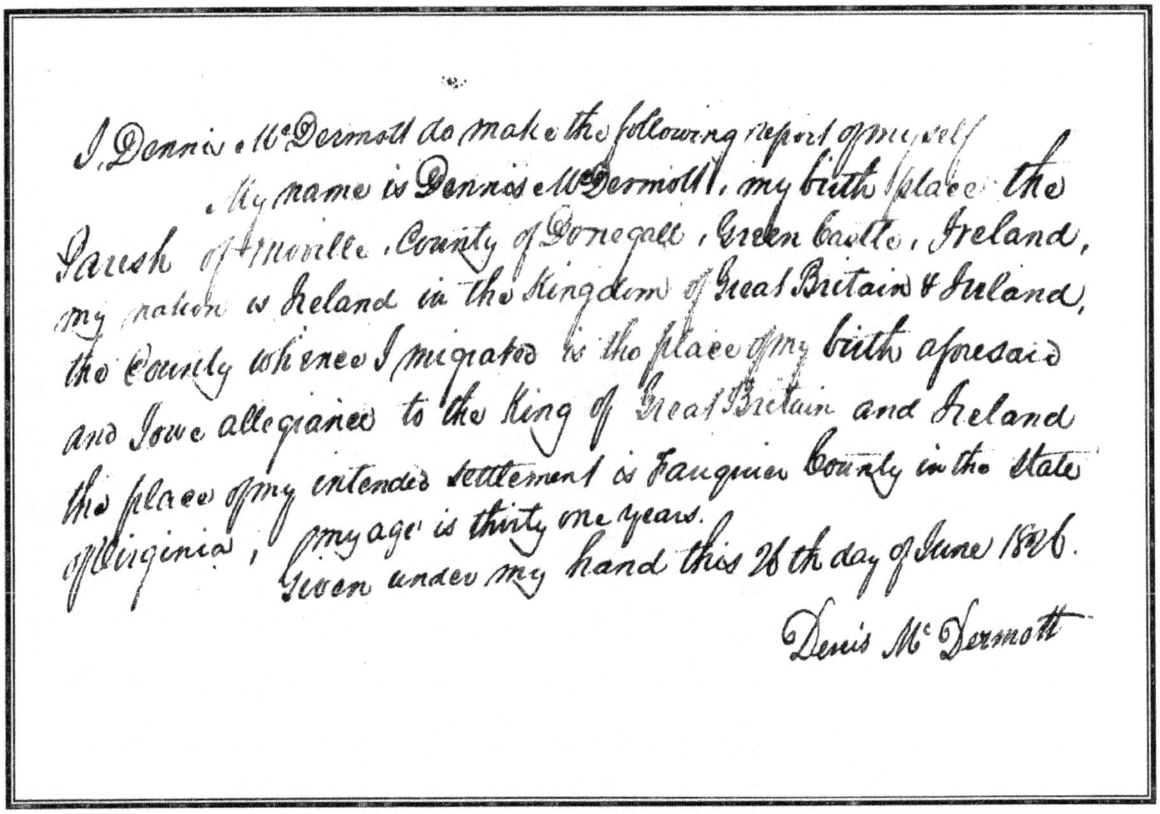

> I, Dennis McDermott do make the following report of myself. My name is Dennis McDermott, my birth place the Parish of Moville, County of Donegall, Green Castle, Ireland, my nation is Ireland in the Kingdom of Great Britain & Ireland, the County whence I migrated is the place of my birth aforesaid and I owe allegiance to the King of Great Britain and Ireland the place of my intended settlement is Fauquier County in the State of Virginia, my age is thirty one years.
> Given under my hand this 26th day of June 1826.
>
> Denis McDermott

Plate 60. Miscellaneous Records, Clerks Loose Papers. Scanned Images from Box 1, Citizenship Papers. 1826-004 Dennis McDermott's Alien Report.

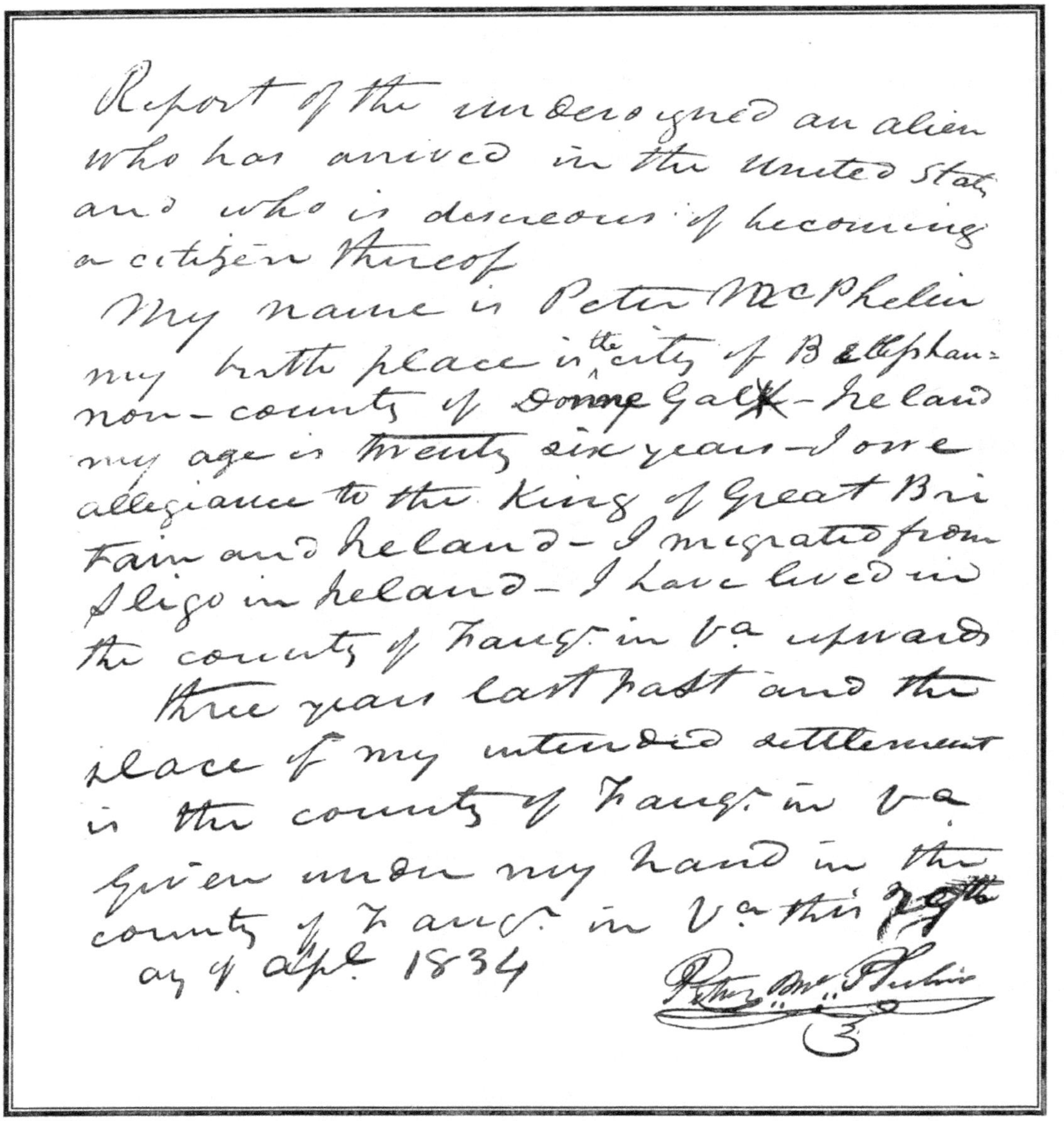

> Report of the undersigned an alien who has arrived in the United States and who is desirous of becoming a citizen thereof
>
> My name is Peter McPhelin my birth place is the city of Ballyshannon — county of ~~Donny~~ Galk — Ireland my age is twenty six years — I owe allegiance to the King of Great Britain and Ireland — I migrated from Sligo in Ireland — I have lived in the county of Fauqr. in Va upwards three years last past and the place of my intended settlement is the county of Fauqr. in Va Given under my hand in the county of Fauqr. in Va this 29th day of Aprl 1834
>
> Peter McPhelin

Plate 61. Miscellaneous Records, County Court Papers.
Scanned Image from Box 23, Naturalizations 1834-001. Peter McPhelin's Alien Report.

Report of the Undersigned an alien who has arrived in the United States, and who is desirous of becoming a citizen thereof.

My name is Ann Jenkins — my birth place is the Tredington in the County of Worcester — England, my age is — forty — years. I owe allegiance to the king of Great Britain and Ireland. I migrated from Liverpool — I have lived in the County of Fauquier eleven months last past and the place of my intended settlement is the County of Fauquier in Virginia.

Given under my hand in the County of Fauquier in Virginia this 3d day of December 1836

Ann Jenkins

Plate 62. Miscellaneous Records, County Court Papers.
Scanned Image from Box 23, Naturalizations 1836-001. Ann Jenkins' Alien Report.

Plate 63. Miscellaneous Records, County Court Papers.
Scanned Image from Box 23, Naturalizations. 1853-001 Joseph Bear's Declaration of Intent.

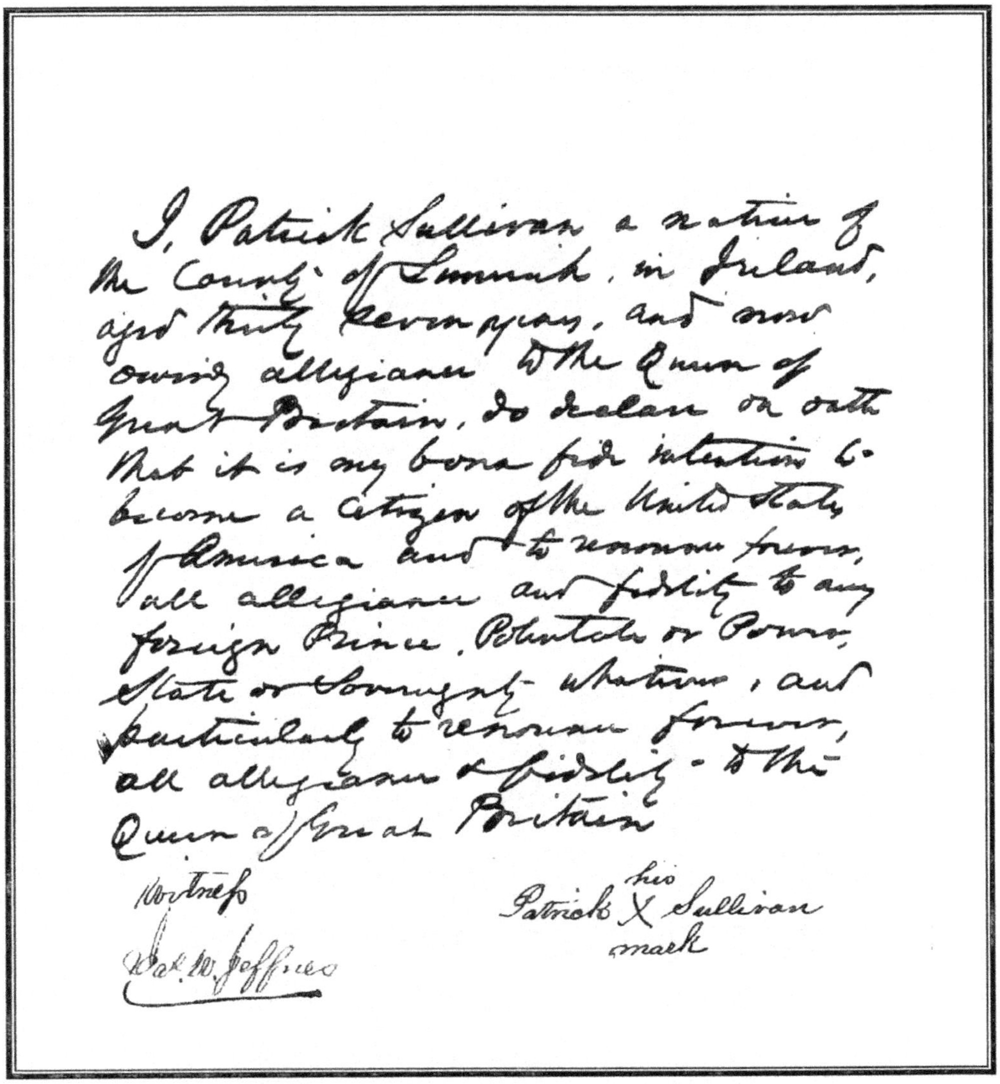

> I, Patrick Sullivan, a native of the County of Limerick, in Ireland, aged thirty seven years, and now owing allegiance to the Queen of Great Britain, do declare on oath that it is my bona fide intention to become a Citizen of the United States of America and to renounce forever, all allegiance and fidelity to any foreign Prince, Potentate or Power, State or Sovereignty whatever, and particularly to renounce forever, all allegiance & fidelity to the Queen of Great Britain
>
> Witness
> Dan. W. Jeffries
>
> Patrick X Sullivan
>   his mark

Plate 64. Miscellaneous Records, County Court Papers.
Scanned Image from Box 23. Naturalizations 1854-006. Patrick Sullivan's Declaration of Intent.

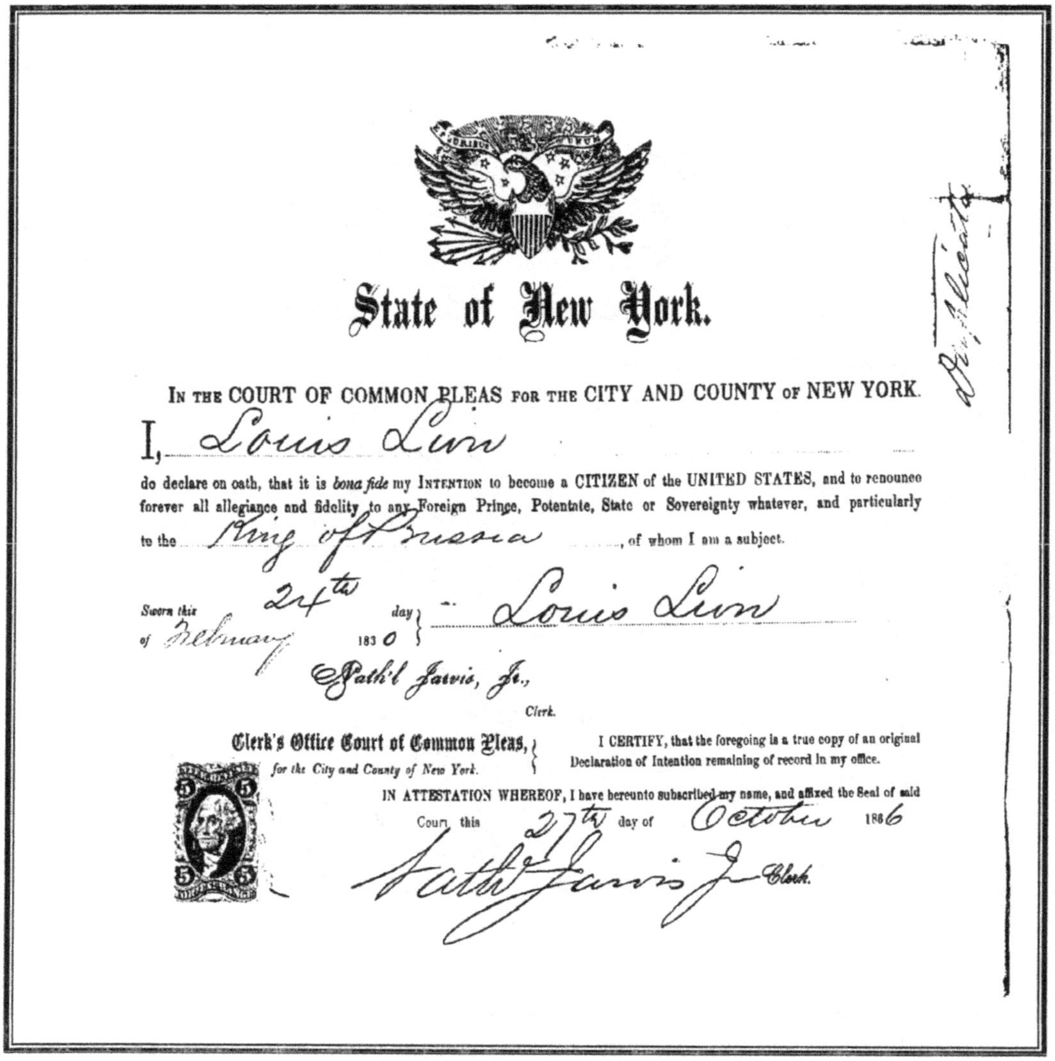

Plate 65. Miscellaneous Records, County Court Papers. Scanned Image from Box 23, Naturalization. 1866-002. Louis Lion's Declaration of Intent.

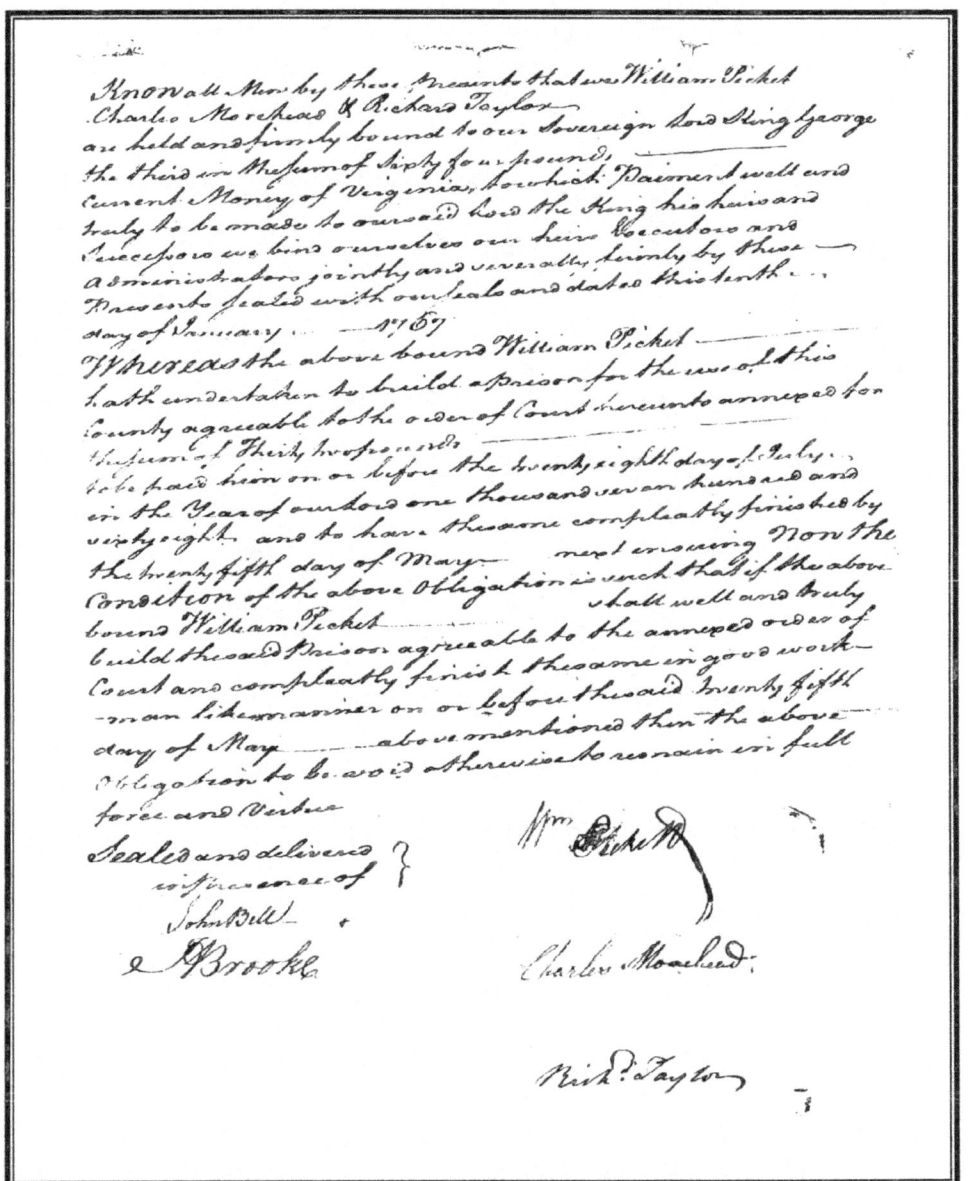

Plate 66. Miscellaneous Records, Clerks Loose Papers. Scanned Image from Box 9, The Jail. 1767-001 William Pickett's Bond to build a prison

In obedience to an order of the worshipful Court of Fauquier dated
august Court 1772 I proceeded to survey the prison Bounds of the said
County — Beginning at a post one of the former Corners of the bounds
Extending thence N°. 29 dr. E. 81 poles thence N° 61 dr. W 19 poles 7
tenths thence S° 29 dr. W 81 poles thence S° 61 dr. E 19 poles 7 tenths
to the beginning Containing — 10 acres —

John Loe }
Joseph Neale } Chainmen

John Knight Surveyor

Plate 67. Miscellaneous Records, Clerks Loose Papers. Scanned Image from Box 9.
The Jail 1771-001 Prison Bounds Survey

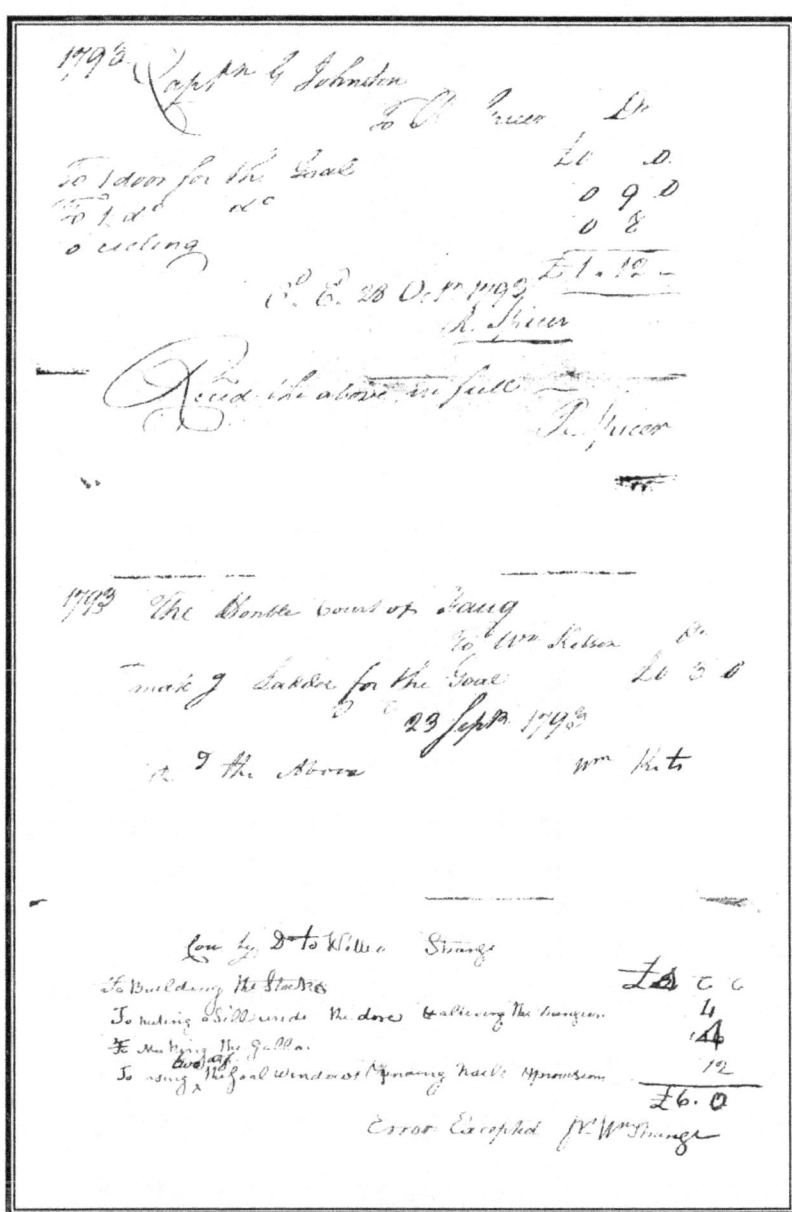

Plate 68. Miscellaneous Records, Clerks Loose Papers. Scanned Image from Box 9. The Jail 1793-001 Three Jail Work Accounts.

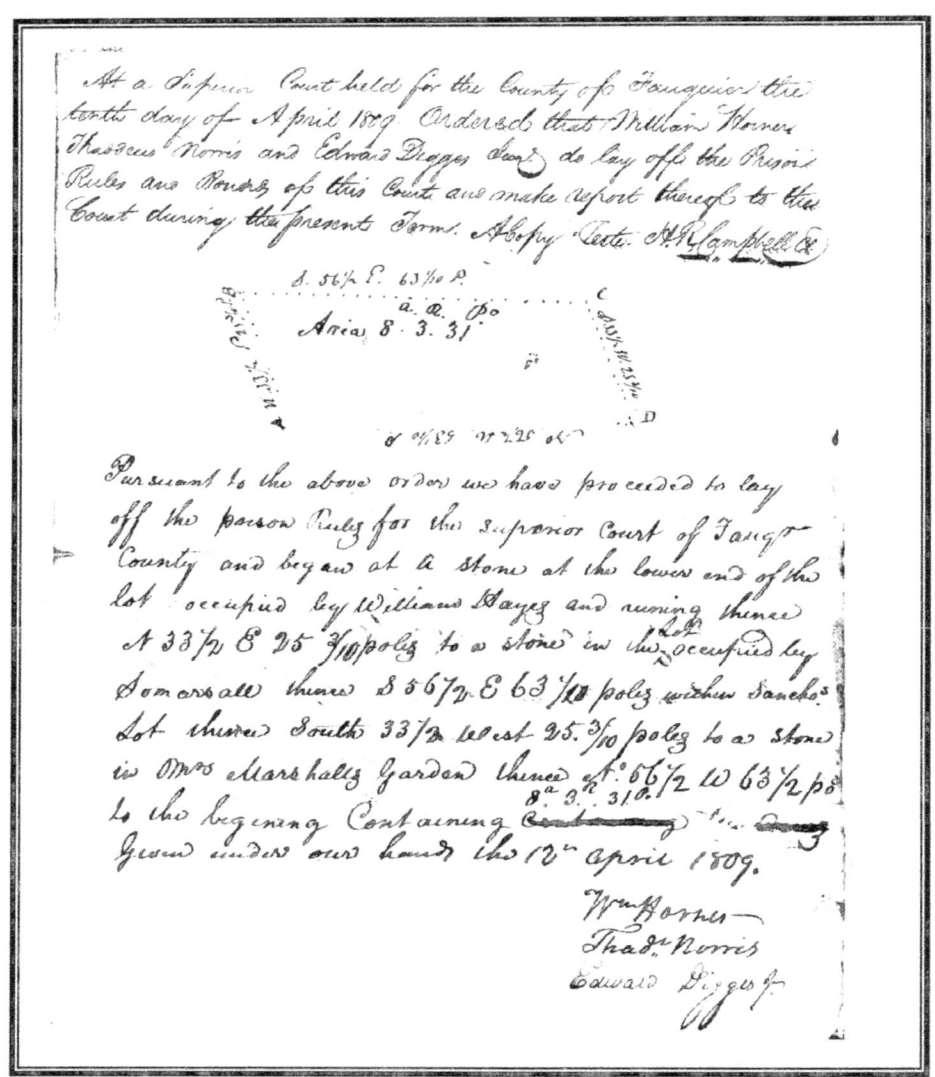

Plate 69. Miscellaneous Records, Clerks Loose Papers. Scanned Image from Box 9.
The Jail 1809-001 Plat & Survey of Prison Bounds

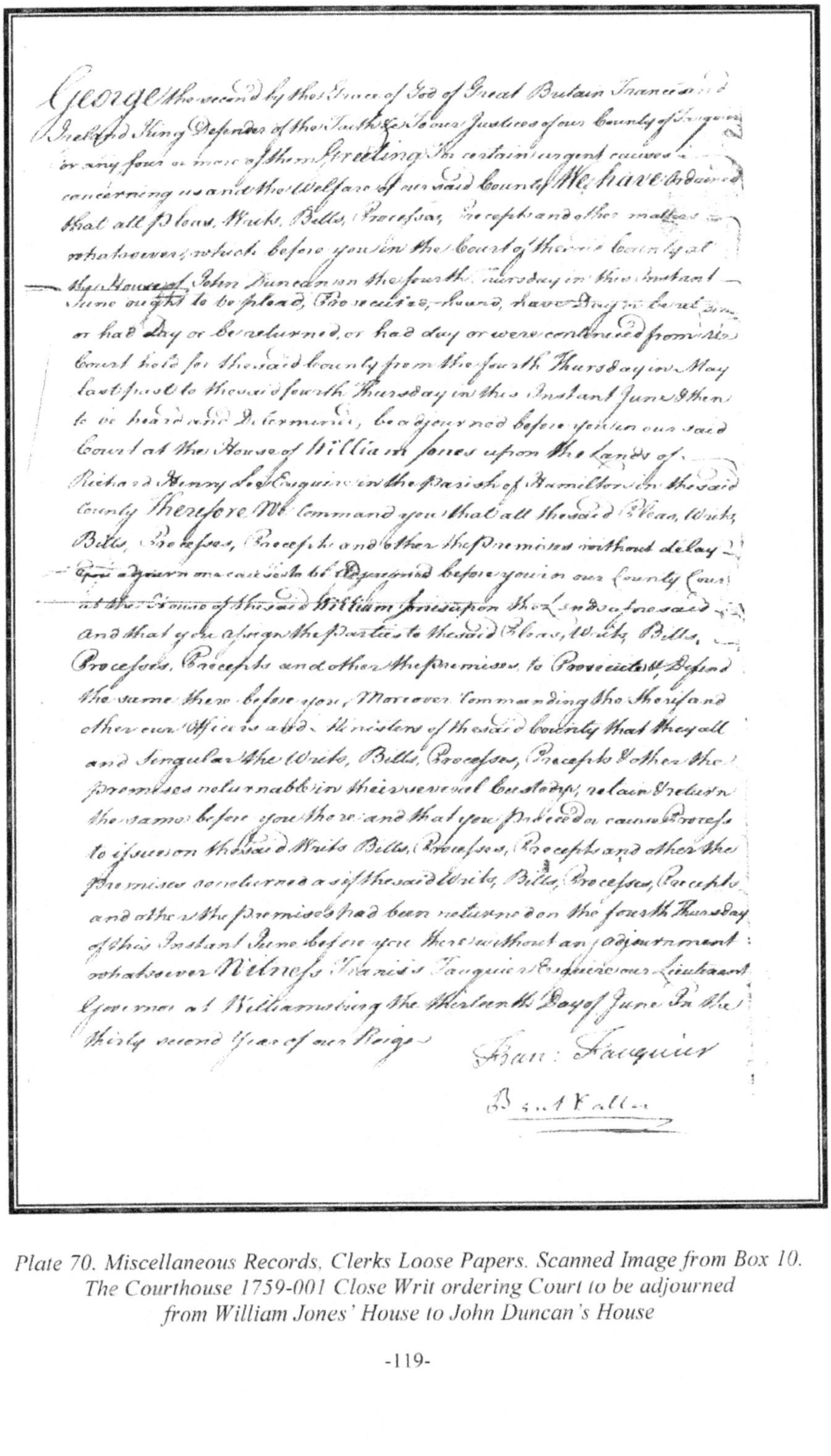
George the second by the Grace of God of Great Britain France and
Ireland King Defender of the Faith &c To our Justices of our County of Fauquier
or any four or more of them Greeting In certain urgent causes
concerning us and the Welfare of our said County We have Ordained
that all Pleas, Writs, Bills, Processes, Precepts and other matters
whatsoever, which before you in the Court of the said County at
the House of John Duncan on the fourth Thursday in this Instant
June ought to be plead, Prosecuted, heard, have Day or be returned
or had Day or be returned, or had day or were continued from the
Court held for the said County from the fourth Thursday in May
last past to the said fourth Thursday in this Instant June & then
to be heard and Determined, be adjourned before you in our said
Court at the House of William Jones upon the Lands of
Richard Henry Lee Esquire in the Parish of Hamilton in the said
County Therefore We Command you that all the said Pleas, Writs,
Bills, Processes, Precepts and other the Premises without delay
you adjourn or cause to be adjourned before you in our County Court
at the House of the said William Jones upon the Lands aforesaid
and that you assign the Parties to the said Pleas, Writs, Bills,
Processes, Precepts and other the premises, to Prosecute & Defend
the same there before you, Moreover Commanding the Sheriff and
other our Officers and Ministers of the said County that they all
and Singular the Writs, Bills, Processes, Precepts & other the
premises returnable in their several Custody, retain & return
the same before you there and that you proceed or cause Process
to issue on the said Writs Bills, Processes, Precepts and other the
Premises so returned as if the said Writs, Bills, Processes, Precepts
and other the premises had been returned on the fourth Thursday
of this Instant June before you there without any adjournment
whatsoever Witness Francis Fauquier Esquire our Lieutenant
Governor at Williamsburg the thirteenth Day of June In the
thirty second Year of our Reign

Fran: Fauquier

Benj Waller

Plate 70. Miscellaneous Records, Clerks Loose Papers. Scanned Image from Box 10. The Courthouse 1759-001 Close Writ ordering Court to be adjourned from William Jones' House to John Duncan's House

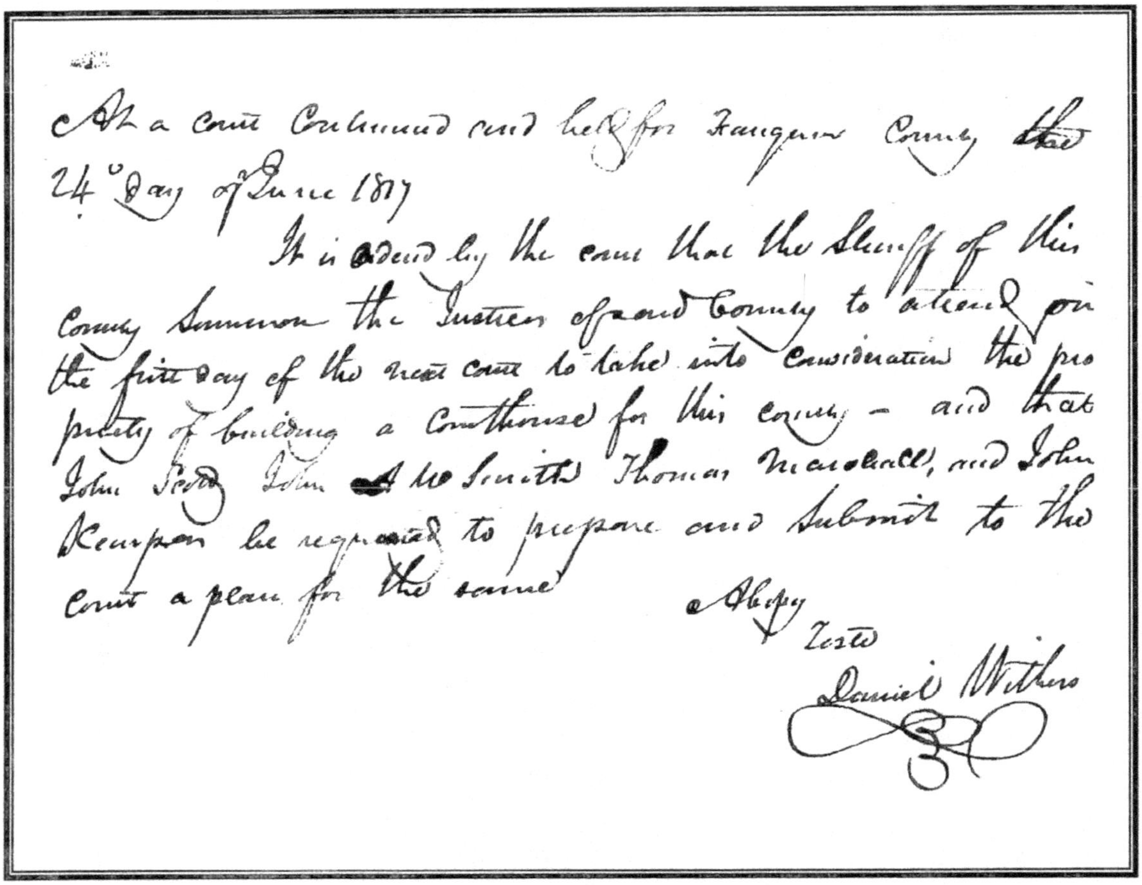

At a Court Continued and held for Fauquier County the 24th Day of June 1817

It is Ordered by the Court that the Sheriff of this County Summon the Justices of said County to attend on the first day of the next Court to take into Consideration the propriety of building a Courthouse for this County – and that John Scott John A W Smith Thomas Marshall, and John Kemper be requested to prepare and Submit to the Court a plan for the same

A Copy
Teste
Daniel Withers

Plate 71. Miscellaneous Records, Clerks Loose Papers. Scanned Image from Box 10.
The Courthouse 1817-002 Order summoning Justices to consider building a new Courthouse.

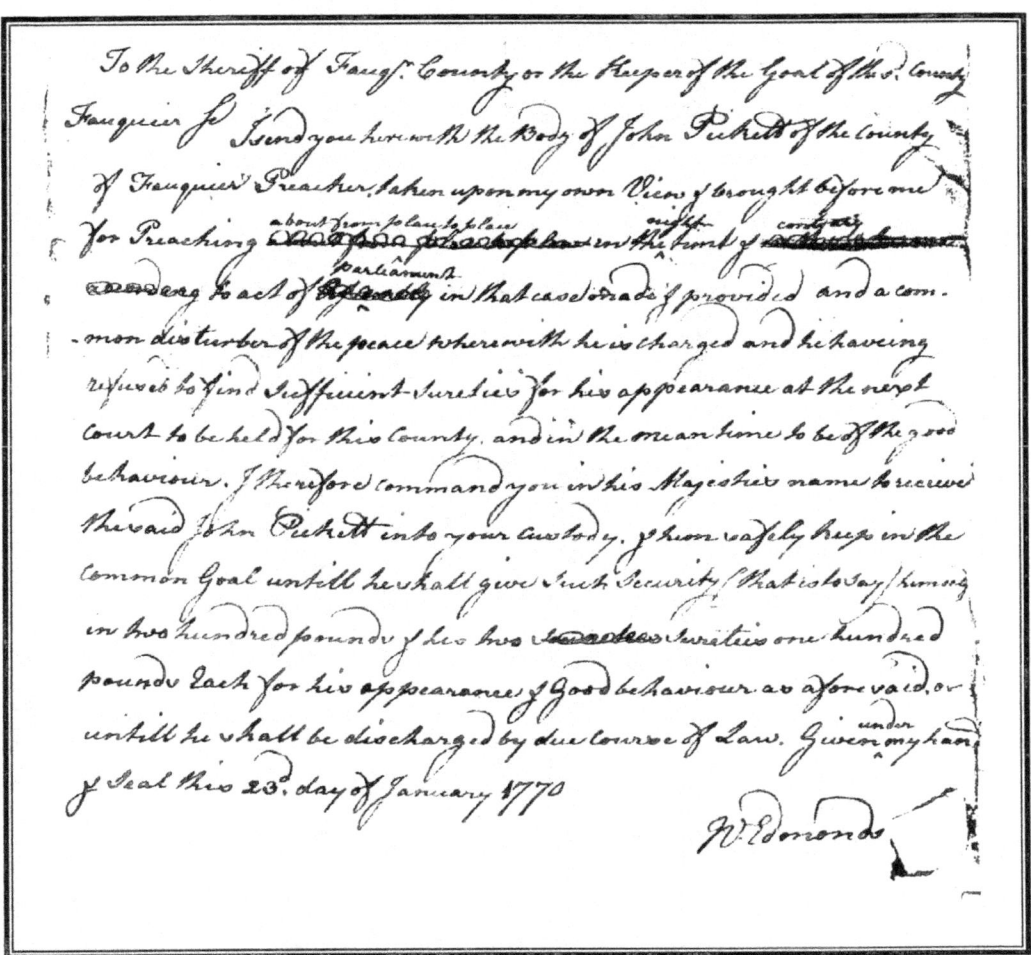

Plate 72. Miscellaneous Records, Clerks Loose Papers. Scanned Image from Box 12.
Interesting Finds 1771-001. John Pickett's Arrest for preaching at night and as a common disturber of the peace.

> Fauquier County to Wit
>
> Whereas I have rec.d information from Hannah Jennings that the following property to wit some Indian Corn in the Ears has within ten days last past, been feloniously taken Stolen & carried away out of possession of the said Hannah living in the County aforesaid and that the said Hannah Jennings hath probable cause to Suspect, and doth suspect that the said Corn are concealed in the House of Isaac Doyle of the said County these are therefore in the name of the Commonwealth to Authorize & require you with necessary & proper assistance to enter in the day time into the place Suspected of the said Isaac Doyl and then there diligently to search for the said Corn and if the said Corn or any part thereof shall be found upon search that you bring the same and also the body of the said Isaac Doyl before me or some Other Justice of the peace for this County to be disposed of and dealt with according to Law Given under my hand & seal this 5th day May 1800 —
>
> Tho. Wirth Seal
>
> To
> Peter Lucas
>   Constable
> to execute & return

Plate 73. Miscellaneous Records, Clerks Loose Papers. Scanned Image from Box 12. Interesting Finds 1800-005. An Early Search Warrant.

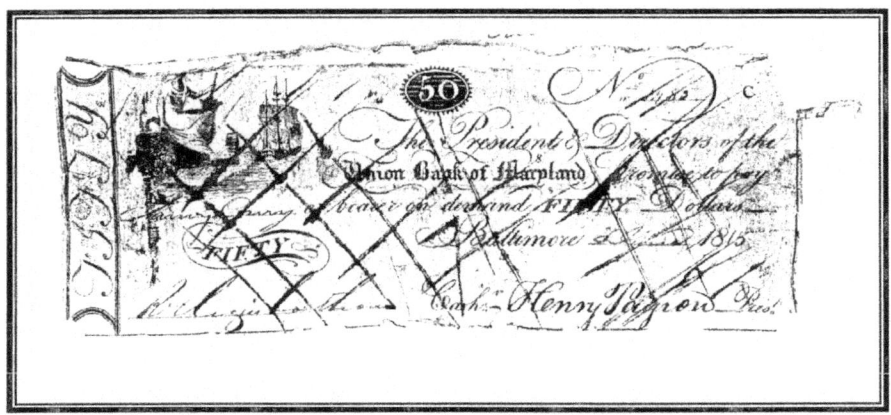

Plate 74. Miscellaneous Records, Clerks Loose Papers. Scanned Image from Box 12. Interesting Finds 1822-003. A Counterfeit $50.00 Bank Note from Ended Causes suit styled Holy & Stuckly v. Chilton.

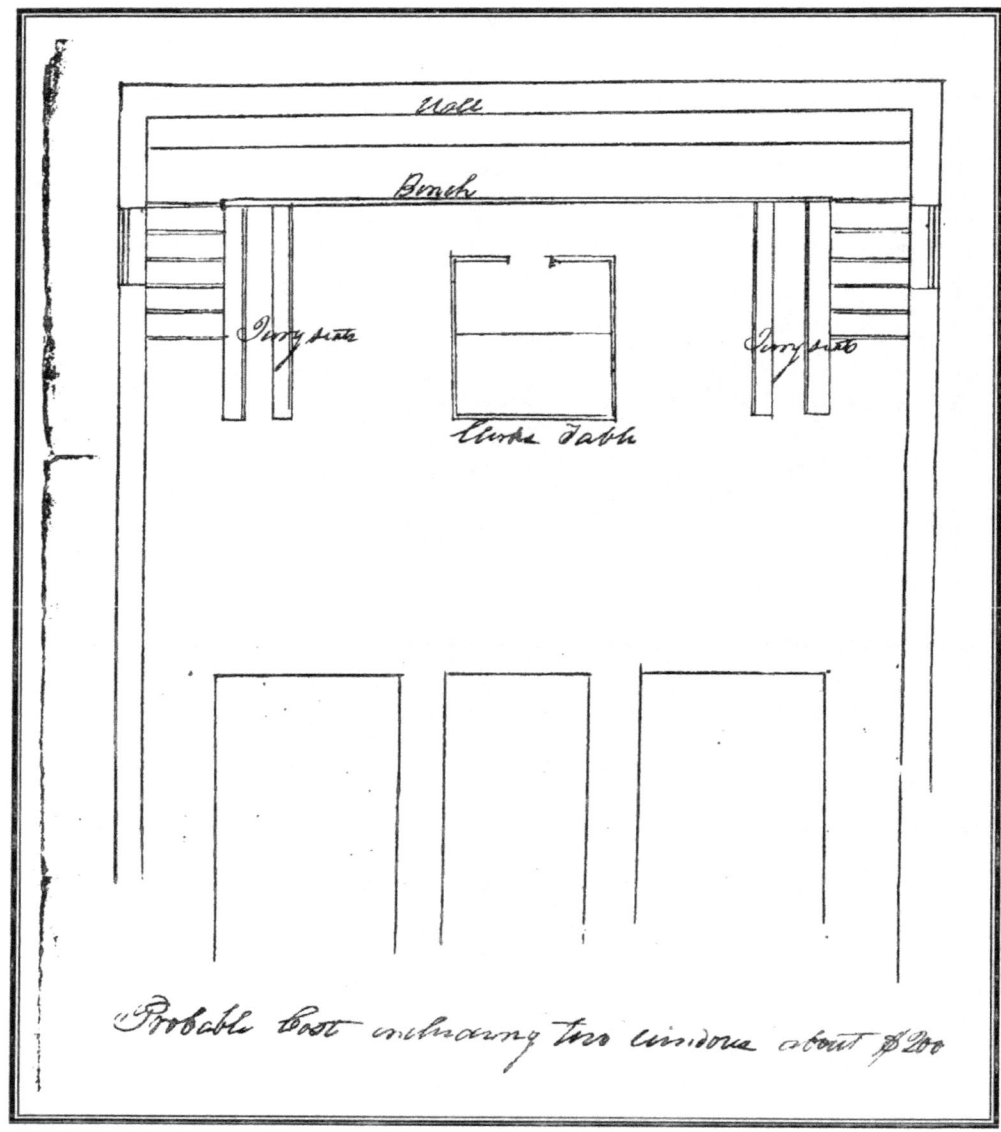

Plate 75. Miscellaneous Records, County Court Papers. Scanned Image from Box 15. The Courthouse 1840-001 Plan of Change in Courthouse Floor Plan

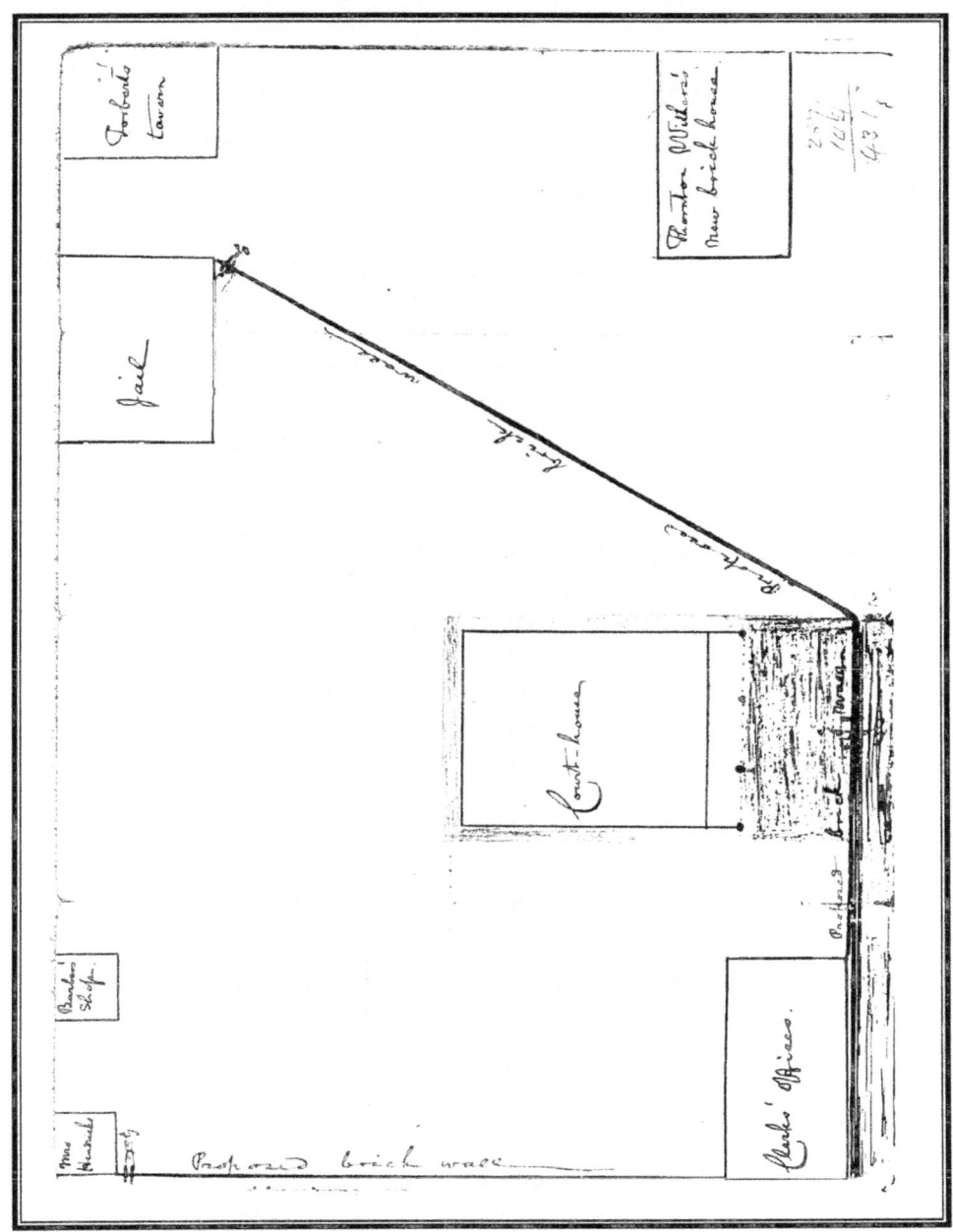

Plate 76. Miscellaneous Records, County Court Papers. Scanned Image from Box 15. The Courthouse 1848-001. Diagram showing how Courthouse and Clerk's Office are to be enclosed by a brick wall.

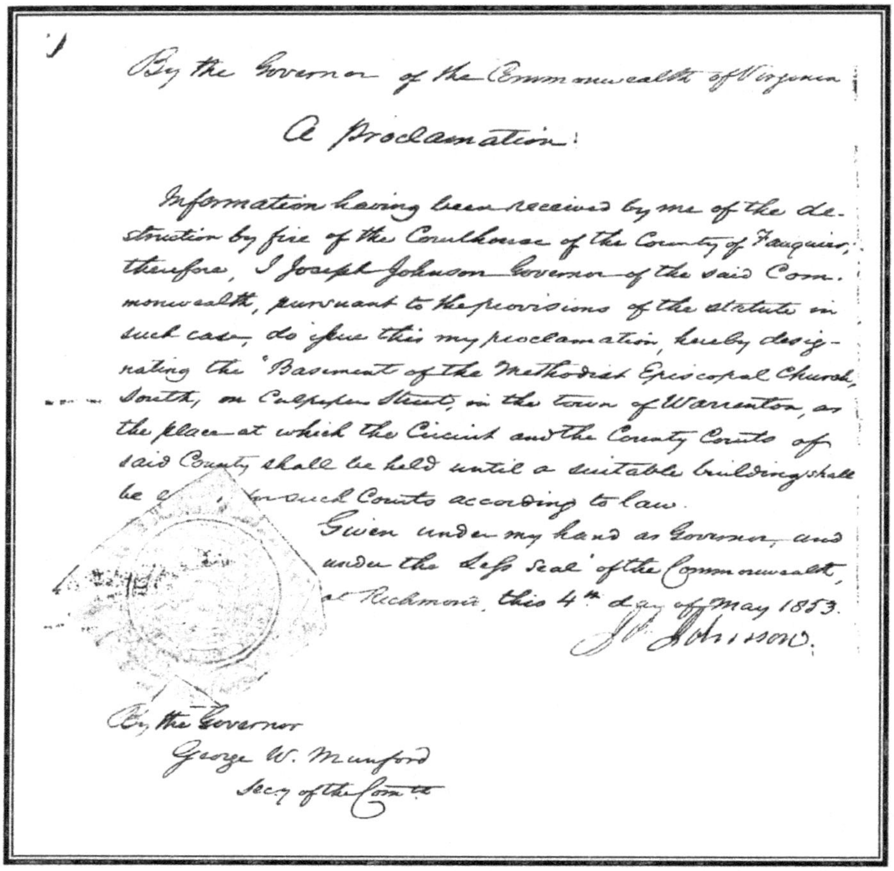

By the Governor of the Commonwealth of Virginia

A Proclamation

Information having been received by me of the destruction by fire of the Courthouse of the County of Fauquier, therefore, I Joseph Johnson Governor of the said Commonwealth, pursuant to the provisions of the statute in such case, do issue this my proclamation, hereby designating the Basement of the Methodist Episcopal Church, South, on Culpeper Street, in the town of Warrenton, as the place at which the Circuit and the County Courts of said County shall be held until a suitable building shall be ____ for such Courts according to law.

Given under my hand as Governor, and under the less seal of the Commonwealth, at Richmond, this 4th day of May 1853.

J? Johnson

By the Governor
George W. Munford
Sec'y of the Com'th

Plate 77. Miscellaneous Records, County Court Papers. Scanned Image from Box 15. The Courthouse 1853-002 1853 Proclamation by Governor Joseph Johnson of Virginia regarding the destruction by fire of the Courthouse of Fauquier County.

Fauquier County, Virginia's Clerks Loose Papers: A Guide to the Records 1759-1919

CHAPTER 12
ORDINARY RECORDS

1. Overview

Eighteenth century ordinaries acted as restaurants, taverns, public houses and inns and served one standard meal to all travelers at a fixed price. Ordinary keepers sold a variety of beverages including liquor and cider. They were expected to keep their establishments in an orderly fashion. Gaming was illegal, whether by games of chance, dice or cards.

Ordinaries were a place to meet, have a friendly drink, gossip and catch up on the news. Often ordinaries were kept in people's homes. While the vast majority of the ordinary keepers were men, there are bonds for women to keep ordinaries in their houses as well. Ordinaries were located through out the county, usually on well traveled roads.

These records, along with those in Mills, Roads & Bridges, give the researcher a greater insight into the daily activities, habits, conduct, behavior and customs of eighteenth and nineteenth century Virginians.

2. The Ordinary Bond

By the time the bond was issued, applicants for ordinaries had already applied for and received a license, good for a year. Licenses could be renewed as long as the ordinary keeper stayed within the law. Bonds were taken out each time a license was issued.

The ordinary bond gives the name of the person entering into the bond, the date and the nature of the conditions or obligations. There is usually a stiff monetary penalty associated with the non-performance of the conditions of the bond. For this reason, applicants found another person to act as a security with them for the performance of the conditions within the bond.

Four conditions had to be met for those operating an ordinary. The first two conditions centered on the provision of food and shelter – for travelers and their animals. The ordinary keeper was responsible for finding and providing good, wholesome and clean lodging and diet for travelers, and for providing stabelage, fodder, and pasturage for horses, as the season required.

The last two conditions demonstrated the Court's concern with behavior. Ordinary keepers were not to allow unlawful gaming in his or her house. On the Sabbath, he or she was not to allow anyone "to Tipple or drink any more than is necessary."

If these conditions were met and kept throughout the term of the license, then the bond was to be null and void. If they were not kept, then the monetary penalty would be forfeited. In addition, suits could be brought against the offending ordinary keeper. They might be charged with selling liquor without a license, running a disorderly house or permitting illegal gaming on their premises.

3. Finding your way around Ordinary Records

Series Title: Ordinary Records
Color Code: Black and Blue Dots on Boxes

Series Dates: 1759-001 to 1850-001
Series Extent: 4 Boxes. *1.6 linear feet.*
Series Arrangement: *Filed by year, thereunder by party.*

Fauquier County, Virginia's Clerks Loose Papers: A Guide to the Records 1759-1919

Series Finding Aid: *Name Index for Ordinary Records 1759-1808*

Types of records in Ordinaries include
- a. Ordinary Bonds and Licenses
- b. Ordinary Accounts
- c. Tavern Fees set by the Court
- d. Peddler Licenses

Ordinary Suits from Commonwealth Causes include
- a. Suits for selling liquor without a license
- b. Suits for illegal gaming
- c. Suits for keeping a disorderly house

4. A Preview of the Ordinary Records Index (1759-1808)

Figure 20 illustrates a representative sampling of the name index for the first box of ordinary records. This index gives only the name of the party who was taking out a bond. It does not index those who acted as securities to the bonds. Only the bonds in the first box have been indexed.

Index #	Surname	Given Name	Date	Type of Record	Location
1800-001	Adams	John & Samuel	1801, 06/12	Merchant License	
1771-001	Allen	Thomas	1771, 10/28	Ordinary Bond	at his house
1760-014	Ashby	John	1760, 02/27	Ordinary Bond	at his dwelling plantation
1807-001	Barbey	Thomas	1807	Grand Jury Presentment for selling liquor w/o a license.	
1796-001	Barnett	Ambrose	1793, 11/--	from List of Ordinary Licenses filed with Court	
1759-004	Hardin	Mark	1759, 08/23	Ordinary Bond	at his house
1763-004	James	Thomas	1763, 09/22	Ordinary Bond	at his house
1786-002	Maddux	Thomas	1786, 03/31	Ordinary Bond	at his house near Fauquier Courthouse
1782-001	Montgomerie	William	1782, 11/25	Ordinary Bond	at house of Joseph Nelson
1768-001	Morgan	John	1768-05/24	Ordinary Bond	at the German Town
1769-004	Neavil	George	1769, 03/28	Ordinary Bond	at his house

Figure 20. Representative examples from the Ordinary Index 1759-1808.

Index #	Surname	Given Name	Date	Type of Record	Location
1802-002	Norris	Thaddeus	1802	from List of Ordinary Licenses filed w/ Clerk	
1771-003	Peake	John	1771, 03/26	Ordinary Bond	at the Courthouse
1800-001	Pendleton	Edmond	1799, 11/18	Merchant License	
1800-001	Stanton	William	1799, 05/01	Merchant License	
1780-001	Turner	John	1780, 07/25	Ordinary Bond	at his house near the Courthouse
1805-002	Verone	Joseph	1805, 02/25	Ordinary Bond	at his house
1759-003	Weaver	Tilman	1759, 09/27	Ordinary Bond	at his house
1761-010	Withers	James	1761, 08/23	Ordinary Bond	at his dwelling plantation
1773-001	Wright	James	1773, 06/28	Ordinary Bond	at the old Glebe

Figure 20. Representative examples from the Ordinary License Index 1759-1808 (Cont.)

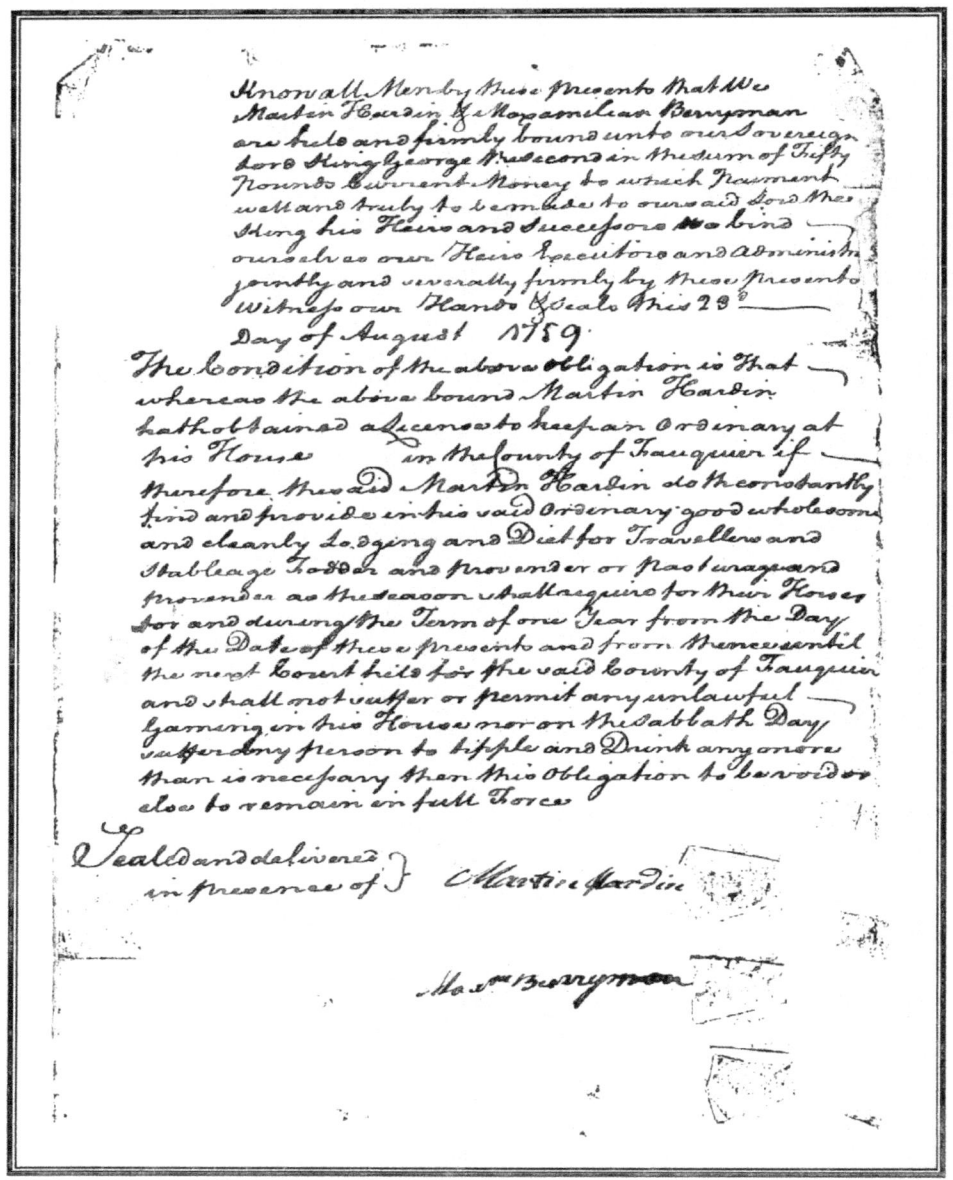

Plate 78. Ordinary Records. Scanned Image from Ordinary Records, Box. 1. Ordinary Records 1759-004. Martin Hardin's Bond to keep an Ordinary.

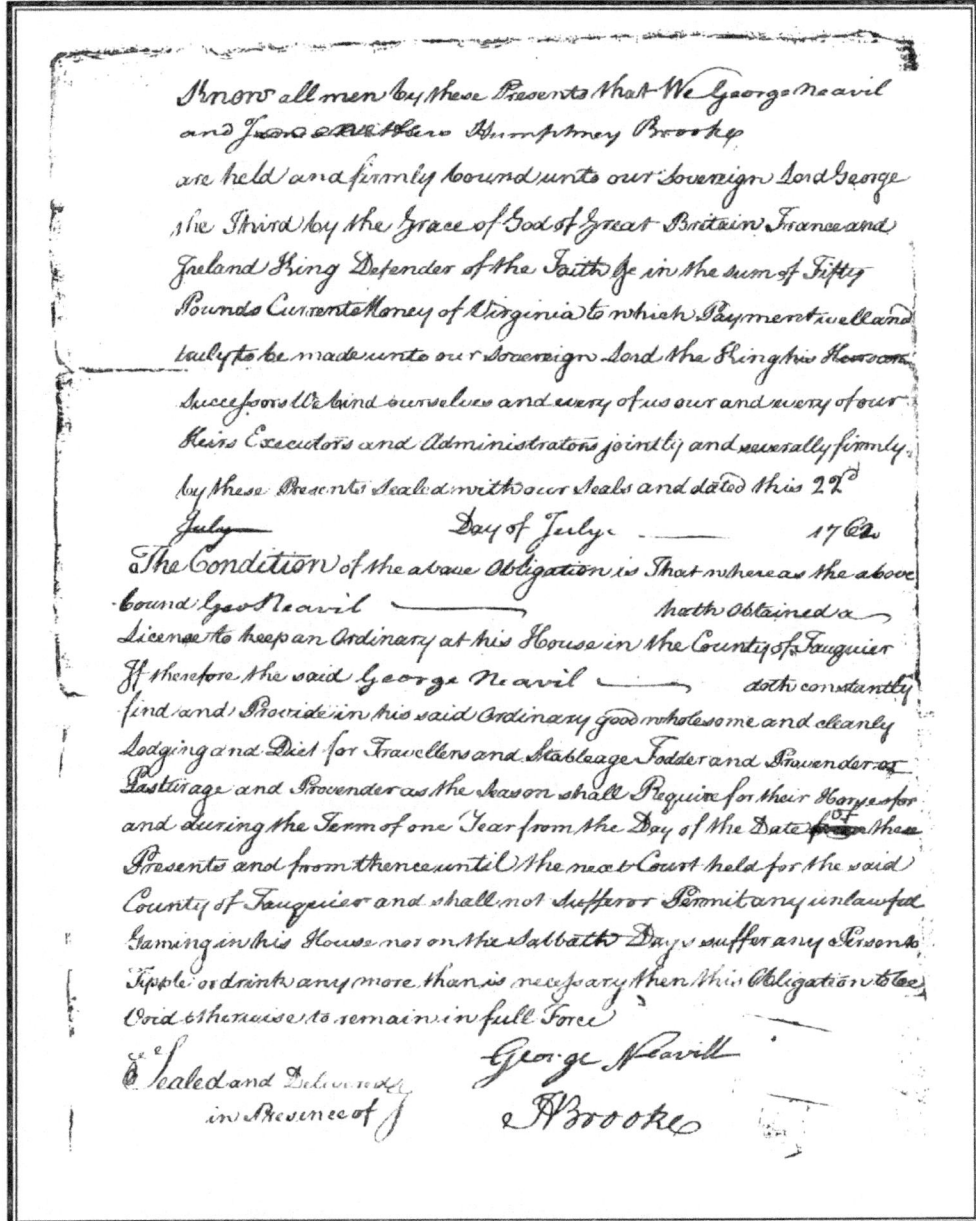

Plate 79. Ordinary Records. Scanned Image from Ordinary Records, Box 1.
Ordinary Record 1762-001 George Neavill's Bond to keep an Ordinary.

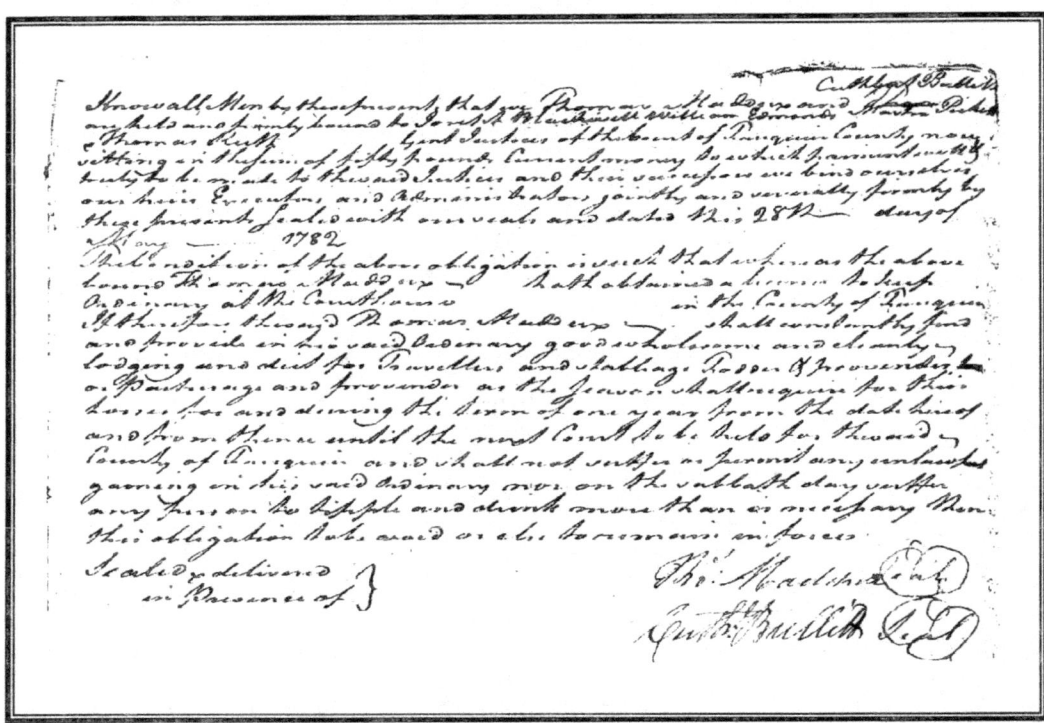

Plate 80. Ordinary Records. Scanned Image from Ordinary Records, Box 1.
Ordinary Record 1782-001 Thomas Maddux's Bond to keep an Ordinary at [Fauquier] Courthouse.

Fauquier County to wit Cuthbert Bullett Gent attorney for the Commonwealth for the County aforesaid who for the Commonwealth informs & prosecutes came here into Court this 22 day of may in the Year of our Lord 1786 and the said Cuthbert Bullett Gent. attorney for the Commonwealth for the County aforesaid, for the Commonwealth giveth the Court here to understand and be informed that, whereas by an act of assembly intitled an act for regulating ordinaries & restraint of tippling houses it is among other things enacted that if any person shall presume to keep a tippling house or retail liquors or sell by retail any wine, beer, cyder, brandy, rum or other spirits or any mixture of such liquor, in any house or booth, arbour, stall, or any other place whatsoever without licence first obtained in mannor as is directed in & by the said act he or she so offending shall forfeit & pay ten pounds current money the one moiety thereof to the King his heirs & successors for and towards the better support of this Government & the Contingent Charges thereof the other moiety to the informer recoverable with Costs in any Court of record in this Commonwealth then colony of Virginia, having cognizance thereof or on failure of present payment or security for payment within six months the party so convicted shall by order of the Court before whom such conviction shall be receive on his or her bare back twenty lashes well laid on at the publick whipping post and which moiety in mann or aforesaid appropriat[...] now is appropriated by law in the same manner to the use of the Commonwealth and that whereas by another act of assembly intitled an act to amend an act for regulating ordinaries & restraint of tippling houses it is among other things enacted that every person keeping a tippling house or retailing liquors contrary to the before recited act shall over & above the penalties inflicted by the said act forfeit & pay the sum of fifty pounds for each & every offence to be recovered with Costs by action of Debt or information in any Court of record one half to the informer & the other half to the Commonwealth or the whole to the Commonwealth where prosecution shall be first instituted on the publick behalf alone — Mary Neale widow — upon the first day of June in the Year of our Lord 1785 at the parish of in the County aforesaid

Plate 81. Ordinary Records. Scanned Image from Ordinary Records, Box 1. Ordinary Record 1788-001. Page 1 of Commonwealth v. Mary Neale, widow.

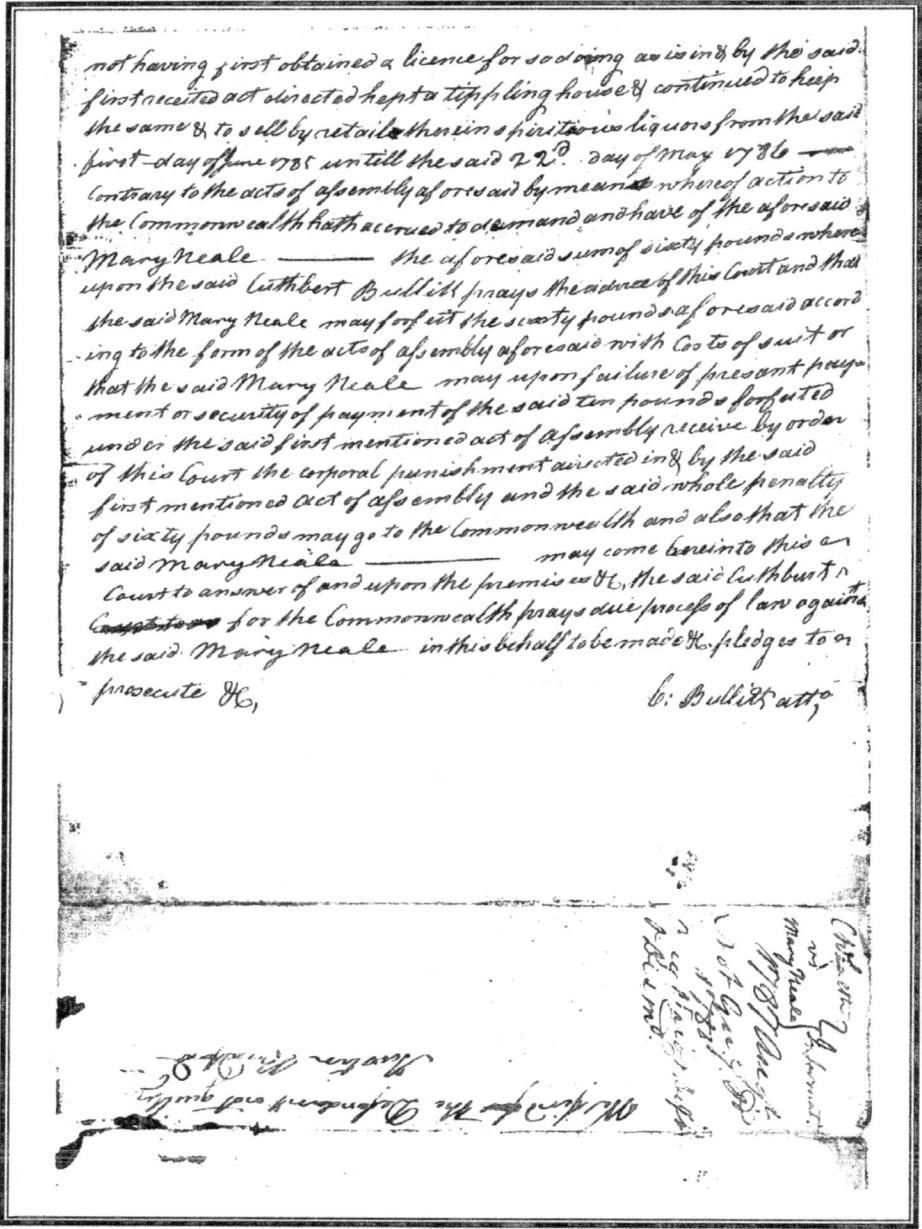

Plate 81 (Cont.) Ordinary Records Scanned Image from Ordinary Records, Box 1. Ordinary Record 1788-001. Page 2 of Commonwealth v. Mary Neale, widow.

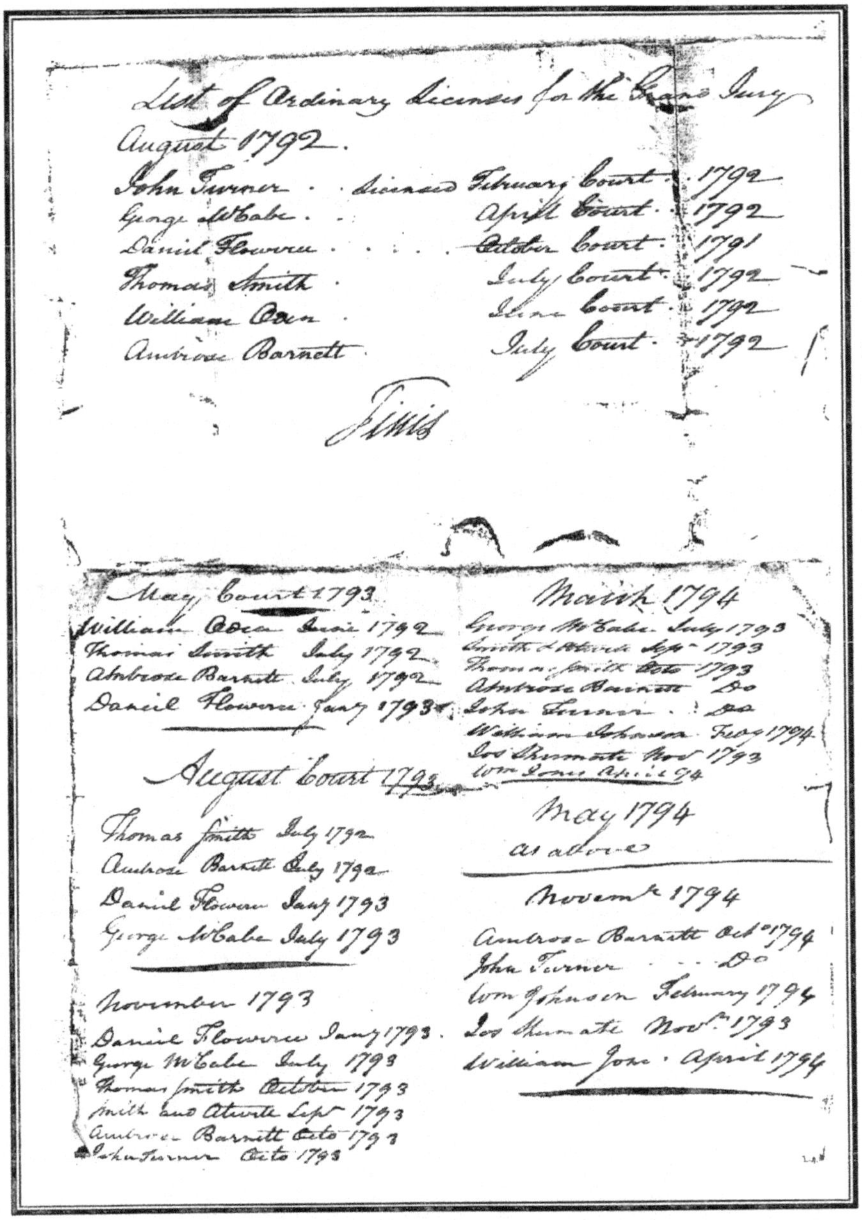

List of Ordinary Licenses for the Grand Jury
August 1792.

John Turner . . licensed February Court . 1792
George McCabe . . April Court . 1792
Daniel Flowree . . . . October Court . 1791
Thomas Smith . July Court . 1792
William Orr . June Court . 1792
Ambrose Barnett . July Court . 1792

Finis

May Court 1793
William Orr June 1792
Thomas Smith July 1792
Ambrose Barnett July 1792
Daniel Flowree Jany 1793

August Court 1793
Thomas Smith July 1792
Ambrose Barnett July 1792
Daniel Flowree Jany 1793
George McCabe July 1793

November 1793
Daniel Flowree Jany 1793.
George McCabe July 1793
Thomas Smith October 1793
Smith and Atwell Sept 1793
Ambrose Barnett Octo 1793
John Turner Octo 1793

March 1794
George McCabe July 1793
Smith & Atwell Sept 1793
Thomas Smith Octo 1793
Ambrose Barnett Do
John Turner . Do
William Johnson Feby 1794
Jos Shumate Nov 1793
Wm Jones April 94

May 1794
as above

Novemr 1794
Ambrose Barnett Octo 1794
John Turner . . Do
Wm Johnson February 1794
Jos Shumate Novr 1793
William Jones . April 1794

Plate 82. Ordinary Records. Scanned Image from Ordinary Records, Box 1.
Ordinary Record 1796-001. List of Ordinary Licenses for the Grand Jury, August 1792- November 1794.

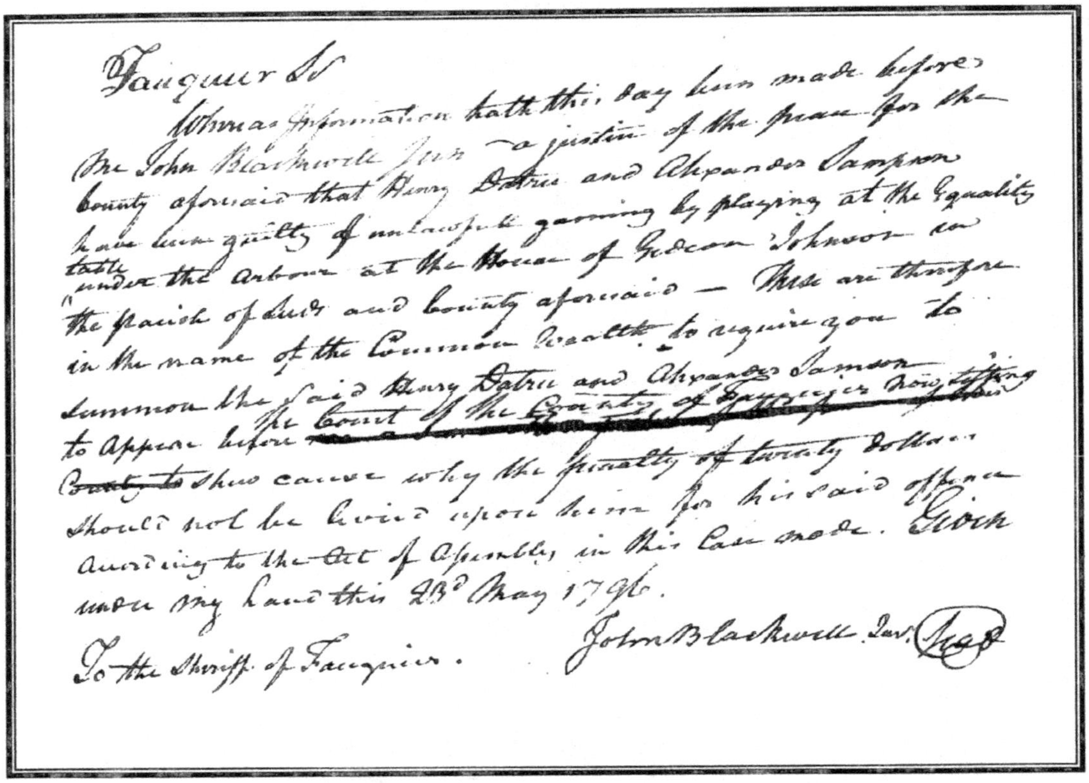
Fauquier Sct
Whereas Information hath this day been made before
me John Blackwell Junr a justice of the peace for the
County aforesaid that Henry Datree and Alexander Sampson
have been guilty of unlawful gaming by playing at the Equality
table under the arbour at the House of Gideon Johnson in
the parish of Leeds and County aforesaid — These are therefore
in the name of the Commonwealth to require you to
summon the said Henry Datree and Alexander Sampson
to appear before the Court of the County of Fauquier now sitting
~~County to~~ shew cause why the penalty of twenty dollars
should not be levied upon him for his said offence
according to the Act of Assembly in this Case made. Given
under my hand this 23d May 1796.
John Blackwell Junr (Seal)
To the Sheriff of Fauquier.

Plate 83. Ordinary Records. Scanned Image from Ordinary Records, Box 1.
Ordinary Record 1796-003. Commonwealth v. Henry Datree and Alexander Sampson.
For unlawful gaming... under the arbor at Gideon Johnston's house.

CHAPTER 13
OVERSEERS OF THE POOR/CHURCHWARDEN RECORDS

1. Overview

During the colonial period, the established Anglican Church and its parish Churchwardens provided for the county's poor. The church tithes and county levies provided the income to maintain and care for poor families. Poor orphans, regardless of race or color, were bound out to families to learn a trade. Boys were indentured until they were twenty-one; girls, until they were eighteen. These indentures enabled poor children to become self-sufficient, responsible adults with marketable skills.

There are several dozen sits brought by the Churchwardens against unmarried women who had children out of wedlock. These women had little trouble naming the father; the Churchwardens then sued these men in order to provide support for the illegitimate children.

After the disestablishment of the Church of England in Virginia, county Overseers of the Poor were charged with the responsibility for the care and maintenance of the county's poor. Many of the poor families went to reside in Poor Houses, built especially for them. Others continued to reside with private families. The Overseers of the Poor provided money for their board, meals, medical needs and clothing.

The Overseers of the Poor continued to provide apprentices to local families from among the poor children, whether they lived with their own families, too poor to support them, or whether they were orphans without any estate to maintain them.

This meant that there was a steady supply of inexpensive labor. During the nineteenth century, the Justices of the County standardized the wages for the apprentice's labor. The wage went to the mother of the apprentice, if alive, until the last year of the indenture. The last year's wage went directly to the apprentice.

The justices also provided ways for apprentices to seek legal redress against cruel or unusual treatment. There were several suits instituted against the man or woman to whom the child was indentured. If the Court agreed that the apprentice had been mistreated, it ruled for the indentures to be rescinded and looked for another family for the child to live with while he or she learned a trade.

Taking care of the county's poor created an infrastructure to supply the poor with basic needs. Doctors were need to care for sick family members. Residents of the Poor House who died were supplied with coffins and burial expenses. Families often needed a means of transportation to the poor house for their meager possessions and themselves. Once in the poor house, families were expected to farm the land to sell produce and goods to maintain themselves.

All of these accounts are reflected in the record base: there are numerous accounts by doctors and merchants for supplying basic necessities to the poor house. Wagon teams had to be hired and paid for transportation costs.

The Overseers of the Poor were expected to meet regularly to see what more could be done to meet the needs of their clientele. Minutes of these meetings were kept and some have survived to find their way into this record series. There are lists of paupers with dates of entry and exit from the poor house. Some of the lists give ages of the house's residents. Many of the paupers are women and children.

This is an often-overlooked set of records probably because the researcher is unaware of the content or the importance of this record base. It brings a fresh insight into the workings of the way eighteenth and nineteenth century Virginians came to grips with those individuals or families living without visible means of support.

Fauquier County, Virginia's Clerks Loose Papers: A Guide to the Records 1759-1919

2. The Apprenticeship Indentures

The Parish Churchwardens, and post Revolutionary War successors the Overseers of the Poor, often bound out children of poor families, poor orphans or children likely to become the County's responsibility to individuals in order to learn a trade.

The customary term for an apprenticeship for boys was until they arrived at legal age, that is, twenty-one. The standard term for girls was until they reached the age of eighteen.

The indenture listed responsibilities for both parties. The apprentice promised to serve faithfully, keep any trade secrets, obey all lawful commands of his "master" and "in all points to behave himself as an honest, dutiful Servant". The master, or individual employing the apprentice, in turn promised to find and provide diet, lodging and apparel, fit and convenient for a service of the apprentice. He also promised to carefully instruct him in a trade or occupation which he gives in the indenture. At the end of the specified term, the apprentice was to receive a suit of clothing and, depending on the trade, a set of tools.

The indentures illustrated on the following pages demonstrate a representative sampling of the types of apprenticeships found in these records.

3. Finding your way around Overseer of the Poor Records (OP Records)

Series Title: Overseers of the Poor/Churchwarden Records
Color Code: Black Dots on Boxes

Series Dates: 1761-001 to 1902-003
Series Extent: 3 Boxes. *1.25 linear feet.*
Series Arrangement: *Filed by Year.*

Series Finding Aid: *Apprentice Indenture Index. Overseers of Poor Index of Records*

Box 1 contains Churchwarden and Overseer of the Poor Apprentice Indentures.
Box 2-3 contain these types of **Miscellaneous Records**
1) Pauper Lists
2) Medical and County claims for the maintenance of the poor
3) Overseer of Poor elections
4) Birth and Death records, Burial Accounts and entrance and departure records
5) Beef, Pork and Foodstuff accounts
6) Petitions for admission into the Poor House
7) Churchwarden and Overseer of Poor suits for Illegitimacy

4. A Preview of the Apprentice Indentures Index from Box 1.

Figure 21 shows representative examples of this index. The Apprentices Indentures are indexed by the name of the apprentice.

Index #	Apprentice	Age	Parent/Guardian	Apprenticed to	to learn the art or trade of
1829-001	Adams, Elias			Fletcher, Stephen	Stone mason and Plasterer
1817-002	Bailey, John	15-16		Turner, Charles	Miller
1889-004	Battles, Myredith			Maddux, T. S.	Farming
1825-005	Ford, Eliza	6	Ford, Juda	Morehead, John	
1825-002	Hunton, William Alexander	15		Berry, Benjamin	Boot & Shoemaker
1889-002	Jackson, Hattie	8	Jackson, Andrew	Christ Church for Females of Baltimore City	Needlework
1828-003	Lee, Henry			Mitchell, Daniel	Cabinet + Wheat Fan maker
1821-001	Lloyd, John		Smallwood, Sarah	Byrne, John	Tanning & Currying until he is 21 which will be 1/1/1825.
1825-004	Martin, Thomas		Martin, Rosey	Martin, Frank (his uncle)	Cooper
1774-01	Metcalfe, John Jr.		Metcalfe, John	Cooper, Apollos	Stonemason, Bricklayer + Plasterer
1808-001	Mozingo, Thomas	18		Pendleton, George	Carpenter
1826-002	Ricketts, William S.			Johnson, William	Hatter
1819-001	Shearman, Maria	7	Shearman, John	Glascock, John	Seamstress
1826-006	Sidebottom, Sam			Reid, Hiram C.	Stonemason, Bricklayer + Plasterer
1798-005	Wadkins, Matthew	14	Wadkins, Hannah	Wadkins, Elijah	Stonemason
1835-02	Woolingham, Washington	8	Woolingham, Polly	Feagans, John	Farming

Figure 21. Examples from the Overseers of the Poor-Churchwardens Record Series. Apprentice Index, Box 1.

5. A Preview of the Overseer of the Poor Index of Records from Miscellaneous OP Records, Boxes 2 and 3.

These records are not indexed by names but by the type of record found in the series. Below are some examples of the Churchwarden and Overseers of the Poor Suits against the fathers of illegitimate children.

Index #	Record Type	Parties in Suit	Synopsis of Suit
1761-004	CW Suit	Churchwardens v. Jemima Brown	Fine levied against Jemima Brown for delivering a bastard child.
1762-005	CW Suit	Churchwardens v. Rachel Duncan	Fine levied against Rachel Duncan for delivering a bastard child.
1766-002	CW Suit	James Delahunt v. Richard Healey	Suit to recover his freedom dues.
1801-001	OP Suit	Commonwealth v. Jesse Fletcher	Mary Willis of Frederick County, single woman, delivered a male bastard likely to be chargeable to the county. She charged Jesse Fletcher, under oath, as father.
1804-002	OP Suit	OP v. William Golden	Sarah Gaugh, single woman, delivered a male bastard child 8/30/1830, likely to be chargeable to the county. She charged William Golden, under oath, as the father.
1768-001	CW Indenture	Elijah Nash to Robert Saunders	Elijah Nash apprenticed to Saunders to learn the trade of carpentry and house joinery.
1760-001	CW Suit	Churchwardens v. Bathsheba Norman	Fine levied against Bathsheba Norman for delivering a base born child.
1799-001	OP Suit	OP v. Sanford Pickett	Hannah Wadkins, single woman, delivered a male bastard 10/21/1798, likely to be chargeable to the county. She charged Sanford Pickett, under oath, as the father.
1755-001	CW Suit	William Wright v. Nicholas Smith	to rescind Apprenticeship due to ill-treatment
1830-002	OP Suit	OP v. William Wright	Susan Evans, single woman, was delivered of male bastard child. She charged William Wright with being the father.

Figure 22. A representative sampling of the types of suits brought by the Churchwardens of the Parish and the Overseers of the Poor in the Overseers of the Poor-Churchwarden Miscellaneous Records, Boxes 2-3.

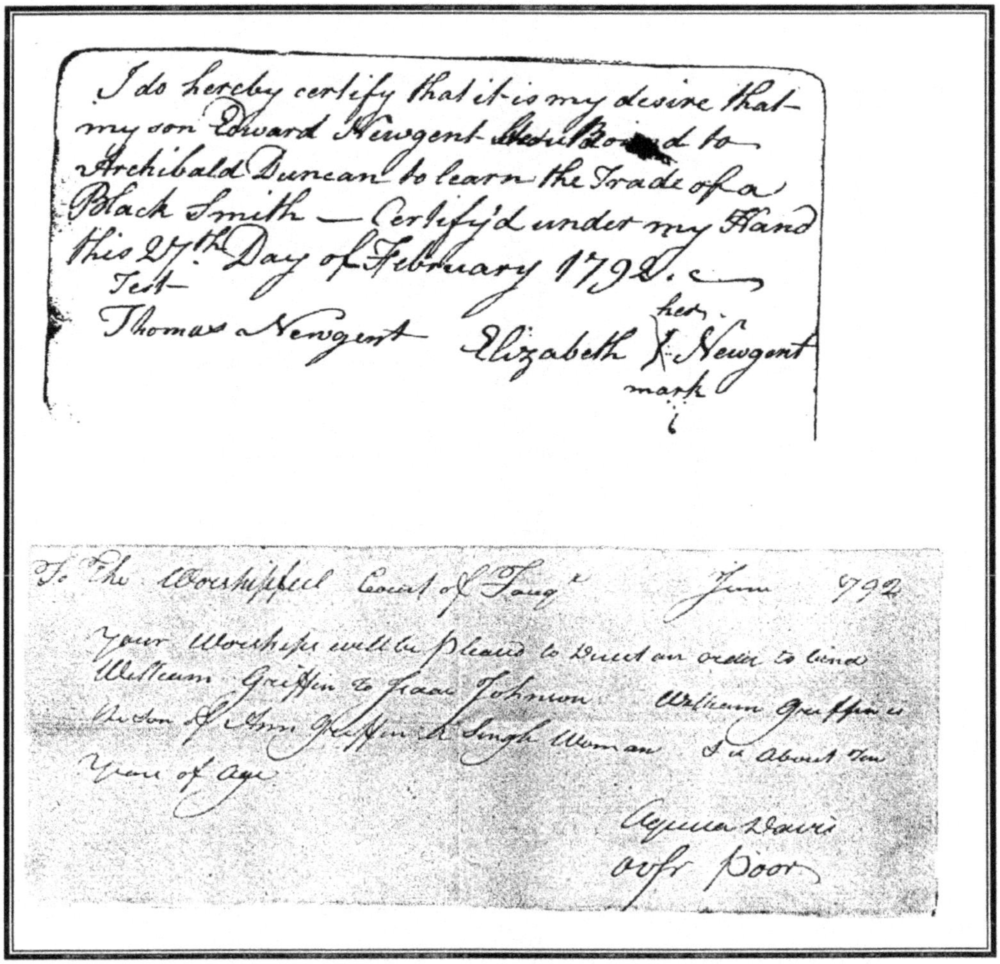

Plate 84. OP/Churchwardens Records. Scanned Image from OP Apprenticeships, Box 1.
Above: 1792-001 Edward Newgent to Archibald Duncan
Below: 1792-002 William Griffin to Isaac Johnson

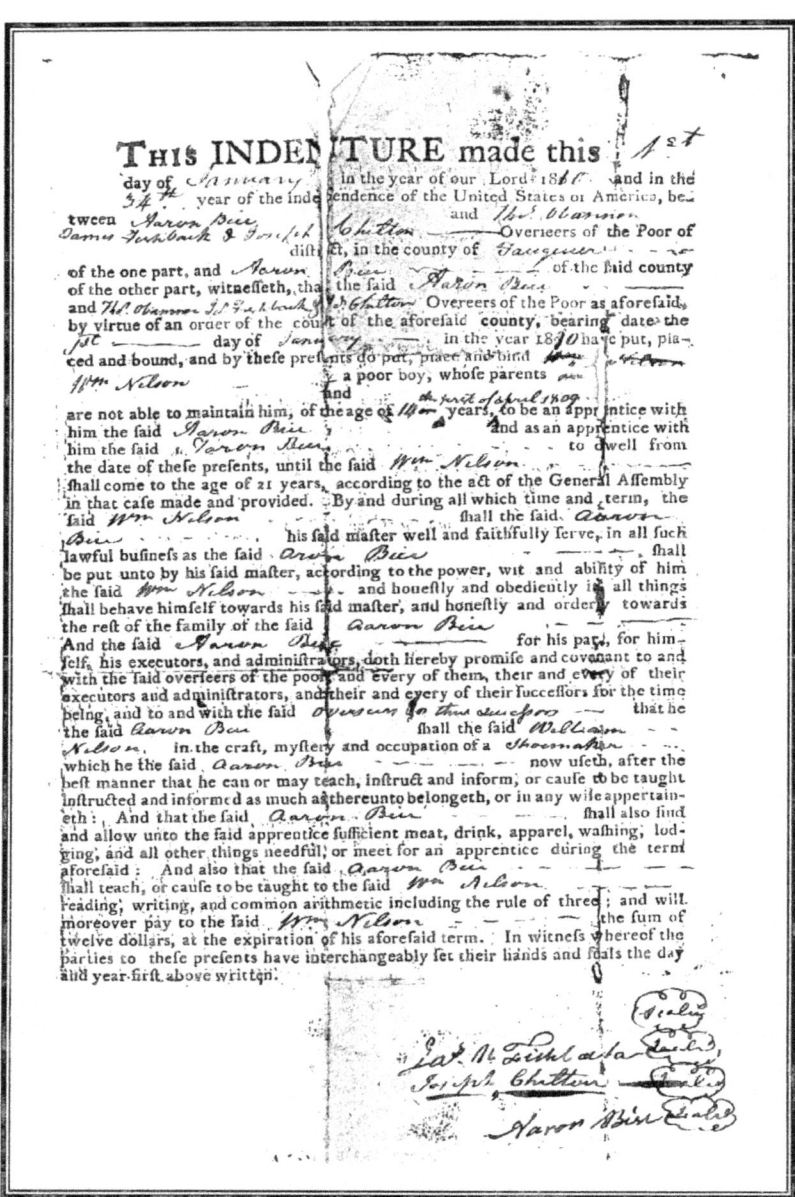

Plate 85. OP/Churchwardens Records. Scanned Image from OP Apprenticeships, Box 1. 1810-001 William Nelson to Aaron Bise

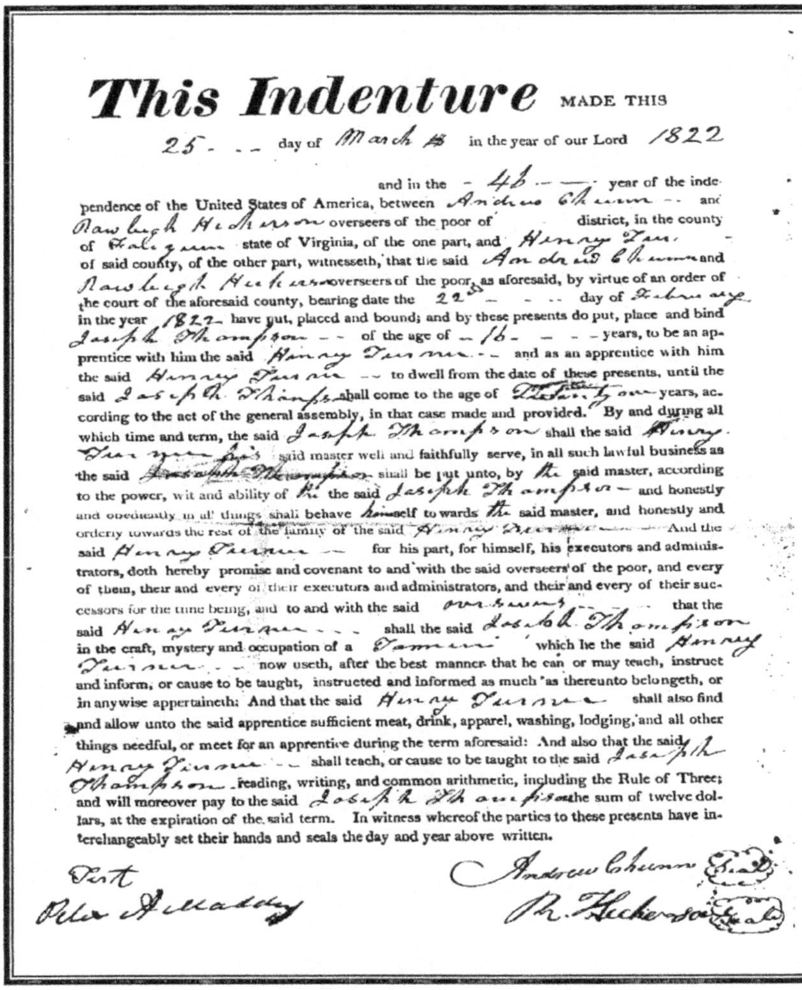

This Indenture MADE THIS 25 day of March in the year of our Lord 1822

and in the 46 year of the independence of the United States of America, between Andrew Chunn and Rawleigh Hickerson overseers of the poor of district, in the county of Fauquier state of Virginia, of the one part, and Henry Turner of said county, of the other part, witnesseth, that the said Andrew Chunn and Rawleigh Hickerson overseers of the poor, as aforesaid, by virtue of an order of the court of the aforesaid county, bearing date the 22d day of February in the year 1822 have put, placed and bound; and by these presents do put, place and bind Joseph Thompson of the age of 16 years, to be an apprentice with him the said Henry Turner and as an apprentice with him the said Henry Turner to dwell from the date of these presents, until the said Joseph Thompson shall come to the age of Twenty one years, according to the act of the general assembly, in that case made and provided. By and during all which time and term, the said Joseph Thompson shall the said Henry Turner his said master well and faithfully serve, in all such lawful business as the said ~~Joseph Thompson~~ shall be put unto, by the said master, according to the power, wit and ability of him the said Joseph Thompson and honestly and obediently in all things shall behave himself towards the said master, and honestly and orderly towards the rest of the family of the said Henry Turner And the said Henry Turner for his part, for himself, his executors and administrators, doth hereby promise and covenant to and with the said overseers of the poor, and every of them, their and every of their executors and administrators, and their and every of their successors for the time being, and to and with the said overseers that the said Henry Turner shall the said Joseph Thompson in the craft, mystery and occupation of a Tanner which he the said Henry Turner now useth, after the best manner that he can or may teach, instruct and inform, or cause to be taught, instructed and informed as much as thereunto belongeth, or in anywise appertaineth: And that the said Henry Turner shall also find and allow unto the said apprentice sufficient meat, drink, apparel, washing, lodging, and all other things needful, or meet for an apprentice during the term aforesaid: And also that the said Henry Turner shall teach, or cause to be taught to the said Joseph Thompson reading, writing, and common arithmetic, including the Rule of Three; and will moreover pay to the said Joseph Thompson the sum of twelve dollars, at the expiration of the said term. In witness whereof the parties to these presents have interchangeably set their hands and seals the day and year above written.

Test
Peter [illegible]

Andrew Chunn (Seal)
R. Hickerson (Seal)

Plate 86. OP/Churchwardens Records. Scanned Image from OP Apprenticeships, Box 1. 1822-001 Joseph Thompson to Henry Turner

```
A List of the Poor of the District No 7 whereof the
Subscribers are Overseers with the allowance to each in Tobco
                                                    lbs Tobo
James Fletcher                                      1000
Charles Garner Junr
Mary Herne                                            75
Simon RedGroves                                      125
Margaret Watson                                      150
Margaret Coley                                       500
Martha Matthews
Ann Brown                                            500
Mary Groves                                          600
Elizabeth Clark                                      300
William Duncan                                       100
Thomas Melony                                        400
Celia Wilkason
Zachariah Vaughan                                      ___
                                                     9800

The above Tobacco may be discharg'd at P.H.
                    William Withers
                    Augustine Jennings
```

Plate 87. OP/Churchwardens Records. Scanned Image from OP, Miscellaneous Records, Box 2. 1788-011 List of the Poor in District # 7.

> Fauquier county to wit
>
> To a Constable of said county
>
> Whereas Nancy Carrol of said county Singlewoman, hath by her examination taken in writing upon oath before me James Pickett one of the commonwealths Justices of the peace for the county aforesaid; declared that on the 21st day of February last past at the house of Joseph Neal in the county aforesaid she the said Nancy Carrol was delivered of a female bastard child, and that the said bastard child is likely to become chargeable to the said county, and hath charged Levi Pickerell of said county shoemaker of having gotten her with child of the said bastard child: And whereas Thomas O'Bannon, one of the Overseers of the poor in the county aforesaid, in order to indemnify the said county in the premises, hath applied to me to issue my warrant for apprehending the said Levi Pickerell: I do therefore hereby command you immediately to apprehend the said Levi Pickerell and to bring him before me or some other of the commonwealth Justices of the peace for the said county, to find sufficient security in the sum of Sixty dollars for his personal appearance at the next court, to be held for the said county of Fauquier and then and there abide by and perform the order of the said court therein, in pursuance of the act of the General Assembly, entitled, An Act providing for the poor, and declaring who shall be deemed vagrants — Given under my hand and seal this 7th day of February in the year 1800 and nine
>
> James Pickett (seal)

Plate 88. OP/Churchwardens Records. Scanned Image from OP/Miscellaneous Records, Box 2. 1809-001. Page 2 of Commonwealth v. Levi Pickerall, who Nancy Carrol alleged was the father of her bastard child.

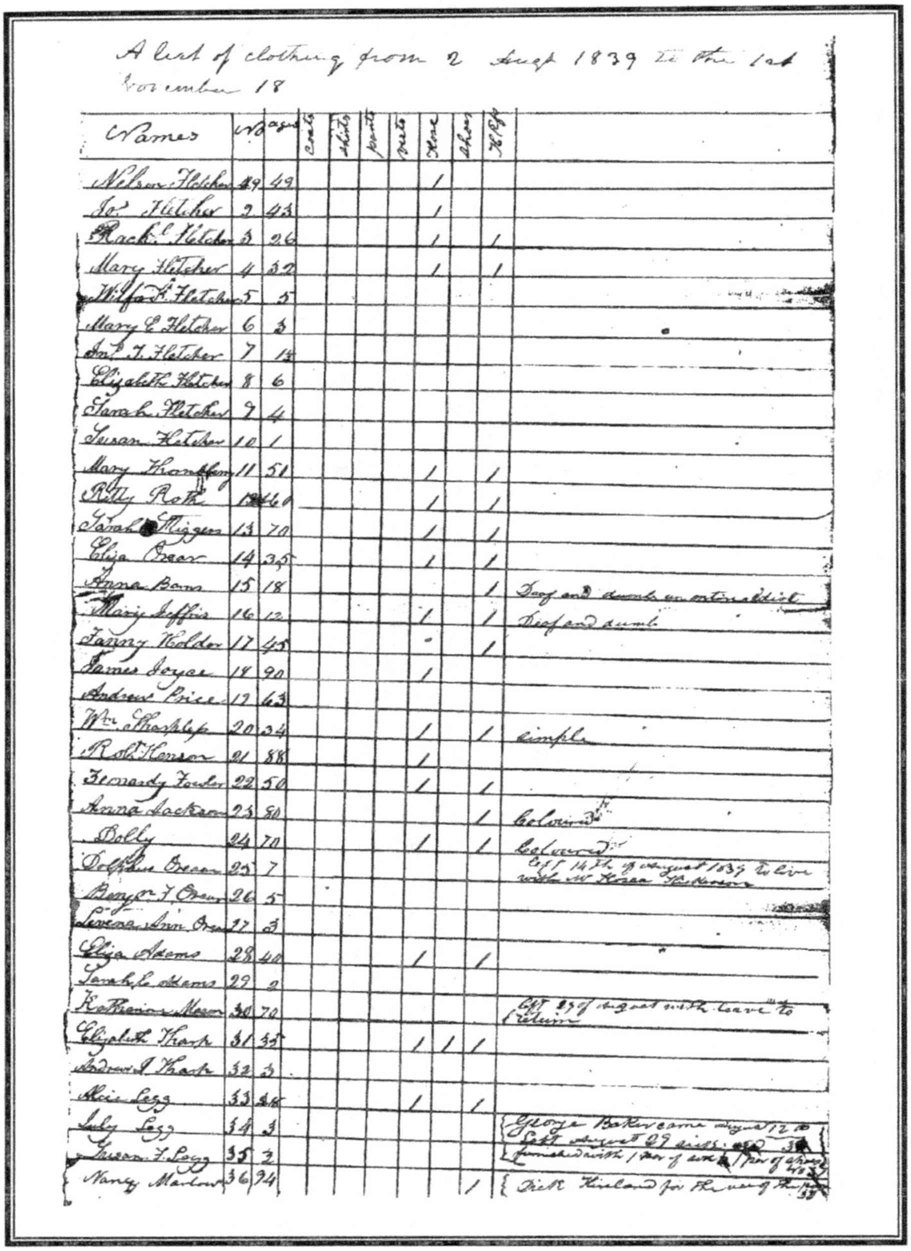

Plate 89. OP/Churchwarden Records. Scanned Image from OP/Miscellaneous Records, Box 2.
1839-028. List of Clothing provided paupers in Poor House in 1839.

Fauquier County, Virginia's Clerks Loose Papers: A Guide to the Records 1759-1919

CHAPTER 14
OVERSIZE RECORDS

1. Overview

The oversize records in the Clerks Loose Papers are records that are too large to fit in the regular brown document boxes used to house the various records series. Large plats, surveys, deeds, bonds, maps and newspapers are all examples of records you might find in these oversize boxes.

One of these boxes also contain records signed by well-known figures in Virginia and United States history. A sampling of names include George and Martha Washington, Augustine Washington, Benjamin Banneker, Richard Henry Lee, Robert Carter, Lady Catharine Fairfax, Thomas Lord Fairfax, George William Fairfax, Thomas Marshall, John Marshall and Thomas Ludwell Lee. These prominent citizens of Virginia all left records in the county's Clerks Loose Papers.

The indices to the appropriate record series (Land or Probate, for example) all contain references directing the researcher to the oversize boxes if such a record is found there.

2. Finding your way around the Oversize Records

Series Title: Oversize Records
Color Code: No Dots on Boxes

Series Dates: 1759-1956
Series Extent: 6 Boxes   *12.5 Linear feet (length-wise) 1.25 linear feet (stacked)*

Boxes 1-3. Oversize Chancery

Oversize Chancery	Box 1	Plats, Deeds, etc too large for regular box storage	1765-001 to 1877-007
Oversize Chancery	Box 2	Plats, Deeds, etc too large for regular box storage	1880-068 to 1912-048
Oversize Chancery	Box 3	Marshall Plats of Leeds Manor	1835-013 to 1900-047

Box 4. Oversize Land Records
   Oversize Deeds, Proprietary Grants, Signatures Series, Fairfax Leases   1724-001 to 1824-011

Box 5. Oversized Other Records 1774-001 to 1956-001
   Oversize Accounts from Ended Causes
   Probate Records – Harmon Rector's Will and 12 Oversize Admr. & Exor. Bonds
   Photostats of Early Plats & Maps from Fauquier County Deed Books and Will Books

Box 6. Oversize Tax & Fiscal and Vital Records
   1788-001 Travers Nash Personal Property List
   1820-001 &c. Nimrod Ashby's Land Tax List
   1875-001   Nelson's District Births and Deaths

Series Arrangement: *Filed by Year*

Series Finding Aid: Chancery Records are indexed in LVA Chancery Index. Land Records are indexed in Land Records and Land Disputes Index. Probate records are indexed in the Consolidated Probate of Clerks Loose Papers and Superior and Circuit Court records.

Illustrations from the Oversize Records include the ones on the front and back cover of this book along with illustrations from Chapter 1.

In the Name of God. Amen I Augustine Washington of the County of King George Gent being Sick and Weak but of Perfect and Disposing Sence and Memory do make my Last Will and Testament in Manner following hereby Revoking all former Will or Wills whatsoever by me heretofore made Imprimis I Give unto my Son Lawrence Washington and his Heirs forever All that Plantation and Tract of Land at Hunting Creek in the County of Prince William Containing by Estimation Two Thousand five Hundred Acres with the Water Mill Adjoining thereto or lying near the same and all the Slaves Cattle and Stocks of all kinds whatsoever and all the Houshold furniture whatsoever now in or upon or which have been Commonly Possessed by my said Son Together with the said Plantation Tract of Land and Mill Item I Give unto my Son Augustine Washington and his Heirs forever all my Lands in the County of Westmorland Except such only as are herein after otherwise Disposed off Together with Twenty five head of Neat Cattle, Forty Hoggs and Twenty Sheep and a Negro Man Named Frank besides those Negroes formerly Given him by his Mother Item I Give unto my said Son Augustine three Young Working Slaves to be Purchased for him out of the first Profits of the Estate _____ Item I Give ____ my Son George Washington and his Heirs the Land I now live on which I Purchased of the Executors of Mr. William Strother Dec'd and One Moiety or half of my Lands lying on deep Run and ten Negro Slaves Item I Give unto my Son Samuel Washington and his Heirs my Land at Chotank in the County of Stafford Containing about ____ hundred Acres and also the other Moiety of my Lands lying on Deep Run Item I Give unto my Son John Washington and his Heirs my Land at the head of Maddox in the County of Westmorland Containing about Seven hund'd Acres Item I Give unto my Son Charles Washington and his Heirs the Land I Purchased of my Son Lawrence Washington of whom Thomas Lewis now lives adjoining to my said Lawrence's Land above Devis'd also I Give unto my said Charles and his Heirs the Land I Purchased of Gabriel Adams in the County of Prince William Containing about Seven hundred Acres Item It is my Will and Desire that all the rest of my Negroes not herein Particularly Divised may be Equally Divided between my Wife and my three Sons Samuel, John and Charles and that Ned, Jack, Bob, Sue and Lucy, may be included in my Wife's Part which Part of my said Wife after her Decease I Desire may be Equally Divided between my Sons George, Samuel, John, and Charles and the Part of my said Negroes so Divised to my Wife I Mean and Intend to be in full Satisfaction and

Plate 90. Oversize Records. Scanned Image of page 1 of Augustine Washington's Will found in Land Disputes 1799-011 Hickerson v. Blackwell Trespass Suit papers.

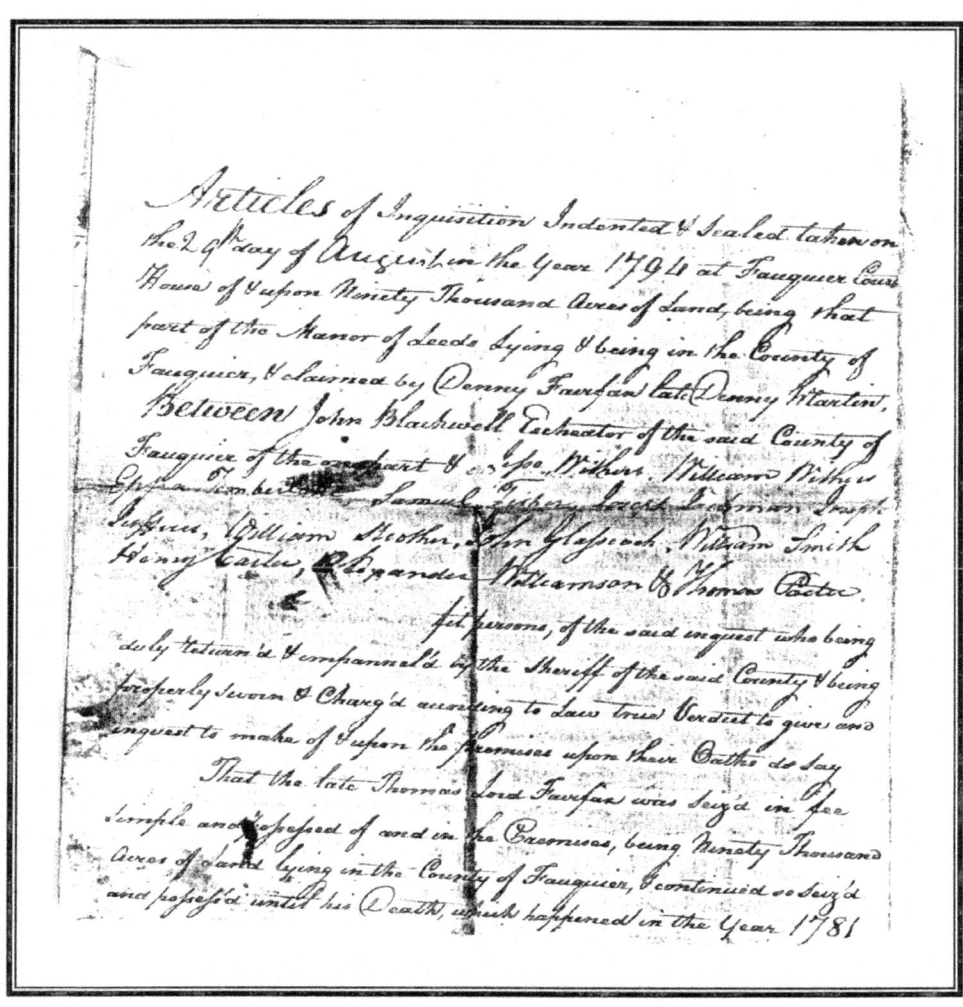

Plate 91. Oversize Records. Scanned Image of page 1 of the Inquest for the Manor of Leeds claimed by Denny Fairfax in Land 1794-005. Escheat of the Manor of Leeds to the Commonwealth.

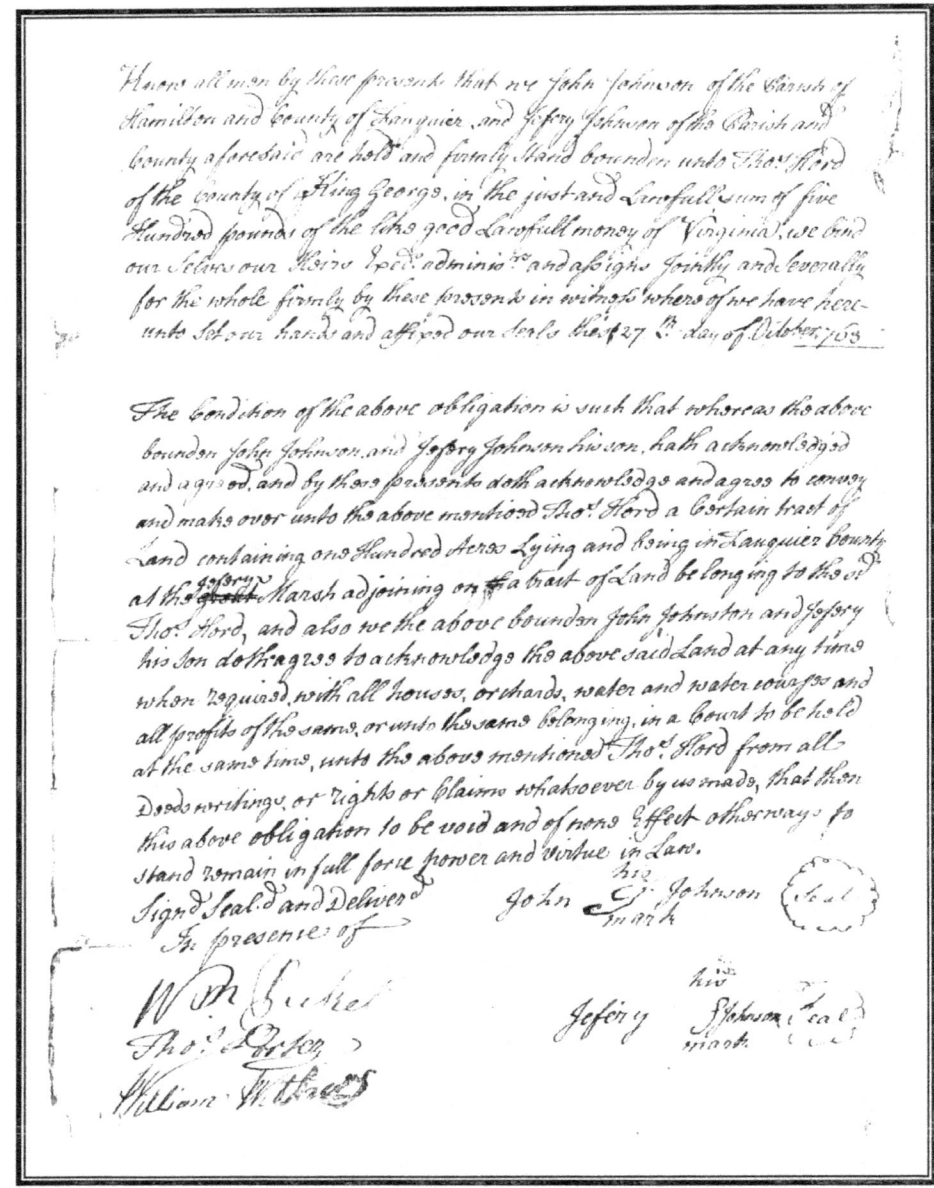

Plate 92. Oversize Records. Signatures. Scanned Image of Land 1763-002. Bond from John and Jeffrey Johnson to Thomas Hord to convey a 100 acre tract at "the Jefery [Johnson] Marsh."

Fauquier County, Virginia's Clerks Loose Papers: A Guide to the Records 1759-1919

CHAPTER 15
PROBATE/FIDUCIARY RECORDS

1. Overview

Probate and Fiduciary Records are those that deal with
1) Administration of estates of deceased persons
2) Validation of Wills
3) Inventories and Appraisements of deceased persons for tax purposes
4) Guardianships of orphans who are under legal age with heritable estates
5) Assignments of Curators or Committees for lunatics with personal property or landed estate.

This series contains a diverse variety of records. There are Ended Causes suits whose parties are Administrators or Executors of a decedent. There are notices of Administrator and Executor appointments, as well as appointments for Committees and Curators for those not capable of looking after their own affair; There are Administrator, Executor and Guardian and Bonds; There are Administrator, Executor and Guardian Accounts; finally there are the traditional probate records - Wills, inventories, appraisements and Sales lists.

In addition, some Clerks Copies of Probate records were filed separately. These records have been placed in their own document box. Some of these records are the original ones and some are office copies of documents needed in a court case or for some other purpose.

2. Finding you way around Probate/Fiduciary Records

Series Title: Probate/Fiduciary Records
Color Code: Yellow Dots on Boxes

Series Dates: 1759-1910
Series Extent: 57 Boxes.

Probate Estate Judgments from Ended Causes	1759-1832	37 Boxes
Probate Estate Judgments: Large Suits from Ended Causes	1816-1831	1 Box
Probate Estate Papers	1762-1872	3 Boxes
Probate: Wills, Inventories &c.	1759-1949	2 Boxes
Probate: Administrator & Executor Bonds	1759-1836	4 Boxes
Probate: Guardian Bonds	1760-1821	2 Boxes
Probate: Clerks Copies	1760-1858	1 Box.
Probate: from Superior Court & Circuit Court Drawers	1832-1910	6 Boxes

Series Arrangement: Filed by year.

Series Finding Aid: There is a Consolidated Probate Index for the Clerks Loose Papers entitled *"Being of Sound Mind..." An Index to Probate Records in the Clerks Loose Papers & Superior/Circuit Court Records 1759-1919*. This index includes *any* probate or fiduciary record found in any of the record series in the Clerks Loose Papers. The index also includes the probate records found in the Superior and Circuit Court records of the County from 1832-1910. These records have been flat filed and placed in archival document boxes. The Superior and Circuit Court probate records make up the records found in the Superior/Circuit Court drawers found in the vault of the Court house basement.

Both sets of County probate records have been indexed and have been made accessible to researchers. Remember, there are now **two** indexes for researchers to use when searching for county probate records. One is the General Index to Wills dating from 1759. The other is this Consolidated Probate Index 1759-1919.

3. A Preview of *"Being of Sound Mind..."* Consolidated Probate Index

Figure 23 shows a representative sampling of the kinds of records that are in this index.

Surname	Given Name	Instrument	Date	County	Fauquier County Record Series	Index #
Adams	Thomas T.	Will	9/22/1856	Fauquier	Chancery	1859-017
Adams	James	Heirs	4/22/1851	Fauquier	Chancery	1861-004
Bowen	Lucy	Gdn. Bond	1806	Fauquier	Probate, Box 49	1806-007
Galloway	Fanny L.	Committee Appointment	6/30/1906	Fauquier	Probate, Box 56 Superior/Circuit Court	1906-004
Jenifer	Walter Hanson	Will	2/4/1786	Charles Co MD.	Chancery	1851-002
Jenkins	Joshua	Heirs	3/27/1780	Fauquier	Military Records	1809-001
Jennings	J. C.	Admr. Bond	4/16/1884	Fauquier	Probate, Box 54 Superior/Circuit Court	1884-001
Jennings	Lewis	Division Of Slaves	12/29/1845	Fauquier	Chancery	1866-029
Primm	John	Plat & Survey Of Division	4/12./1872	Fauquier	Chancery	1894-067
Shipp	Betsey	Gdn. Bond	1778	Fauquier	Probate, Box 48	1778-002
Shipe	J. R.	Estate Committed To Sheriff	4/4/1899	Fauquier	Probate, Box 55 Superior/Circuit Court	1899-002
Shultz	Benjamin	Admtrx. Bond	1808	Fauquier	Probate, Box 46	1808-016
Washington	Augustine	Will	5/6/1743	King George Co. VA.	Land Disputes	1799-011
Washington	George	Will	1/20/1800	Fairfax Co. VA.	Land Disputes	1812-009

Figure 23. Examples of names, Instruments and Record Series in "Being of Sound Mind..." the Consolidated Probate Index.

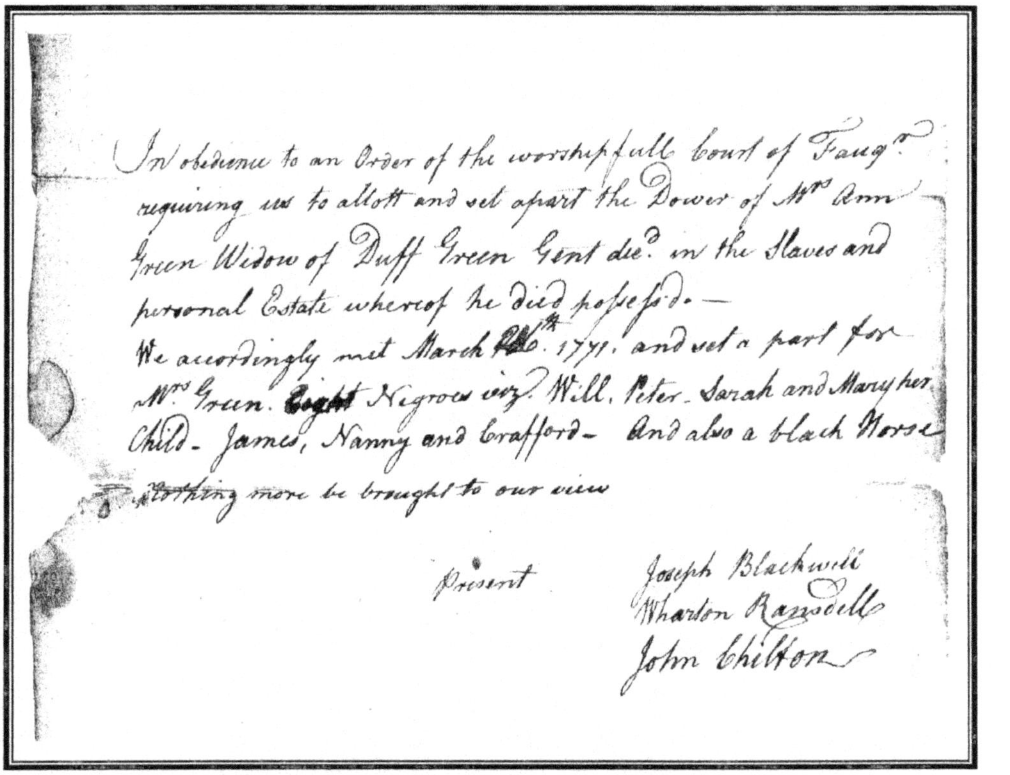

> In obedience to an Order of the worshipfull Court of Fauqr. requiring us to allott and set apart the Dower of Mrs Ann Green Widow of Duff Green Gent decd. in the Slaves and personal Estate whereof he died possesd.—
> We accordingly met March __th 1771. and set a part for Mrs Green. ~~Eight~~ Negroes viz? Will. Peter. Sarah and Mary her Child. James, Nanny and Crafford— And also a black Horse nothing more be brought to our view
>
> Present
>
> Joseph Blackwell
> Wharton Ransdell
> John Chilton

Plate 93. Probate. Scanned Image from Box 39, Wills, &c. 1771-001. Dower Allotment to Mrs. Ann Green

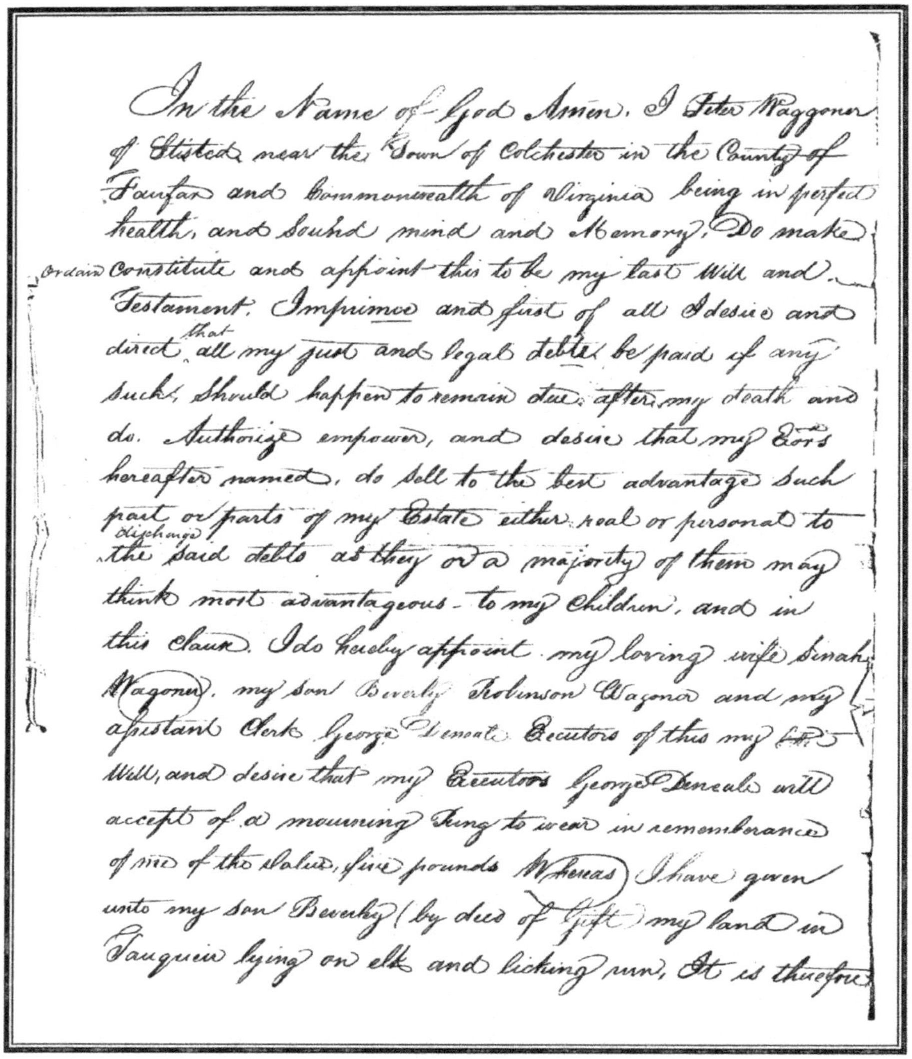

> In the Name of God Amen. I Peter Waggoner of Stisted near the Town of Colchester in the County of Fairfax and Commonwealth of Virginia being in perfect health, and sound mind and Memory, Do make ordain Constitute and appoint this to be my last Will and Testament. Imprimis and first of all I desire and direct that all my just and legal debts be paid if any such, should happen to remain due after my death and do Authorize empower, and desire that my Exors hereafter named, do sell to the best advantage such part or parts of my Estate either real or personal to discharge the said debts as they or a majority of them may think most advantageous to my Children, and in this Clause. I do hereby appoint my loving wife Sinah Wagoner, my son Beverly Robinson Wagoner and my Assistant Clerk George Deneale Executors of this my last Will, and desire that my Executors George Deneale will accept of a mourning Ring to wear in remembrance of me of the Value, five pounds Whereas I have given unto my son Beverly (by deed of Gift) my land in Fauquier lying on elk and licking run, It is therefore

Plate 94. Probate. Scanned Image from Box 39, Wills &c. 1793-006. Page 1 of Peter Waggoner's Will.

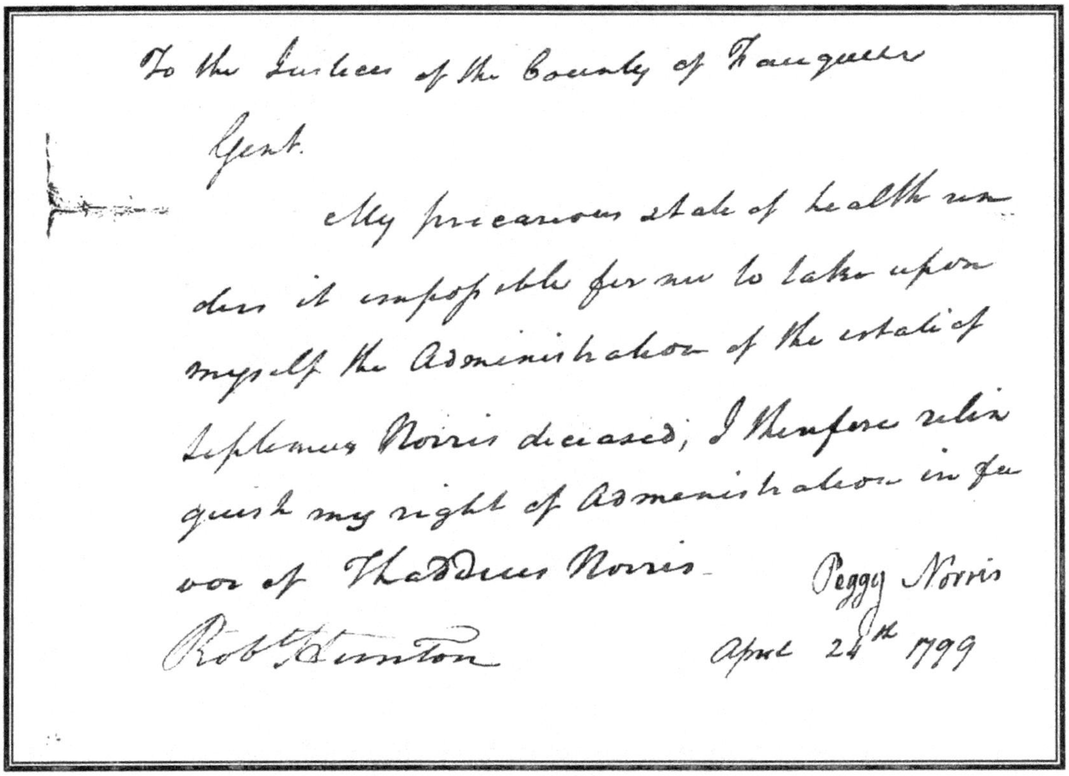

To the Justices of the County of Fauquier
Gent.

My precarious state of health renders it impossible for me to take upon myself the Administration of the estate of Septimus Norris deceased; I therefore relinquish my right of Administration in favor of Thaddeus Norris.

Robt Hinton

Peggy Norris
April 24th 1799

Plate 95. Probate. Scanned Image from Box 39, Wills &c. 1799-002. Peggy Norris' Relinquishment of Administration of Estate of Septimus Norris, decd. to her son Thaddeus Norris.

> In pursuance of an order of court for the appraisement of personal Estate of Wm Smith deceased we whose names are undersigned have proceeded to appraise and Inventory the said Estate as follows at the dwelling house of the said William Smith

Negro Nace	$100	One young Bay	£20
Tom	90	One negro & gear	2.4
Joseph	100	five Setts of plow gear	2
Jacob	90	115 feet of Plank	1/7
Patience	70	four flax Brakes	/10
Cumboo	40	Sixteen Sheep @ 10/	8
Judah	60	8 Cows with their Calves	120
Frank	60	One Bull	6
Sampson	50	Two Steers	15
Manuel	45	Two Small Steers	3/12
Lewis	125	Three heifers	6
Lydia	45	One Cow	4/10
David	90	One wheat fan	9/8
Rose	36	Seven Tubs & one half bushel	/18
Jenny	36	72 Bushels of flax Seed	1
Milly	30	four Stacks of hay	6
Scipio	36	48 hogs and 52 Pigs	60
Charles	36	Blacksmiths Tools & Bellows	12
Harrison	25	9 Shovel plows & for stocks	3
Kingston	20	Eight hoes	/12
Clary	60	three scythes and Cradles	1/10
Hannah	60	Seven Sheep brakes	/14
Phillis & Child	40	Twenty two tubs & Casks	3
Ben	20	three plow plates	/18
One Black horse	15	three Jugs & one Butter pot	/15
One white Do	15	three Spades & three augers	/18
One Black riding Do	20	One lock Chain	/12
One Bay Do	15	four Axes	1/10

Plate 96. Probate. Scanned Image from Box 39, Wills &c. 1810-002. Page 1 of William Smith's Inventory and Appraisement.

Account of Sales of Charles Duncan's Estate, sold on the 13th, 14th, 15th and 16th days of October 1818.

Purchaser Names	Articles Sold	Price sold for $	cts
Travers Duncan	To negro man Priamus	440	"
Mariah Duncan	" negro Sarah and her child Abby	466	"
Gillard Duncan changed to S. Duncan	" woman Suckey and child Lucinda & Emily	820	"
Edmund Duncan	" negro boy Tom	520	"
	" old Winkey	0	4
Gillard Duncan	" boy Reuben (sold at Jan.y Court 7th Nov.r 1818)	613	"
Willed to Mrs. Duncan	" Sophia & children viz. Sary, Peter, Robert & John		
Zachariah Dulany	" unmarked white back spoted rump black face cow & calf	29	50
" "	" Red and white bobtail cow and calf	96	"
Willed to Mrs. Dulany	" white back speckled face cow & calf	"	"
John Jeffries	" white back speckled rump red face cow and calf	30	"
Willed to Mrs. Duncan	" pale red and white cow speck under each eye & calf	"	"
Alex B Nelson	" red cow, white tail & dark face and calf	14	50
Willed to Miss Maria Duncan	" Red cow & calf	"	"
John Jeffries	" one broken horned cow & calf	32	"
" "	" dark red black face cow & calf	33	"
		3013	"

Plate 97. Probate. Scanned Image from Box 39, Wills &c. 1818-005. Page 1 of Charles Duncan's Sales Account.

KNOW all Men by these Presents, That We Elizabeth Shadrack Samuel Earle & Charles Morehead are held and firmly bound to Thomas Harrison William Blackwell John Wright, Henry & Yelverton Peyton

Gent. Justices of the Court of Fauquier County, now sitting, in the Sum of Five hundred pounds

To the Payment whereof well and truly to be made to the said Justices, and their Successors, we bind ourselves, and each of us, our and each of our Heirs, Executors, and Administrators, jointly and severally, firmly by these Presents. Sealed with our Seals, the 27th Day of Sep. in the Year of our Lord One Thousand Seven Hundred and and in the 39. Year of the Reign of our Sovereign Lord GEORGE the Second.

THE Condition of this Obligation is such, That if the above bound Elizabeth Shadrack Executrix of the Last Will and Testament of John Shadrack Deceased, do make, or cause to be made, a true and perfect Inventory of all and singular the Goods, Chattels and Credits of the said Deceased, which have, or shall come to the Hands, Possession or Knowledge of the said Elizabeth or into the Hands and Possession of any other Person or Persons for her. and the same so made, do exhibit unto the County Court of Fauquier at such Time as she shall be thereunto required by the said Court; and the same Goods, Chattels, and Credits, and all other the Goods, Chattels, and Credits of the said Deceas'd, which at any Time after shall come to the Hands, Possession, or Knowledge of the said Elizabeth or into the Hands and Possession of any other Person or Persons for her do well and truely administer according to Law: And further to make a true and just Account of her Actings and Doings therein, when thereto required by the said Court; and also, shall well and truely pay and deliver all the Legacies contained and specified in the said Testament, as far as the said Goods, Chattels and Credits, will thereunto extend, and the Law shall charge: Then this Obligation to be void and of none Effect, or else to remain in full Force and Virtue.

Sealed and Delivered in the Presence of }

Eliz^a her mark Shadrack

Sam Earle

Charles Morehead

Plate 98. Probate. Scanned Image from Box 44. Administrator & Executor Bonds. 1759-005. John Shadrack's Extrx. Bond.

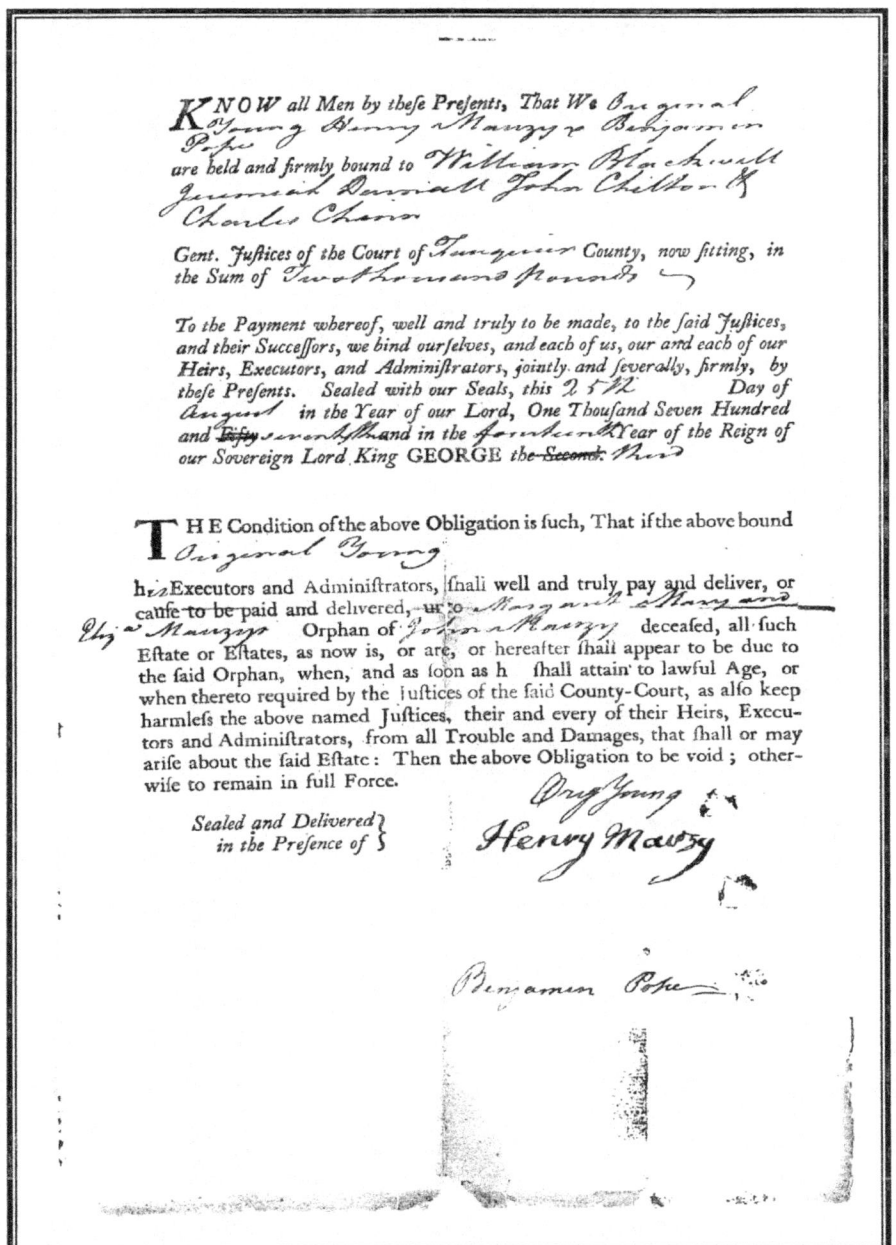

Plate 99. Probate. Scanned Image from Box 49, Guardian Bonds. 1807-002 Margaret and Elizabeth Mauzeys' Guardian Bond.

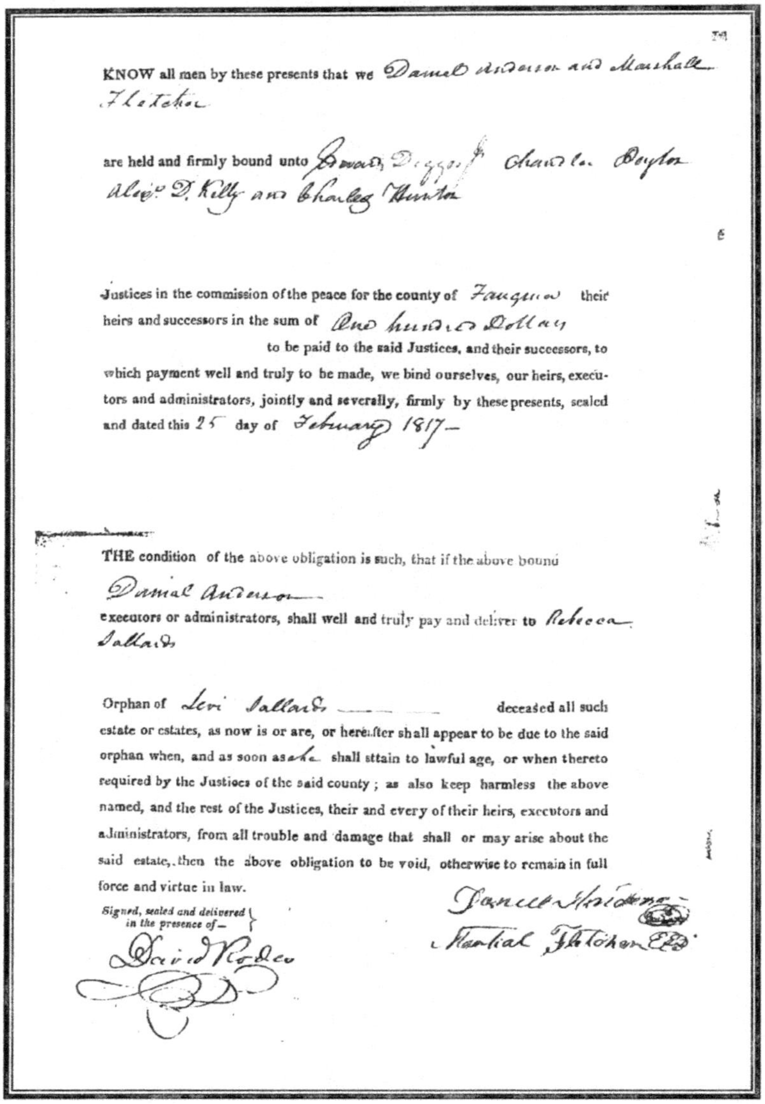

KNOW all men by these presents that we *Daniel Anderson and Marshall Fletcher*

are held and firmly bound unto *Edward Diggs, Chandler Boyton, Alexr. D. Kelly and Charles Hunton*

Justices in the commission of the peace for the county of *Fauquier* their heirs and successors in the sum of *One hundred Dollars* to be paid to the said Justices, and their successors, to which payment well and truly to be made, we bind ourselves, our heirs, executors and administrators, jointly and severally, firmly by these presents, sealed and dated this *25* day of *February 1817* —

THE condition of the above obligation is such, that if the above bound *Daniel Anderson* executors or administrators, shall well and truly pay and deliver to *Rebecca Sallards*

Orphan of *Levi Sallards* deceased all such estate or estates, as now is or are, or hereafter shall appear to be due to the said orphan when, and as soon as *he* shall attain to lawful age, or when thereto required by the Justices of the said county; as also keep harmless the above named, and the rest of the Justices, their and every of their heirs, executors and administrators, from all trouble and damage that shall or may arise about the said estate, then the above obligation to be void, otherwise to remain in full force and virtue in law.

Signed, sealed and delivered in the presence of —

David Rodes

Daniel Anderson
Marshall Fletcher

Plate 100. Probate. Scanned Image from Box 49, Guardian Bonds. 1817-022. Rebecca Sallard's Guardian Bond.

Fauquier County, Virginia's Clerks Loose Papers: A Guide to the Records 1759-1919

CHAPTER 16
SCHOOL RECORDS

1. Overview

There are five boxes of records relating to the schools of Fauquier County. Among the records found in this series are school master's accounts and suits that date to 1760. These school master suits came from Ended Causes. The school superintendent's reports and receipts for school maintenance and other receipts for teachers were found, stored together, in a woodruff drawer labeled simply "schools".

These records contain information that furnish the researcher with a fresh insight into the education of children in eighteenth and nineteenth century Fauquier. There are school master accounts in the eighteenth century and reports and receipts, in the nineteenth century that will enhance our knowledge of the county's public and private school system.

Many of these records are large and in very fragile condition. Handle with care!

2. Finding your way around School Records

Series Title: School Records
Color Code: Bright fluorescent Yellow Dots on Boxes

Series Date: 1760-1896
Series Extent: 5 Boxes. *2.08 linear feet.*
Series Arrangement: Filed by year.

Series Finding Aid: These records have not been indexed.

Types of Records found in Box 1 of School Records (1760-1836) include:
   a. School Master suits and Accounts from Ended Causes
   b. School Superintendent Reports

Types of Records found in Box 2 of School Records (1837-1876) include more Superintendent Reports.

Types of Records found in Box 3 of School Records (1893-1896) include
   a. Receipts for Teachers
   b. Receipts for maintenance of the schools in Fauquier County.

> I Josiah Fishback, will take the care, and tuition of an English School, at Longbranch Institution for the term of Twelve Months (five) days in each Week, Beginning the second Monday in January 1820, and ending the 20th day of December following of Spelling, Reading, Writing, Cyphering, English Grammar and Geography, at twelve Dollars ⅌ year for each Scholar, where due attention will be given.
>
> We the undermentioned Subscribers do promise and oblige ourselves to furnish the school with a Sufficiency of Wood in due Season, and to pay the said Fishback the above mentioned price for tuition. Whereunto we set our hands and Number of Scholars this 20th day of Decr. 1819

Subscriber	No.	Subscriber	No.
X John Fishback	2	X Thomas Gregg	
X Samuel Fleming	1	X W B Sampson	
X James Pickitt	3		
X Richard Clark	1		
X Joseph Haines	2		
X Isaac Sinclair	2		
X William Flynn	2		
X Cuthbert Owens	1		
X William Ball	2		
X Uriah McKnight	1½		
X William Milton	2		
X Daniel Hains	½		
X Dudley Bayliss	1		
X Thomas Whiting	1½		

Plate 101. School Records. Scanned Image from Box 1, School Master Suits, &c. 1828-001 Josiah Fishback's Schoolmaster's Account from a Tuition suit styled Fishback v. Ball's Admr.

Fauquier County, Virginia's Clerks Loose Papers: A Guide to the Records 1759-1919

CHAPTER 17
SHERIFF'S RECORDS

1. Overview

The records relating to the Sheriff of the County have all been taken from Ended Causes. Many are accounts with either the Commonwealth or with Fauquier County. Among the records here are medical accounts for attending sick prisoners; escape warrants to apprehend those who had escaped its confines; runaway accounts; prison bound bounds; guard accounts for guarding prisoners in the jail; and a variety of suits involving the Sheriff.

They present the researcher with a unique opportunity to understand how the county handled law enforcement in the eighteenth and nineteenth century.

2. Finding your way around Sheriff's Records.

Series Title: Sheriff's Records
Color Code: Green and Black Dots on Boxes

Series Dates: 1760-1840
Series Extent: 1 Box. *0.5 linear feet.*
Series Arrangement: Filed by year.

Series Finding Aid: These records have not been indexed.

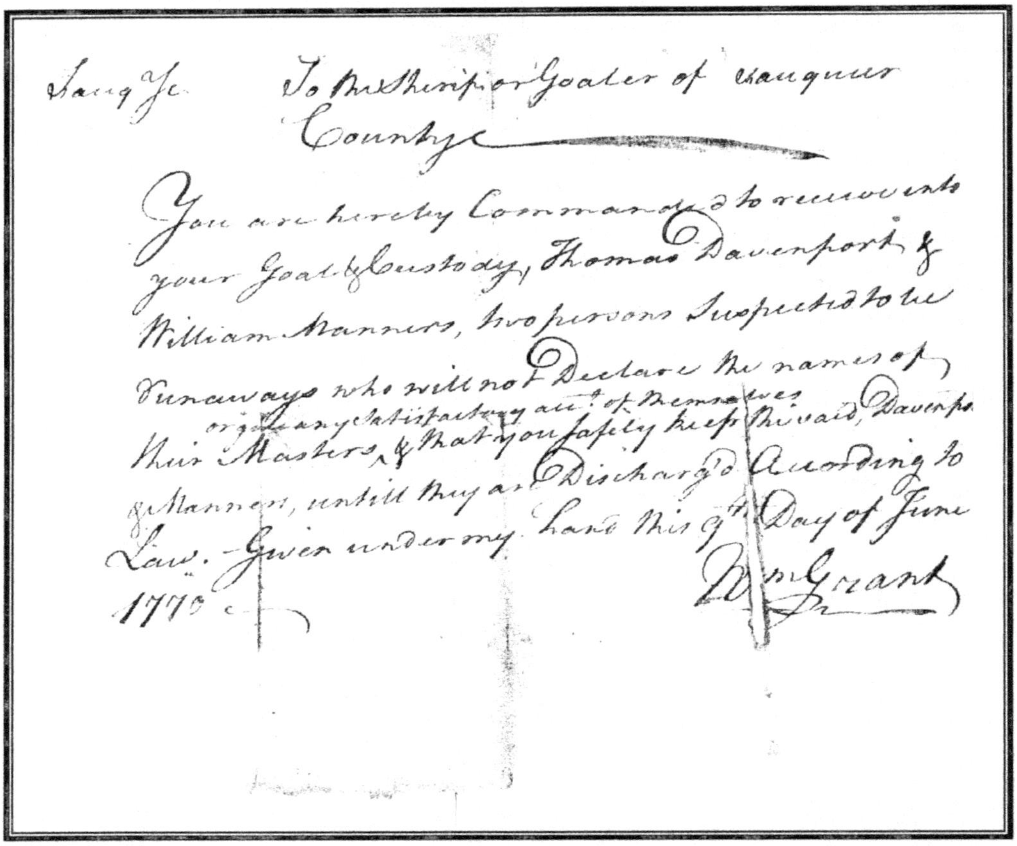

Fauq ss. To the Sheriff or Goaler of Fauquier County

You are hereby Commanded to receive into your Goal & Custody, Thomas Davenport & William Manners, two persons Suspected to be Runaways who will not Declare the names of their Masters or give any satisfactory acc.t of themselves, & that you safely keep the said Davenport & Manners, untill they are Discharg'd According to Law. Given under my hand this 9th Day of June 1770.

Wm Grant

Plate 102. Sheriff's Records. Scanned Image from Box 1.
1770-002 An Escape Warrant for Runaways.

CHAPTER 18
TAX & FISCAL RECORDS

1. Overview

The tax and fiscal records in the Clerks Loose Papers range from 1759-1849. They include early tithable lists, 1785 lists of whites and dwellings, personal property lists and land tax lists covering both the colonial and Commonwealth time periods. They represent the work done by the county's tax collectors when the county was formed in 1759. The lists track the colonial period until independence. They then chart the years of the eighteenth century and nineteenth century until they end in 1849. In 1850, Land and Property Books replaced the lists.

2. Fauquier County's Colonial Tax Lists (1759-1782)

When Fauquier was formed from Prince William in 1759, the British colonies of North America were engaged in part of a European conflict called the Seven Years War. While Britain and Prussia faced of against France and Austria in the European phase, the colonists and their Indian allies squared off against the French and *their* Indian allies here in America. The war was fought along the frontiers and in Canada.

When the war broke out along Virginia's frontier in 1756, the colony found that it needed to secure its own frontier in order to keep open the gateway to lands in the fertile Ohio Valley. Virginia's tobacco planters were looking for fertile lands to replace their worn-out ones. As settlers pushed the bounds of Virginia's frontier westward into the Ohio valley, they ran into stiffened Indian resistance. The Algonquin, becoming increasingly alarmed at the loss of their hunting and sacred burial grounds, decided to fight back.

During this conflict, Virginia's colonial legislature had two goals in looking for money. First, the legislators wanted to protect, defend and secure the frontier against an increasingly hostile Indian and French foe. Secondly, and even more important, they wanted to provide funding on the local county infrastructure. This funding took the form of a county levy.

Each county had public expenses. The poor needed to be maintained; so, too did the public jail and courthouse. The clerk of the county court kept an account for these and other expenses, which he meticulously recorded in the county's minute books. Justices appointed men of impeccable reputations to take lists of the county's "tithables", as the colonial taxpayers were called. The tithables then paid their share of the county levy with tobacco at a rate established by the colonial legislature.

There are five tithable lists for Fauquier County, found in the Clerks Loose Papers, which have survived from the French and Indian War period. The five lists were all taken in 1759, during the year the county was formed. Unfortunately, only Thomas Marshall's 1759 list of tithables appears to be complete. The other four lists are not. While tithable lists were certainly made and taxes were collected between 1760 and 1763, Fauquier's lists did not survive for the remaining part of the French and Indian War.

Fortunately, there are six other colonial tax lists, in the Clerk's Loose Papers, that date from 1765-1775. During this period, Virginia and her colonial neighbors were officially at peace with their neighbors. Virginia's 1765 tax legislation dealt primarily with the collection of the public levy on the county level. In 1768, the legislature revised the colonial tax code. Duties on tithables, slaves, tobacco, carriage wheels, writs and ordinary licenses continued since the legislature considered these taxes enough to cover the needs of local government.

By 1775, the tax situation had changed. The colonists were growing daily more restive under British control. Lexington, Concord, Bunker Hill and been fought. The Continental Congress had met in Philadelphia. Virginian George Washington had been sent to Boston to take charge of the troops there. It appeared to many that open rebellion and a fight for independence was becoming a reality.

Now, the Virginia's colonial legislature needed money to pay a militia to defend the frontiers and to fight against the British. There were taxes on wheeled vehicles, on ordinary licenses, marriage licenses, writs, and on land. Since there was not enough public money in Virginia's treasury to pay for its defense, the Treasurer was authorized to issue Treasury notes to fund the war.

Only one 1775 Tithable list was found in the Clerk's Loose Papers. William Grant's Tithable list is simply a list of the tithes owing taxes. The list includes slaves. The 1777 list, taken by John Moffett, more accurately reflects the 1775 tax legislation. This list included the Tithes, land and wheeled carriages in Leeds Parish.

There are two surviving lists for 1778. Thomas Keith's list and William Pickett's list name both tithes and Negro slaves.

Five Lists survive for 1782. These are lists giving names of all white tithes responsible for paying taxes and members in their household that are under 21 (usually between the ages of sixteen and twenty-one). Negro slaves are named, along with the number of horses, cattle, Billiard Tables and Ordinary Licenses.

3. The 1785 Fauquier County State Census

There are 12 Lists of Whites and Dwellings, taken in 1785 that were found in the county's Clerks Loose Papers. These lists give the taxpayer, the number of tithes in his household, the number and dimension of his dwelling house(s) and the number of other buildings on his property.

These lists represent a find of inestimable value to researchers interested in the early residents of the county. Their existence unknown and unsuspected, they lay in drawers housing the Clerks Loose Papers, in the Courthouse vault, for nearly 200 years.

4. Personal Property Tax Lists and the Land Books in the Clerks Loose Papers

There were two types of taxes collected in Fauquier County during the late eighteenth and nineteenth century. One was a personal property tax – collected on a variety of property – from slaves to clocks to piano fortes. The list expanded or shrunk according to the economic needs of the times.

The property lists between 1782-1810 may list members of the household who are between the ages of sixteen and twenty-one. These lists are especially useful for pinning down hard-to-locate family members of an ancestor. Slaves may also be named and placed in to age groupings found in the list.

The 1815 personal property tax list, with new taxes assessed to pay for the War of 1812, is noteworthy because it placed taxes on additional property not found in previous property lists. Mills and Ordinaries rejoined the list. Duties on "Ice Houses for private use" and "houses in the country" were now included. So were levies on licenses for Merchants, Attorneys and Physicians.

The second list involved the assessment of land, whether by fee simple or by lease. Unfortunately, Fauquier's land books are not as complete, from year to year, as are the personal property books. The land books that *are* extant, however, gives information about 1) the residence of the land holder, 2) whether the land is owned outright (i.e. in fee simple) or is a leasehold, 3) the amount of acreage in the holding, 4) the value of the land per acre, 5) the total value, 6) the tax owed on the land and 7) any remarks about the nature of the holding. The remarks often included a purchase or sale of the land during that year. Values in the early lists are in English pounds, shillings and pence. Then, in the early nineteenth century, there is a transition to dollars and cents.

By 1813 or thereabouts, the land books included a location for the property. The acreage was located in a number of ways. The land might be adjacent to a landholder, who was named; or, it might be on or near a run, Creek, River or other body of water.

Then, in 1820, another change was made in the way the land taxes were collected. The values of buildings on the land were to be assessed for the first time. Now the county was able to assess value not only on the land but on the buildings as well.

5. The copies of the Property and Land Books in the Clerks Loose Papers

There were several copies of these tax records. The list taker made one. The Clerk of the Court made a copy for the Court's use. The Clerk then made another copy and sent it along to the Commissioner of Public Accounts in Richmond.

Each of the extant land and property tax lists in the Clerks Loose Papers have "Original", "for the Clerk" or words to that effect on their covers. It appears, then that these were the Clerk's office copies. He differentiated his lists from the ones going to the Commissioner of Public Accounts by stating that his were "for the Clerk". It is interesting to note that the tax lists in the Clerks Loose Papers, are not quite the same as the copies that went to Richmond. The copies in the Clerks Loose Papers are more detailed and may be more complete than the copies that went to Richmond.

It also should be noted that the Clerks Loose Papers tax lists do not contain all of the land and property lists. There are some years, especially in the 1800-1815 period, where there is an extant property book but not an extant land book. At other times, there are land books but no property tax lists.

While the lists in Richmond have all been microfilmed, **none of the lists in the Clerks Loose Papers have.** It is always wise to compare the two copies to note the differences

6. The Insolvent Lists

There are insolvent or delinquent tax lists naming those who had not yet paid their taxes. These lists should be examined closely because there are names of those who didn't pay their taxes because they had removed from the state. One of the years may list them as insolvent or delinquent; the following year may then contain a comment like "removed to Kentuck" or some other place of abode.

In addition to the six boxes of Insolvents from the Clerks Loose Papers, there are County Court papers containing Insolvent Lists filed between 1832-1886, placed here for consistency in the historical record base.

7. The Value of the Tax and Fiscal Record Series

A county's tax and fiscal records are among the most valuable papers found in the Clerks Loose Papers. These records prove residence and give the researcher new insights into the economic status of their ancestor. Early records, if extant, are especially valuable since they could help locate someone whose whereabouts were previously unknown.

While inherently valuable to the family researcher, these records also have value to the historical researcher. The land records provide insight into the assessment process of both the land itself and the buildings located on the holding. Tracking the values of the land and its buildings and the total value of the holding allows researchers to compute the assessment rate, especially over time. The values of the buildings themselves help preservationists date changes to historic properties.

The land lists also are helpful in distinguishing between leasehold and fee simple lands and between landholders who actually live in Fauquier and those who reside elsewhere. There is often information about the leasehold that includes the name of the lessor. Since the Manor of Leeds comprised the Fairfax and later Marshall leaseholds, these records are especially valuable for sorting out original holders.

Fauquier County, Virginia's Clerks Loose Papers: A Guide to the Records 1759-1919

The personal property lists give information about the person's property, economic statue and standing within the community. They sometimes include, as has already been mentioned, other members of the household between the ages of sixteen and twenty-one. They include names of slaves.

The insolvent tax lists may be one of the most underutilized resources in this series. These lists can give clues to when families first moved from the county. They may provide pointers to their destinations. Used with Power of Attorneys in the Deeds, the insolvent lists may provide the family researcher with evidence concerning his ancestors' whereabouts whether in Fauquier or somewhere else.

When the information on eighteenth century slaves is put together with other records like Bills of Sale, Deeds of Gifts or Probate records like Wills, Inventories or Sales Lists, the African American researcher may have more clues to assemble the pieces of an eighteenth and early nineteenth century family history.

The early original colonial tax lists and the 1785 State Census for Fauquier will eventually re-write the history of the county and its residents. These lists present entirely new information about those who called Fauquier their home during one of the most turbulent periods of our history.

8. Finding your way around Tax and Fiscal Records

Series Title: Tax and Fiscal Records
Color Code: Red Dots on Boxes

Series Dates: 1759-1849
Series Extent: 30 Boxes.
Series Arrangement: *Filed by year.*

Series Finding Aid: These records have not been indexed.

Boxes 1-18	Personal property and Land Tax Lists 1783-1849.
	NOTE: Box 1 also contains 12 lists from the 1785 Fauquier County State Census.
Box 19	Tithables 1759 to 1787 (Original Lists)
Boxes 20-24	Insolvent Lists between 1798-1851
Box 25	Insolvent Lists from Sheriff's Records 1784-1823
Box 26-29	Miscellaneous Court Records and County Accounts 1759-1827
Box 30	Tithables 1759-1787 (Copies of Lists in Box 19)
Boxes 31-37	County Court Papers Insolvents 1832-1886

> A List of the Tithables in Fauquier County in the Year 1759. Taken by Thos Marshall

At Churchill's Quarter	Rodham Tullos
John Churchill	Joshua Tullos } 3
Henry Churchill	Rodham Tullos Junr
William Hunton	John Ferguson ... 1
Tharnack Grey	Simon Cummins } 2
John Ship, Edwd Harrison	Alexr Cummins
Edward Fields	Richd Minatt ... 1
Alexr Smith	James Drummond } 2
Negr Ulyses, Will	John Drummond
Boatswain, Nell, Guy	At Alexr Dr
Tom, Dick, French	Robert Green
Phillis, Moses, Warner	Negr Parson, James } 6
Lucy, Sarah, China	Tom, Carmen, Pegg
Harper, Jack, Jeffery	William Blackwell
Peter, Charles, Jenny	Saml Blackwell
Phillis, Cutterus, Moll	Isaac Taylor } 10
Brister, Cate, Margery	Negr Addison, Phillis
Bess, Guy, George	Susanah, Caesar, Moll
Doll, Cato, Diana, Hannah	Banger, Caesar
Andrew, Ratliff, Tawney	William Ferguson ... 1
Nell, Nanny, Sarah, Thos	John Matthews } 3
Joan Total 49	Mrs Margt Irons

Plate 103. Tax & Fiscal. Scanned Image, 1759-001.
Page 1 of Thomas Marshall's List of Tithables.

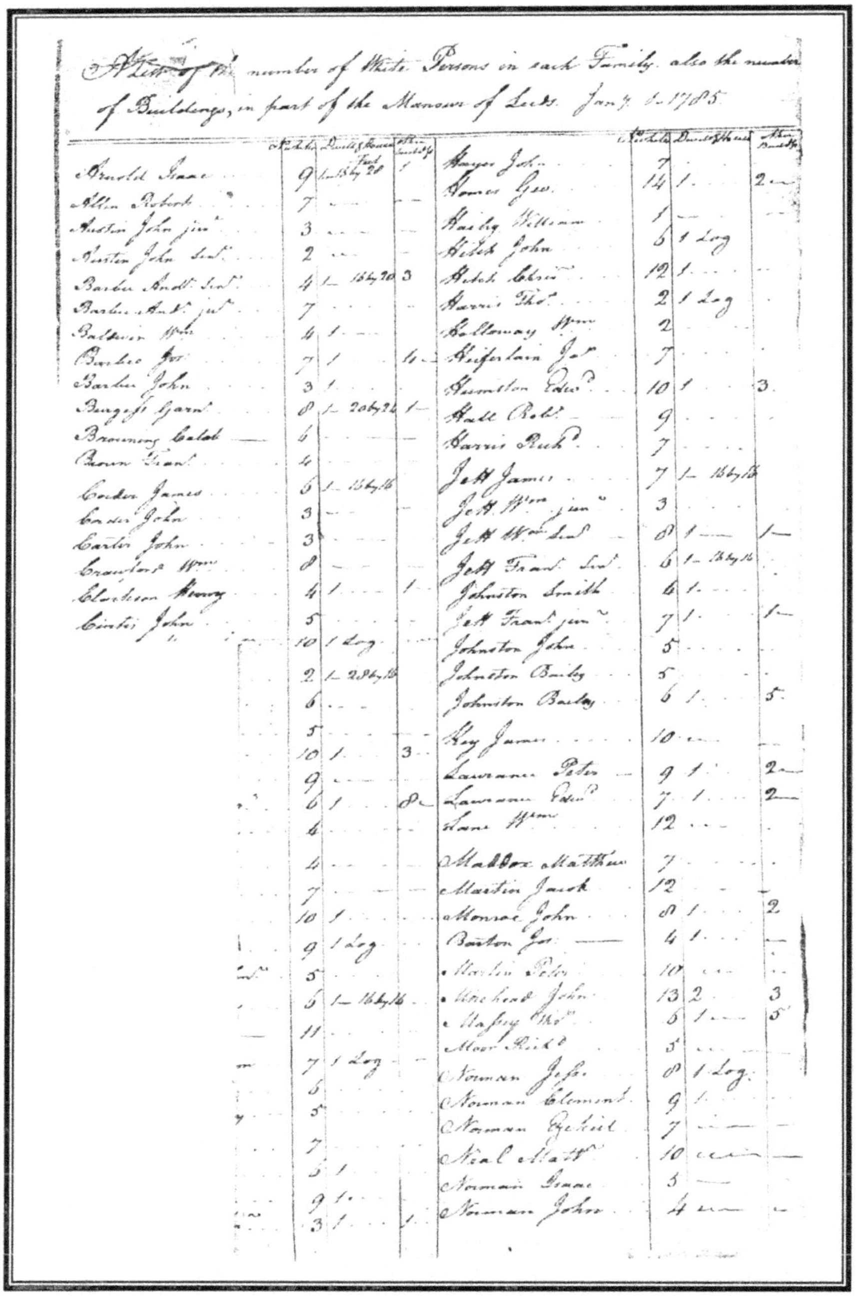

A List of the number of White Persons in each Family also the number of Buildings, in part of the Manour of Leeds. Jany 1st 1785

Name	Whites	Dwell. Houses	Other Buildings	Name	Whites	Dwell. Houses	Other Buildings
Arnold Isaac	9	1-18 by 20	1	Harper John	7		
Allen Robert	7			Homes Geo	14	1	2
Austin John jun	3			Harley William	1		
Austin John Senr	2			Hitch John	5	1 Log	
Barber Andw Senr	4	1-16 by 20	3	Hitch Abra	12	1	
Barber Andw jun	7			Harris Thos	2	1 Log	
Baldwin Wm	4	1		Holloway Wm	2		
Barker Jos	7	1	4	Heiferlain Jas	7		
Barber John	3	1		Hamilton Edwd	10	1	3
Burgess Garnt	8	1-20 by 24	1	Hall Robt	9		
Browning Caleb	4			Harris Richd	7		
Brown Frans	4			Jett James	7	1-16 by 16	
Corder James	5	1-18 by 16		Jett Wm jun	3		
Corder John	3			Jett Wm Senr	8	1	1
Carter John	3			Jett Frans Senr	6	1-16 by 16	
Crawford Wm	8			Johnston Smith	6	1	
Clarkson Henry	4	1	1	Jett Frans jun	7	1	1
Cirtis John	5			Johnston John	5		
	10	1 Log		Johnston Bailey	5		
	2	1-28 by 16		Johnston Bailey	6	1	5
	6			Key James	10		
	5			Lawrance Peter	9	1	2
	10	1	3	Lawrance Edwd	7	1	2
	9			Lane Wm	12		
	6	1	8	Maddox Matthew	7		
	4			Martin Jacob	12		
	4			Monroe John	8	1	2
	7			Barton Jos	4	1	
	10	1		Martin Peter	10		
	9	1 Log		Morehead John	13	2	3
	5			Massey Thos	6	1	5
	5	1-16 by 16		Moor Richd	5		
	11			Norman Jos	8	1 Log	
	7	1 Log		Norman Clement	9	1	
	6			Norman Ezekiel	7		
	5			Neal Matt	10		
	7			Norman Isaac	5		
	5	1		Norman John	4		
	9	1					
	3	1	1				

Plate 104. Tax & Fiscal Records. Scanned Image from Box 1, Tax Lists. 1785-005. Page 1 of the Leeds Manor, Fauquier County State Census.

Name	[White]	Dwellings & Houses	Other Houses
Norman William	9		
Ogleby Thos.	4		
Philips Moses	2		
Robinson James	6		
Rush Randall	2		
Randall John	7	1 Log	2
Reade John	8		
Randall Geo.	1		
Rigsy Richd	10	1	1
Robinson John senr.	2		
Robinson William	10		
Smith William	4		
Smith Mary	5	1	1
Shavo Geo.	1		
Shavo John	1		
Smith John	7		
Smith Jarrott	4		
Smith William jr	8		
Shumate John	8	1 Log	
Settle Joel	6		
Snyder Henry	13		
Smith John	7		
Shackleford Benj.	10	1 Sky 22	
Thompson Jesse	9		
Wheatley William	8		
Withers James	11	1	5
Wigfield Richd	7		

Capt Shackleford
L.S. Sends 18
1785
3

A Shackleford

Plate 104. (Cont.) Tax & Fiscal Records. Scanned Image from Box 1, Tax Lists. 1785-005. Page 2 of the Leeds Manor, Fauquier County State Census

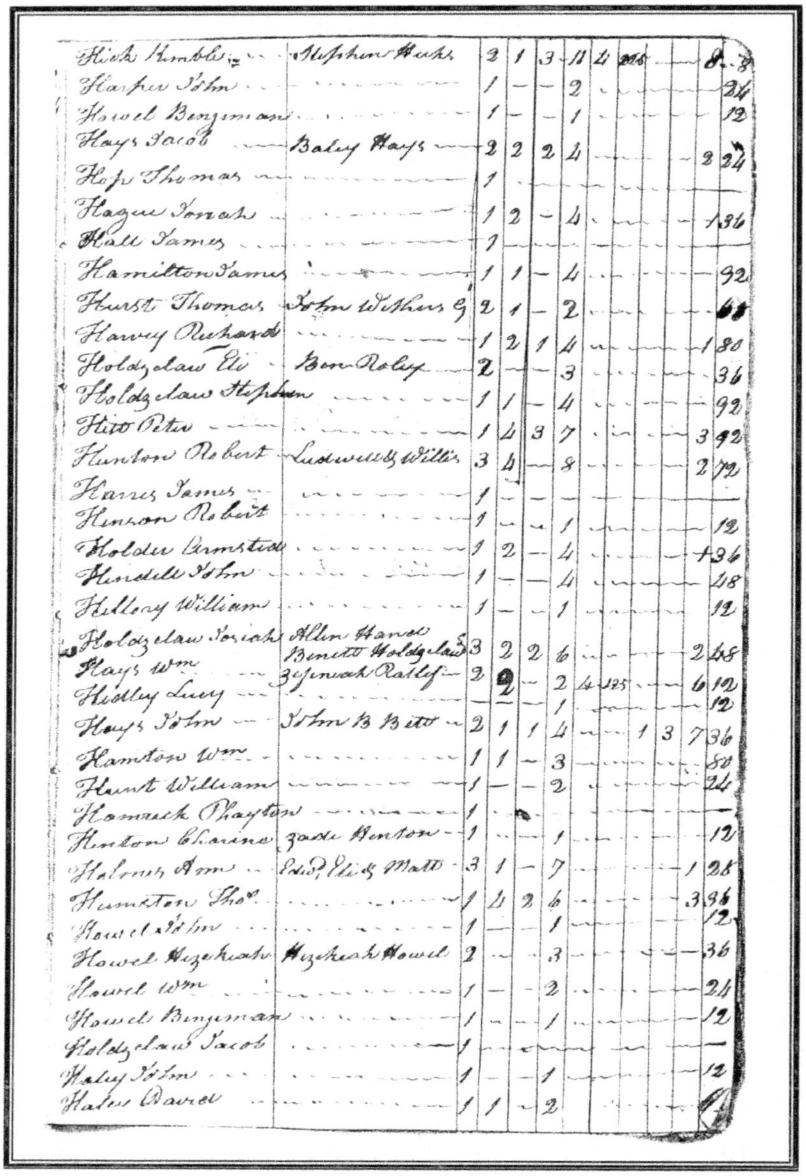

Plate 105. Tax & Fiscal Records. Scanned Image from Box 8, Tax Lists. 1809-001. A page from Thomas Robinson's 1809 Personal Property Tax List.

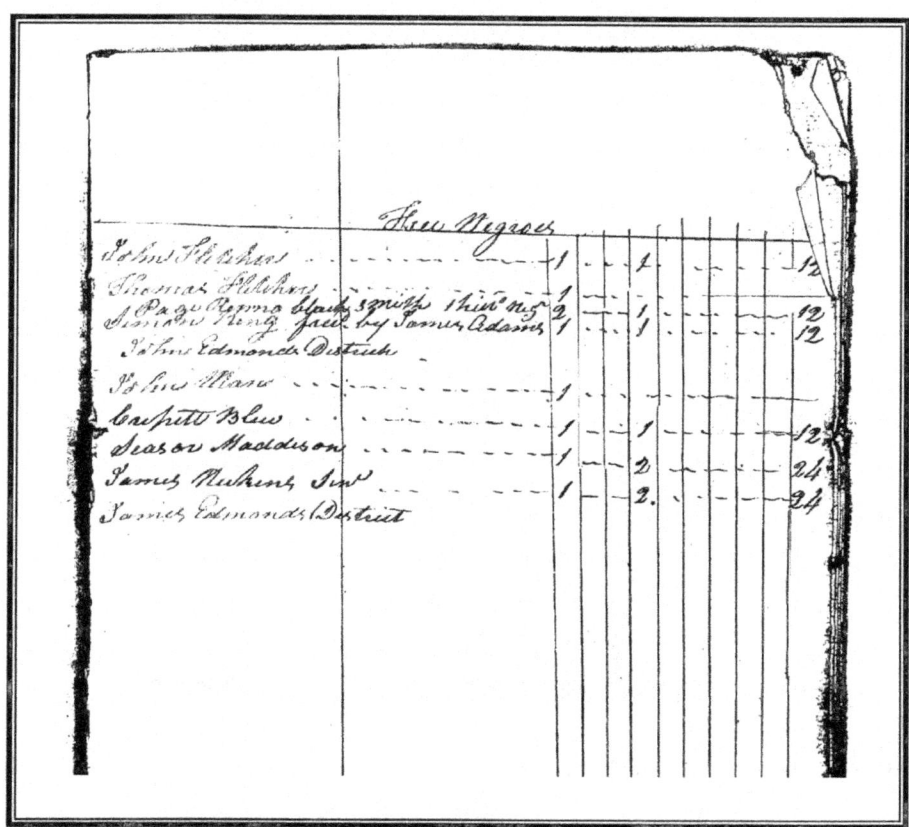

Plate 106. Tax & Fiscal Records. Scanned Image from Box 8, Tax Lists. 1809-001. Page from the back of Thomas Robinson's Tax List giving names of Free Negroes in his District.

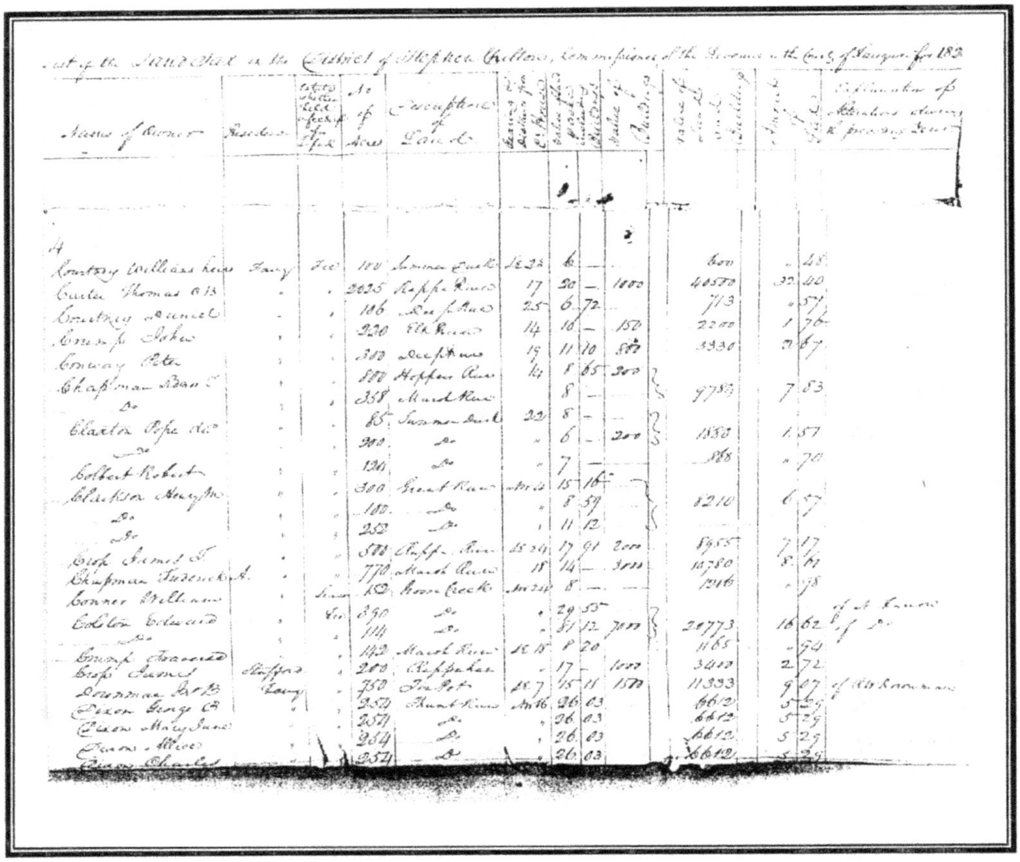

Plate 107. Tax & Fiscal Records. Scanned Image from Box 12, Tax Lists. 1825-001 A page from Stephen Chilton's 1825 Land Book.

Fauquier County, Virginia's Clerks Loose Papers: A Guide to the Records 1759-1919

CHAPTER 19
VITAL RECORDS

1. Overview

Vital Records in the Clerks Loose Papers include Marriages, Births and Deaths. The bulk of this series is comprised of marriage bonds and consents. Thirty-four of the marriage bonds were previously unknown. These 1784 marriage bonds were found among the Administrator, Executor and Guardian Bonds. There are also a variety of other marriage bonds, licenses, written consents and Minister returns filed in the papers between 1795-1901.

In addition, there are several records that relate to births and deaths of early residents of the County.

2. Finding you way around Vital Records

Series Title: Vital Records
Color Code: Black and Yellow Dots on Boxes

Series Dates: 1784-1901
Series Extent: 1 Box. *0.5 linear feet.*
Series Arrangement: *Filed by year.*

Series Finding Aids: There is a Marriage Records Index sorted by Males and Females.

3. A Preview of the Marriage Record Index

Figures 24 and 25 below show a sampling of the Marriage Index, sorted by Names of Males, then by Females.

Index #	Name (M)	Name (F)	Instrument	Date	Bondsmen	Witnesses	Consent
1784-001	Allen, John	Threlkeld, Mary	Marriage Bond	11/23/1784	Allen, John; Threlkeld, Wm.		
1800-003	Brady, Patrick	Bowie, Sallie	Marriage Bond	8/23/1800	Brady, Patrick Foote, Wm.	Lake, Wm. (consent) Foster, Wm. (consent)	By parents John Sr. + Cynthia Bowie
1806-001	Davis, Wm. F. R. (Rev.)	-----	Minister Returns	1/1805 to 1/1806			
1784-017	Levy, Judith	McGraw, Jemima, Daughter of Jemima	Marriage Bond	10/16/1784	Levy, Judith Ridley, John	Brooke, G. (bond + consent)	by mother Jemima McGraw
1784-019	Marshall, Thomas	Jett, Francis	Marriage Bond	12/7/1784	Jett, Daniel Marshall, Thomas	Brooke, G. (bond)	
1803-002	Winn, Minor	Harrison, Eleanor	Marriage Contract	6/2/1803			

Figure 24. A representative sampling from the Marriage Records Index, sorted by Male names.

Index #	Name (M)	Name (F)	Instrument	Date	Bondsmen	Witnesses	Consent
1784-020	Bawmer, Susanna	McCormack, John	Marriage Bond	2/20/1784	McCormick, John; Bower, Peter	Brooke, H. (bond)	
1784-003	Carroll, Mary Ann	Bartlett, Benjamin	Marriage Bond	9/29/1784	Bartlett, Benjamin; Haynie, Wm.	Brooke, G.	
1867-007	Ellis, M. J.	Ash, B. H.	Consent to Marriage License	9/17/1867			by father Nathan P. Ellis
1784-029	Horton, Elizabeth	Stadler, Jacob	Marriage Bond	7/26/1784	Bradford, Alexander; Stadler, Jacob	Brooke, G. (bond)	
1784-018	Marshall, Mary Ann	Marshall, Humphrey	Marriage Bond	9/12/1784	Marshall, Humphrey; Marshall, James Markham	Brooke, G. (bond)	
1867-004	Nickens, Nancy	Williams, Joe (colored)	Consent to Marriage License	3/8/1867			by Nancy Nickens' parents
1816-001	Smith, Rebecca	Welsh, Alexander	Marriage Contract	2/29/1816			
1801-001	Wheeler, Catharine	Rockingbaugh, Jacob	Marriage Bond	3/24/1801	Chenaunit, Elijah; Rockingbaugh, Jacob	Brawner, Bazzel (consent) Brawner, Meredith (consent)	by Catharine Wheeler "of legal age"

Figure 24. A representative sampling of the Marriage Records Index, sorted by Female names.

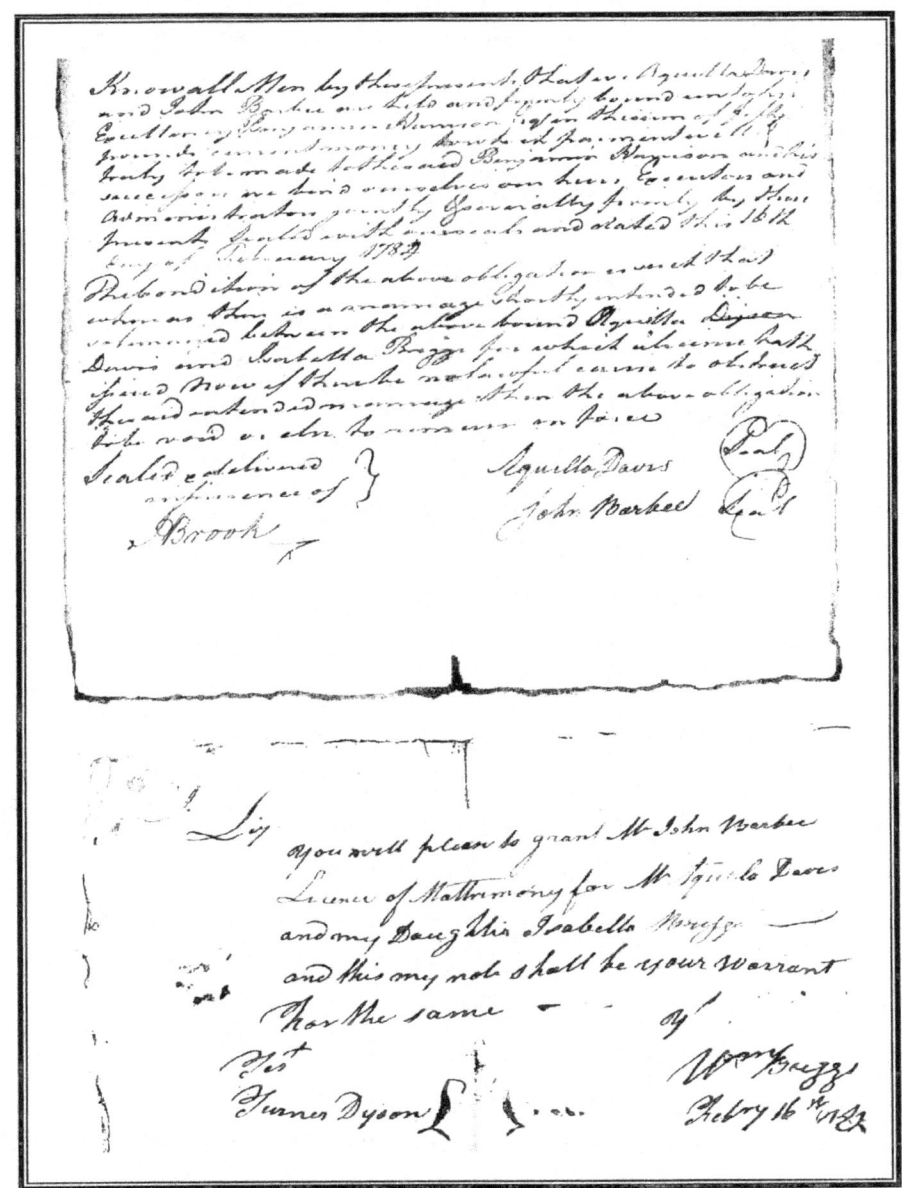

Plate 108. Vital Records. Scanned Image of 1784-007 Marriage Bond & Consent. 2/16/1784 Aquilla Davis to Isabella Briggs, daughter William Briggs (consent)

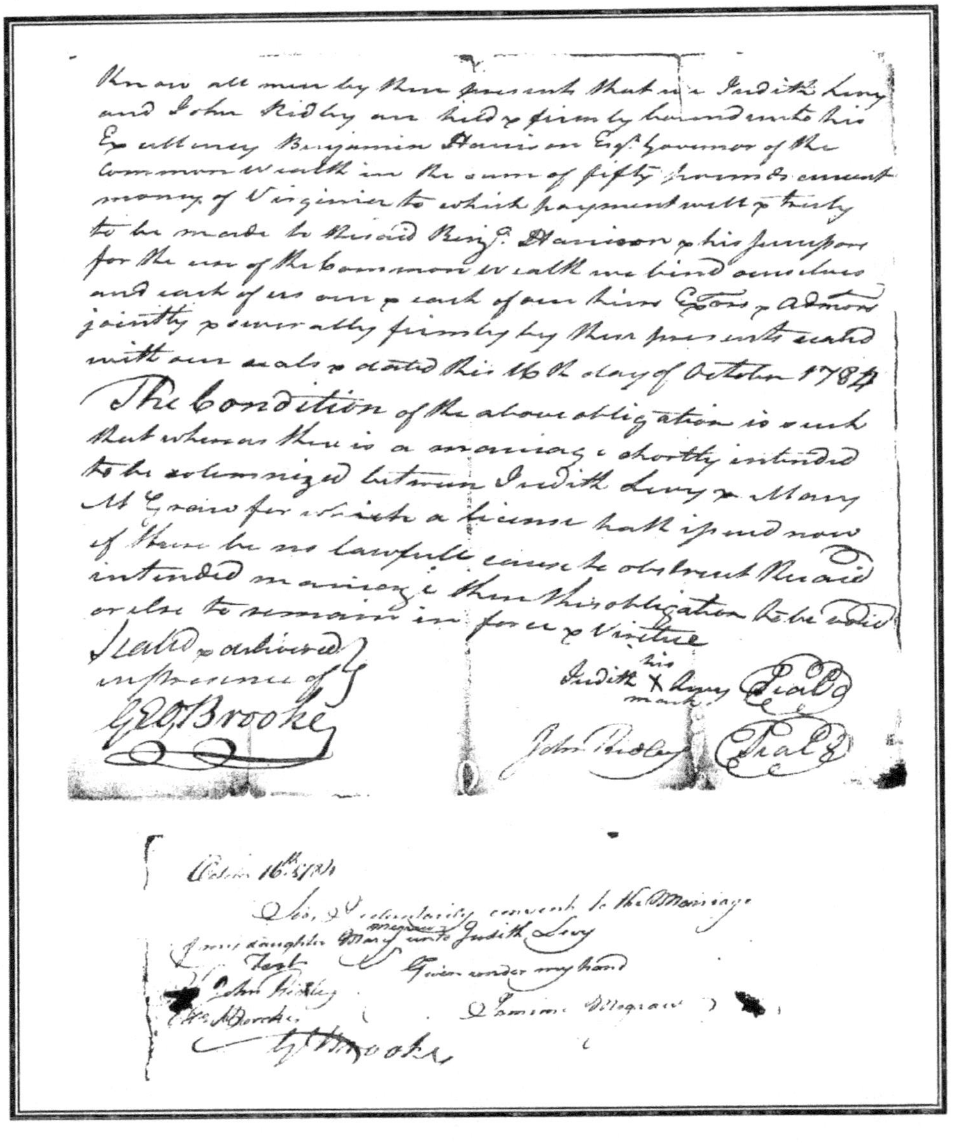
Know all men by these presents that we Judith Levy and John Ridley are held & firmly bound unto his Excellency Benjamin Harrison Esq. Governor of the Commonwealth in the sum of fifty pounds current money of Virginia to which payment well & truly to be made to the said Benj.a Harrison & his successors for the use of the Commonwealth we bind ourselves and each of us our & each of our heirs Exors & admors jointly & severally firmly by these presents sealed with our seals & dated this 16th day of October 1784

The Condition of the above obligation is such that whereas there is a marriage shortly intended to be solemnized between Judith Levy & Mary McGraw for which a license hath issued now if there be no lawfull cause to obstruct the said intended marriage then this obligation to be void or else to remain in force & virtue

Sealed & delivered in presence of
G.W. Brooke

Judith his X mark Levy (Seal)
John Ridley (Seal)

October 16th 1784
Sir, I voluntarily consent to the Marriage of my daughter Mary McGraw unto Judith Levy
Given under my hand
Test
John Ridley
Wm. Brooke
Jemima McGraw
G. Brooke

Plate 109. Vital Records. Scanned Image of 1784-017 Marriage Bond & Consent. 10/16/1784. Judith [Judah] Levy to Mary McGraw, daughter Jemima McGraw (consent)

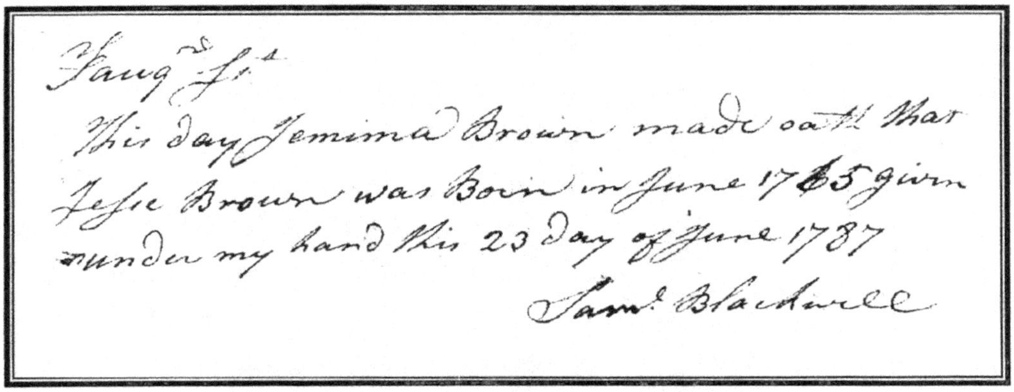

> Fauq'r ss.
> This day Jemima Brown made oath that
> Jesse Brown was Born in June 1765 given
> under my hand this 23 day of June 1787
>
> Sam'l Blackwell

Plate 110. Vital Records. Scanned Image of 1787-001 Jesse Brown's Birth Record.

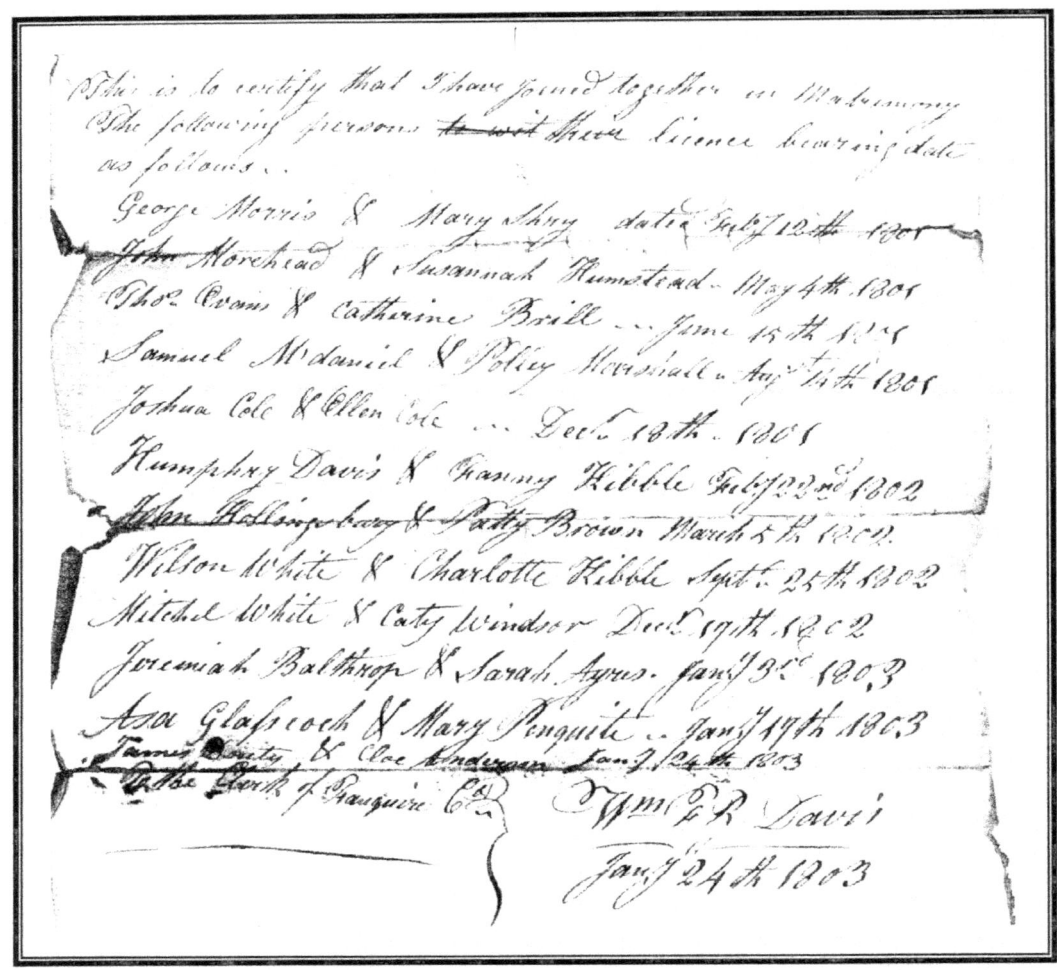

Plate 111. Vital Records. Scanned Image of 1803-001.
William F. R. Davis' Minister Returns for February 1801 to January 1803.

Fauquier County, Virginia's Clerks Loose Papers: A Guide to the Records 1759-1919

QUICK REFERENCE "POINTERS"/INDEX

This "Quick Reference" is meant to help readers promptly find areas of immediate interest to them. Chapter 1 informs the reader about the Preservation Grant Program available through the Library of Virginia and gives some history of the papers uncovered during the several grants awarded to Fauquier County. For a thorough grounding in the make-up of the Clerks Loose Papers, play close attention to the information in Chapter 2. An Introduction to the Records. This chapter will help you understand the record base, the arrangement of folders and the database.

Chapter 4. Chancery Records.
- For a discussion of what Chancery is and how it works, see pages 19-20.
- For definitions of legal terms associated with Chancery suits, see pages 20-22.
- For the way folders are filed, arranged and organized, see pages 22-24.
- For information regarding the Library of Virginia Chancery Index and the abbreviations used therein, see page 25-27.
- **This series has been indexed following the form set by the LVA State Chancery Index.**

Chapter 5. Dead Papers, Ended Causes & Judgments
- For a discussion of the steps involved in a **Civil** case, see pages 35-37.
- For a discussion of the steps involved in a **Criminal** case, see pages 37-38.
- For definition of the legal terms associated with Civil and Criminal cases, see pages 38-39.
- **This series has not been indexed.**

Chapter 6. Free Negro & Slave Records (after 1865 Negro Records)
- For a discussion of the types of records in this record series, see pages 45-48.
- For a discussion of the value of these records for African Americans, see pages 48-49.
- For a discussion of the law, Slavery and the Free Negro, see pages 49.
- For a preview of the Indices associated with this series, see pages 51.
- **There are three Name indices associated with this record series, created and compiled by the author:**
    1) **African-American Transactions and Conveyances from the Clerks Loose Papers**
    2) **African-American Suits and other Records from the Clerks Loose Papers**
    3) **African-American Records from the County Court Papers 1832-1904**

Chapter 7. Land Records (Conveyances) and Land Disputes
- For a discussion of the types of records in this series, see pages 57-60.
- For a discussion of the Marshall Ejectment Suits found in Circuit Superior Court papers, see page 60.
- For the ways folders are filed, arranged and organized in this series, see pages 61-62.
- For a discussion of the Land Dispute Index, see page 63.
- For the Grantor-Grantee Deed index, called "Recorded Deeds, filed separately from conveyances found in Land Disputes; see page 63-64.
- For the Grantor-Grantee Deed Index, called "Clerk's Copies (found in a drawer marked "Unrecorded Deeds"), see pages 65.
- For the Land Dispute Index, see page 66.
- **There are three Indices associated with this record series, created and compiled by the author:**
    1) **Grantor & Grantee Deed Index for Deeds &c.**
    2) **Grantor & Grantee Deed Index for Clerks Copies/Unrecorded Deeds**
    3) **Plaintiff & Defendant Land Dispute Index**

Chapter 9. Military Records
- For a general overview of the records in this series, see page 79.
- For a preview of the Military Records Party index, see page 80.
- **There is a Military Records Index, sorted by Party, created and compiled by the author.**

Fauquier County, Virginia's Clerks Loose Papers: A Guide to the Records 1759-1919

Chapter 14. Probate/Fiduciary Records
- For a general overview of the types of records in this series, see, page 151.
- **There is a Consolidated Probate Index for all probate records found in the Clerks Loose Papers from 1759-1919.** This index has been created and compiled by the author. It includes probate records found in Chancery, Land Disputes, Military Records and the Probate record series of the Clerks Loose Papers. It also includes any probate record found in the Superior and Circuit Court papers between 1832-1910.

Indices from the Clerks Loose Papers:
1) **The LVA Chancery Index** is the intellectual property of the Library of Virginia.

2) The remaining indices, listed below, are the intellectual property of the author of this guide and are copyrighted accordingly.
   - From the Free Negro & Slave Records. Printed copies of these indices will be available for research use in the fall, 2001.
     - **African-American Transactions and Conveyances from the Clerks Loose Papers**
     - **African-American Suits and other Records from the Clerks Loose Papers**
     - **African-American Records from the County Court Papers 1832-1904**

   - From the Land Records and Land Disputes Record Series. Printed copies of these indices are available in the Fauquier County Circuit Court record room for research use.
     - **Grantor & Grantee Deed Index for Deeds &c.**
     - **Grantor & Grantee Deed Index for Clerks Copies**
     - **Plaintiff & Defendant Land Dispute Index**

   - From the Probate/Fiduciary Records Series: **Consolidated Probate Index 1759-1919**. A printed copy of this index will be available for research use July 2001. Willow Bend Books will publish this index.

3) In addition, eight small indices have been created and are the intellectual property of the author of this guide and copyrighted accordingly. These indexes are printed copies and are all available in the Fauquier County Circuit Court record room for research use.

   - **Military Records Party Index**, taken from the first two boxes of Military Records.

   - **Name Index for Mill Petitioners and Viewers**

   - **Name Index for Road Petitioners, Viewers, Surveyors and Overseers**, taken from the first box of Roads & Bridge Records.

   - **Naturalization Index** taken from the Citizenship and Naturalization Boxes found in the Miscellaneous Records record series, including Naturalizations from the County Court records.

   - **Name Index for Ordinary Keepers**, taken from the first box of Ordinary Records.

   - **Apprenticeship Index**, taken from the Overseers of the Poor Record Series.

   - **Marriage Records Index for Males and Females**, taken from the Vital Records record series.

Fauquier County, Virginia's Clerks Loose Papers: A Guide to the Records 1759-1919

NAME INDEX

Surname	Given Name	pg #
ADAMS		
Adams	Charles	91
Adams	Elias	139
Adams	Eliza	146
Adams	James	152
Adams	John	128
Adams	Samuel	128
Adams	Thomas T.	152
Adams	Sarah C.	146
ALLASON		
Allason	William	91
ALLEN		
Allen	John	175
Allen	Joseph	66
Allen	Robert	170
Allen	Thomas	128
ANDERSON		
Anderson	Adeline	88
Anderson	Cloe	180
Anderson	Daniel	160
Anderson	E. S.	88
Anderson	John	89
ARELL		
Arell	Richard	66
ARNOLD		
Arnold	Elijah	67, 68
Arnold	Humphrey	63
Arnold	Isaac	63, 170
ASBURY		
Asbury	Henry	104
ASH		
Ash	B. H.	176
ASHBY		
Ashby	John	128
Ashby	John (Captain)	80
Ashby	William C.	54
AUSTIN		
Austin	John Jr.	170
Austin	John Sr.	170

NAME INDEX

Surname	Given Name	pg #
BAILEY		
Bailey	Carr	12
Bailey	John	139
Bailey	Joseph	32
Bailey	William	80
BAKER		
Baker	J. H.	86
Baker	Richard	65
BALL		
Ball	Benjamin	65
Ball	Daniel F.	88
Ball	Edward	62, 73
Ball	James	62
Ball	William	62, 162
BALTHROPE		
Balthrope	Jeremiah	180
BANNAKER		
Bannaker	Benjamin	1, 5, 6, 9
BARBEE		
Barbee	Andrew Jr.	170
Barbee	Andrew Sr.	170
Barbee	John	177
BARBEY		
Barbey	Thomas	128
BARNETT		
Barnett	Ambrose	25, 128, 135
BARNS		
Barns	Ann	146
BARTLETT		
Bartlett	Benjamin	176
BATTLES		
Battles	Myredith	139
BAWMER		
Bawmer	Susanna	176
BAYLISS		
Bayliss	Dudley	162

Fauquier County, Virginia's Clerks Loose Papers: A Guide to the Records 1759-1919

NAME INDEX

Surname	Given Name	pg #
BEACH		
Beach	Peter	93
BEANE		
Beane	Joseph	51
BEAR		
Bear	Joseph	112
BELL		
Bell	John	4
BERNARD		
Bernard	Richard	4
Bernard	William	4
BERRY		
Berry	Benjamin	139
Berry	Joseph	64
Berry	Joseph Sr.	64
BERRYMAN		
Berryman	Maxm.	130
BIRCH		
Birch,	Thomas & Sons	3
BISE		
Bise	Aaron	142
BLACKWELL		
Blackwell	John Junr.	136
Blackwell	Joseph	12, 16, 22, 25, 27 28, 66, 98, 153
Blackwell	Saml	169, 179
Blackwell	Samuel	1, 2, 4, 13, 65
Blackwell	Thomas	44
Blackwell	William	158, 169
BLUE		
Blue	Cupid	51
Blue	Cupitt	173
BOGGESS		
Boggess	Henley	89

NAME INDEX

Surname	Given Name	pg #
BOOKER		
Booker	Sarah	80, 84
BOWEN		
Bowen	James	66
Bowen	Lucy	152
BOWER		
Bower	Peter	176
BOWIE		
Bowie	Cynthia	175
Bowie	John Sr.	175
Bowie	Sally	175
BRADFORD		
Bradford	Alexander	176
Bradford	Wm.	84
BRADY		
Brady	Patrick	175
BRAGG		
Bragg	Charles F.	88
BRAWMER		
Brawmer	Bazzel	176
Brawmer	Meredith	176
BRAY		
Bray	Timothy	80
BRIGGS		
Briggs	David	25
Briggs	Isabella	177
Briggs	William	177
BRILL		
Brill	Catherine	180
BRONAUGH		
Bronaugh	John T.	33
BROOK		
Brook	H.	131
BROOKE		
Brooke	G.	175, 176, 178
Brooke	Geo	178

Fauquier County, Virginia's Clerks Loose Papers: A Guide to the Records 1759-1919

NAME INDEX

Surname	Given Name	pg #
BROOKE (Cont.)		
Brooke	H.	176
Brooke	Humphry	100
BROWN		
Brown	Ann	144
Brown	Fran^s	170
Brown	Jemima	140, 170
Brown	Jesse	179
Brown	John	93
Brown	Louisa	13
Brown	Patty	180
Brown	Thomas	65
BROWNING		
Browning	Caleb	170
BUCKNER		
Buckner	Judith	64
Buckner	Richard	64
Buckner	Thornton	41
BULLITT		
Bullitt	C.	134
Bullitt	Cuthbert	61
Bullitt	Cuth^t	132
BULLOCK		
Bullock	Richard	4
BURGES		
Burges	Garner	25
BURGESS		
Burgess	Edward	25, 29
Burgess	Garn^r	170
Burgess	M. F.	88
BUTLER		
Butler	John	93
BYRNE		
Byrne	John	139
Byrne	Uriah	65
CALLOW		
Callow	John R.	107

NAME INDEX

Surname	Given Name	pg #
CARPER		
Carper	David	88
CARROL		
Carrol	Nancy	145
CARROLL		
Carroll	Mary Ann	176
CARTER		
Carter	Charles	1, 2
Carter	John	170
Carter	John	170
Carter	Landon	1
Carter	Moore F.	66
Carter	Robert	2, 75
Carter	Thomas	13
Carter	Thomas O. B.	174
CATLETT		
Catlett	Peter	63, 64
Catlett	Susan	63
CELEY		
Celey	Margaret	144
CHAMBERS		
Chambers	Joseph	13, 64
CHAPMAN		
Chapman	[Illegible]	174
Chapman	Frederick A.	174
CHENAUNIT		
Chenaunit	Elijah	176
CHICHESTER		
Chichester	Richard McCarty	66
CHILTON		
Chilton	Captain	85
Chilton	John	153
Chilton	Joseph	66, 142
CHUNN		
Chunn	Andrew	143

Fauquier County, Virginia's Clerks Loose Papers: A Guide to the Records 1759-1919

NAME INDEX

Surname	Given Name	pg #
CHURCHILL		
Churchill	Armistead	91
Churchill	Henry	169
Churchill	John	89, 169
CISON		
Cison	Roger	100
CLARK		
Clark	Elizabeth	144
Clark	Richard	162
CLARKSON		
Clarkson	Henry	170, 174
CLAXTON		
Claxton	Pope (decd.)	174
Claxton	Robert	13
CLEMENTS		
Clements	Charles	84
COLBERT		
Colbert	Robert	174
COLE		
Cole	Ellen	180
Cole	Joshua	180
COLES		
Coles	George	89
COLLINS		
Collins	Jno.	84
COLSTON		
Colston	Edward	174
CONNER		
Conner	Joseph	88
Conner	William	174
CONWAY		
Conway	Peter	174
COOK		
Cook	Fannie	88
Cook	Mary	84

NAME INDEX

Surname	Given Name	pg #
COOKSEY		
Cooksey	John	93
COOPER		
Cooper	Appollos	139
CORBIN		
Corbin	Gawin	1
CORDELL		
Cordell	David	104
CORDER		
Corder	Charles	13
Corder	James	170
Corder	John	170
CORNHILL		
Cornhill	Mary	84
CORTNEY		
Cortney	W^m	93
COURTNEY		
Courtney	Daniel	174
Courtney	William Heirs	174
COVINGTON		
Covington	W^m	84
COX		
Cox	Charles	90
CRAWFORD		
Crawford	W^m	170
CROP		
Crop	James	174
Crop	James T.	174
CROSBY		
Crosby	George	104
CRUMP		
Crump	Benjamin	4
Crump	John	4, 16, 66, 174
Crump	Traverse	174
Crump	Travis	66

Name Index

Surname	Given Name	pg #
CRUPPER		
Crupper	John	104
CUMMINS		
Cummins	Alex^r	169
Cummins	Simon	169
CUNNINGHAM		
Cunningham	Elis^h	84
Cunningham	Elizabeth	80
DAGG		
Dagg	John	4
DATREE		
Datree	Henry	136
DAVENPORT		
Davenport	Thomas	164
DAVIS		
Davis	Aquilla	141, 177
Davis	G. C.	96
Davis	Humphrey	180
Davis	Lucy A. (Mrs.)	88
Davis	William F. R.	175, 180
DAVISON		
Davison	James	41
DAWSON		
Dawson	Benjamin	63, 78
DEARING		
Dearing	John	90
DEBUTTS		
DeButts	Parson	72
DELAHUNT		
Delahunt	James	140
DIGGES		
Digges	John Jr.	160
DIGGS		
Diggs	Edward Jr.	118

Name Index

Surname	Given Name	pg #
DILLARD		
Dillard	Mary	84
DIXON		
Dixon	Alice	174
Dixon	Charles	174
Dixon	Mary Jane	174
Dixon	Peter	54
Dixon	Roger	101
DODD		
Dodd	John	90
DORAM		
Doram	Bill	54
DOUTY		
Douty	James	180
DOWNMAN		
Downman	Jno. B.	174
Downman	R. H.	87
Downman	Robt	174
DOYLE		
Doyle	Isaac	122
DRUMMOND		
Drummond	James	169
Drummond	John	169
DULANY		
Dulany	Zachariah	157
DULING		
Duling	William	62, 65
DUNCAN		
Duncan	Archibald	141
Duncan	Charles	51, 90, 92, 157
Duncan	Dillard	157
Duncan	Edmund	157
Duncan	John	119
Duncan	Mariah	157
Duncan	Olivia	51
Duncan	Rachel	140
Duncan	Traverse	157
Duncan	William	144

Fauquier County, Virginia's Clerks Loose Papers: A Guide to the Records 1759-1919

NAME INDEX

Surname	Given Name	pg #
DYSON		
Dyson	Turner	177
EARLE		
Earle	Saml	158
EASTHAM		
Eastham	George	23
Eastham	Susan	23
EDMONDS		
Edmonds	Elias	64
Edmonds	W.	121
EDWARDS		
Edwards	John	13, 91
EGAN		
Egan	Barnaby	72
ELLIOTT		
Elliott	Elizabeth	63
ELLIS		
Ellis	M. J.	176
Ellis	Nathan P.	176
EMBREY		
Embrey	Stanton	53
Embrey	W. W.	88
Embrey	William	53
ESKRIDGE		
Eskridge	George	104
EUSTACE		
Eustace	William	16
EVANS		
Evans	John	90
Evans	Susan	140
FAIRFAX		
Fairfax	Denny	63, 66, 69, 70, 149
Fairfax	George William	2
Fairfax	Hampton	54
Fairfax	Lady Catharine	1, 2, 10
Fairfax	Lord Thomas	1, 2, 13, 64, 65, 66, 74, 75

NAME INDEX

Surname	Given Name	pg #
FALLIS		
Fallis	Thomas	90, 95
FANT		
Fant	Henry M.	33
FARMER		
Farmer	Nelson P.	88
FARROW		
Farrow	N.	174
FAUQUIER		
Fauquier	Francis	2, 17, 119
FEAGANS		
Feagans	Polly	139
FERGUSON		
Ferguson	John	169
FIELD		
Field	John	91
FIELDS		
Fields	Charles W.	88
FISHBACK		
Fishback	Ja^s	142
Fishback	John	162
Fishback	Josiah	162
FISHER		
Fisher	Samuel	64
FLEMING		
Fleming	Samuel	162
FLETCHER		
Fletcher	Elizabeth	146
Fletcher	James	104, 144
Fletcher	Jesse	140
Fletcher	Jno. T.	146
Fletcher	John	173
Fletcher	Jos.	146
Fletcher	Marshall	160
Fletcher	Mary	146
Fletcher	Mary C.	146
Fletcher	Mary Emily (Mrs.)	88

Fauquier County, Virginia's Clerks Loose Papers: A Guide to the Records 1759-1919

NAME INDEX

Surname	Given Name	pg #
FLETCHER (Cont.)		
Fletcher	Nelson	146
Fletcher	Rach¹	146
Fletcher	Sarah	146
Fletcher	Stephen	139
Fletcher	Susan	146
Fletcher	Thomas	173
Fletcher	Wilford H.	146
FLOWEREE		
Floweree	Daniel	135
FLYNN		
Flynn	William	162
FOOTE		
Foote	Wᵐ	175
FORD		
Ford	Asa	54
Ford	Eliza	139
Ford	Juda	139
FOSTER		
Foster	Frederick	84
Foster	Henson	78
Foster	Wᵐ	175
FOWLER		
Fowler	Zeonandy	146
FREEMAN		
Freeman	James	25
FRENCH		
French	George	65
FURGUSON		
Furguson	Robert	84
GALLOWAY		
Galloway	Fanny L.	152
GARNER		
Garner	Charles	80
Garner	Charles Junʳ	144
Garner	John	14

NAME INDEX

Surname	Given Name	pg #
GENT		
Gent	Mary	25
GEORGE		
George	Parnach	169
George	Weedon	90
GIBSON		
Gibson	David	104
Gibson	Isaac	91
GILLISON		
Gillison	John (Major)	80
GLASCOCK		
Glascock	Asa	180
Glascock	Benjamin	64
Glascock	John	139
Glascock	Joseph	64
Glascock	Nimrod	88
Glascock	Peter	63
GOLDEN		
Golden	William	140
GOOCH		
Gooch	William	13
GORAM		
Goram	Harrison	54
GOULDING		
Goulding	William	84
GRANT		
Grant	J.	93
Grant	William	166
Grant	Wᵐ	164
GRAY		
Gray	Thaddeus	88
GREEN		
Green	Ann (Mrs.)	14, 153
Green	John	78
Green	Robert	169

Fauquier County, Virginia's Clerks Loose Papers: A Guide to the Records 1759-1919

NAME INDEX

Surname	Given Name	pg #
GREGG		
Gregg	Thomas	162
GRIFFIN		
Griffin	William	141
GRIGSBY		
Grigsby	Aaron	16
Grigsby	Nathaniel	66
Grigsby	Samuel	91
Grigsby	William	25
GRIMSLEY		
Grimsley	Zachariah	334
GROVES		
Groves	Albert	88
Groves	Mary	144
HACKLEY		
Hackley	Lott	93
HAGUE		
Hague	Jonah	172
HAINS		
Hains	Daniel	162
Hains	Joseph	162
HALEY		
Haley	David	172
Haley	John	172
HALL		
Hall	James	172
Hall	Robert	170
HAMILTON		
Hamilton	George	87
Hamilton	James	172
HAMPTON		
Hampton	William	91
HAMRICK		
Hamrick	Phayton	172
HAMTON		
Hamton	Edward	169

NAME INDEX

Surname	Given Name	pg #
HAMTON (Cont.)		
Hamton	W^m	172
HANBACK		
Hanback	Silas B.	88
HAND		
Hand	Allen	172
HARDIN		
Hardin	Mark	128
Hardin	Martin	130
HARGROVE		
Hargrove	Ann	84
HARPER		
Harper	John	172
HARRIS		
Harris	Bartlett	54
Harris	Daniel	94
Harris	James	172
Harris	Rich^d	170
Harris	Thos	170
HARRISON		
Harrison	Eleanor	175
Harrison	John	104
Harrison	Maria	55
Harrison	Thomas	16, 158
HARVEY		
Harvey	Richard	172
HATHAWAY		
Hathaway	James	25
HAY		
Hay	Thomas	64
HAYES		
Hayes	James	84
Hayes	Thomas	64
HAYNIE		
Haynie	William	176

Fauquier County, Virginia's Clerks Loose Papers: A Guide to the Records 1759-1919

NAME INDEX

Surname	Given Name	pg #
HAYS		
Hays	Baley	172
Hays	Jacob	172
Hays	John	172
Hays	W^m	172
HEALEY		
Healey	Richard	140
HEFERLAIN		
Heferlain	Ja^s	170
HEFLIN		
Heflin	James E.	88
HELM		
Helm	Elizabeth	25
Helm	Thomas	25
HENRY		
Henry	George	65
Henry	John	93
HENSON		
Henson	Robert	172
Henson	Robt.	146
HEREFORD		
Hereford	Francis	16
HEWITT		
Hewitt	Richard	88
HICKERSON		
Hickerson	Joseph	1, 2, 3, 4, 13, 65
Hickerson	R.	143
HICKS		
Hicks	Kimble	172
Hicks	Stephen	172
HILLERY		
Hillery	William	172
HINTON		
Hinton	Clarina	172
Hinton	Zade	172

NAME INDEX

Surname	Given Name	pg #
HISLEY		
Hisley	Lucy	172
HITCH		
Hitch	Clem	170
Hitch	John	170
Hitch	Nathan	63
HITT		
Hitt	Peter	34, 172
HODGES		
Hodges	Jes	84
HOLDER		
Holder	Armistead	172
Holder	Fanny	146
HOLDZCLAW		
Holdzclaw	Benett	172
Holdzclaw	Eli	172
Holdzclaw	Jacob	172
Holdzclaw	Josiah	172
HOLLINGSBURG		
Hollingsburg	John	180
HOLLOWAY		
Holloway	W^m	170
HOLMES		
Holmes	Ann	172
Holmes	Edwd	172
Holmes	Eli	172
Holmes	Matt	172
HOLTZCLAW		
Holtzclaw	C. W.	88
HOMES		
Homes	Geo.	170
HOOE		
Hooe	Henry	72
HOOMES		
Hoomes	N.	96

Name Index

Surname	Given Name	pg #
HOP		
Hop	Thomas	172
HOPPER		
Hopper	Thomas	100
HOPPIN		
Hoppin	Charles A.	4
HORD		
Hord	Thomas	98, 99, 150
HORNER		
Horner	Wm	32
HORTON		
Horton	Elizabeth	176
HOWEL		
Howel	Benjamin	172
Howel	Hezekiah	172
Howel	Hezekiah	172
Howel	John	172
Howel	Wm	172
HOWELL		
Howell	Jemima	84
HUME		
Hume	Andrew	66
HUMSTEAD		
Humstead	Susannah	180
HUMSTON		
Humston	Edwd	170
Humston	Thos	172
HUNDELL [HUDNALL?]		
Hundell	John	172
HUNT		
Hunt	William	172
HUNTON		
Hunton	Charles	160
Hunton	Ludwell	172
Hunton	Robert	172
Hunton	Robt	155

Name Index

Surname	Given Name	pg #
HUNTON (Cont.)		
Hunton	Thos	41
Hunton	William	41, 169
HURST		
Hurst	Thomas	172
HYLAND		
Hyland	Ferguson	84
JACKSON		
Jackson	Andrew	139
Jackson	Anna	146
Jackson	Hattie	139
Jackson	Joseph	91
JACOBS		
Jacobs	Maxwell [?]	93
JAMES		
James	Edmond T.	88
James	Thomas	65, 102, 128
JEFFERSON		
Jefferson	Thomas	5, 6
JEFFRIES		
Jeffries	John	157
JEFFRIS		
Jeffris	Mary	146
JENIFER		
Jenifer	Walter Hanson	152
JENKINS		
Jenkins	Ann	80, 111
Jenkins	George	54
Jenkins	Joshua	81, 85, 152
Jenkins	Josiah	80
Jenkins	Thomas	81
JENNINGS		
Jennings	Augustine	144
Jennings	Hannah	122
Jennings	J. C.	152
Jennings	Lewis	152
Jennings	William	105

Fauquier County, Virginia's Clerks Loose Papers: A Guide to the Records 1759-1919

NAME INDEX

Surname	Given Name	pg #
JETT		
Jett	Daniel	175
Jett	Francis	175
Jett	Fran^s Junr	170
Jett	Fran^s Senr	170
Jett	James	170
Jett	Wm Junr	170
Jett	Wm Senr	170
JOHNS		
Johns	Bushrod	13
JOHNSON		
Johnson	Gideon	41
Johnson	Gideon (Captain)	117
Johnson	Isaac	141
Johnson	Jeffrey	150
Johnson	John	150
Johnson	Joseph	126
Johnson	Smith	88
Johnson	William	139
Johnson	W^m	135
JOHNSTON		
Johnston	Bailey	170
Johnston	Bailey	170
Johnston	Gideon	136
Johnston	John	170
Johnston	Smith	170
JONES		
Jones	James	53
Jones	William	119, 135
JUDD		
Judd	Isaac	64
KAMPER		
Kamper	Henry	102
KEITH		
Keith	John	91
Keith	Thomas	166
Keith	Thos	166
KELLY		
Kelly	Alex^r D.	160

NAME INDEX

Surname	Given Name	pg #
KEMPER		
Kemper	Henry	53
Kemper	John	66, 81, 120
Kemper	Joshua T.	88
KENNARD		
Kennard	Lucinda	88
KERNES		
Kernes	Mary	81
KERNS		
Kerns	Mary	86, 144
KESTERSON		
Kesterson	William	169
KEY		
Key	James	170
KIBBLE		
Kibble	Charlotte	180
Kibble	Fanny	180
KINCAID		
Kincaid	John W. (Lt.)	81
KING		
King	Simon	173
KIRK		
Kirk	Thos	122
KITSON		
Kitson	W^m	117
KNIGHT		
Knight	Peter	63
KNOX		
Knox	Thomas P.	105
LAWRANCE		
Lawrance	Edwd	170
Lawrance	Peter	170

Fauquier County, Virginia's Clerks Loose Papers: A Guide to the Records 1759-1919

NAME INDEX

Surname	Given Name	pg #
LAKE		
Lake	W^m	175
LAWRENCE		
Lawrence	William	104
LAWS		
Laws	W^m	170
LEACH		
Leach	Bartlett	104
Leach	Thos	104
Leach	Wm M.	88
LEE		
Lee	Ann	1
Lee	Henry	1, 2, 83, 139
Lee	Molly	1
Lee	Richard Henry	1, 2
Lee	Thomas	43, 44
Lee	Thomas Ludwell	1, 2
LEGG		
Legg	Alcie	146
Legg	July [Judy?]	146
Legg	Susan F.	146
LEONARD		
Leonard	Robert	84
LEVIE		
Levie	Judah	12, 27, 28
LEVY		
Levy	Jemima	22
Levy	Judah	178
Levy	Judas	22, 25
Levy	Judith [Judah]	175
LEWIS		
Lewis	Robert	1, 3
LION		
Lion	Louis	114
LLOYD		
Lloyd	John	139

NAME INDEX

Surname	Given Name	pg #
LOIS		
Lois	John	116
LOMAX		
Lomax	John	66
LOVE		
Love	Samuel	91
Love	Samuel	91
MADDISON		
Maddison	Seasor	173
MADDOX		
Maddox	Matthew	170
MADDUX		
Maddux	Peter A.	143
Maddux	T. S.	139
Maddux	Thomas	128, 132
MAN		
Man	John	173
MANNERS		
Manners	William	164
MARLOW		
Marlow	Nancy	146
MARR		
Marr	Daniel	64
Marr	John	64
MARSHALL		
Marshall	Charles	2
Marshall	Humphrey	176
Marshall	James	67, 68, 97
Marshall	James M.	66, 69
Marshall	James Markham	176
Marshall	John	1, 2, 67, 68, 97
Marshall	Mary Ann	176
Marshall	Polley	180
Marshall	Thomas	1, 2, 85, 120, 165, 168, 175

-194-

Fauquier County, Virginia's Clerks Loose Papers: A Guide to the Records 1759-1919

NAME INDEX

Surname	Given Name	pg #
MARTIN		
Martin	Frank	139
Martin	Jacob	170
Martin	Peter	170
Martin	Rosey	139
Martin	Thomas	139
MASON		
Mason	Katharine	146
MASSEY		
Massey	Thos	170
MATHEW		
Mathew	Thomas	104
MATTHEWS		
Matthews	John	169
Matthews	Martha	144
MAUZEY		
Mauzey	Elizabeth	159
Mauzey	John	103, 159
Mauzey	Margaret	159
MAUZY		
Mauzy	Henry	159
Mauzy	Peter	4
McBEE		
McBee	Fanny	76
McCABE		
McCabe	George	135
McCARTY		
McCarty	Mary	84
McCLINTICK		
McClintick	Alice	84
McCORMACK		
McCormack	John	176
McDANIEL		
McDaniel	Samuel	180
McDERMOTT		
McDermott	Dennis	109

NAME INDEX

Surname	Given Name	pg #
McGRAW		
McGraw	James	27
McGraw	Jemima	175, 178
McGraw	Jemima (Mrs.)	175, 178
McKNIGHT		
McKnight	Uriah	162
McPHELIN		
McPhelin	Peter	110
MELDRUM		
Meldrum	Michael	75
MELONY		
Melony	Thomas	144
METCALFE		
Metcalfe	John	139
Metcalfe	John Junr	139
Metcalfe	W^m	104
MICHAEL		
Michael	Daniel	66
MILLER		
Miller	G. Allen	88
Miller	Simon	64
MILTON		
Milton	William	162
MINATT		
Minatt	Rich^d	169
MINTER		
Minter	Joseph	42
MITCHELL		
Mitchell	Daniel	139
MOFFETT		
Moffett	James	88
Moffett	John	166
MONTGOMERIE		
Montgomerie	William	128

NAME INDEX

Surname	Given Name	pg #
MONROE		
Monroe	James	1, 2, 16, 18
Monroe	John	170
MOOR		
Moor	Rich^d	170
MOORE		
Moore	J. M.	87
MOORHEAD		
Moorhead	Charles	115
MOREHEAD		
Morehead	Charles	115, 158
Morehead	George	78
Morehead	John	128, 139, 170, 180
MORGAN		
Morgan	John	128
Morgan	Simon (Lt.)	80
MORRIS		
Morris	George	180
MOUNTJOY		
Mountjoy	William	4
MOZINGO		
Mozingo	Thomas	139
MUNFORD		
Munford	George W.	126
MURDOCK		
Murdock	Jeremiah	74
MURRAY		
Murray	James & Co.	105
NASH		
Nash	Elijah	140
NEAL		
Neal	Matt^w	170
NEALE		
Neale	Joseph	116
Neale	Mary	133, 134

NAME INDEX

Surname	Given Name	pg #
NEAVIL		
Neavil	George	128
NEAVILL		
Neavill	George	90, 94, 128, 131
Neavill	George (Captain)	30
NELSON		
Nelson	Alex B.	157
Nelson	William	142
NEWGENT		
Newgent	Edward	141
Newgent	Elizabeth	141
Newgent	Thomas	141
NICKENS		
Nickens	James Senr	173
Nickens	Nancy	176
NICKINS		
Nickins	Thomas	54
NORMAN		
Norman	Bathsheba	140
Norman	Clement	170
Norman	Ezekiel	170
Norman	Isaac	170
Norman	Jesse	170
Norman	John	170
NORRIS		
Norris	Peggy	155
Norris	Septimus	155
Norris	Thaddeus	129, 155
Norris	Thad^s	118
ODEN		
Oden	William	135
OGLEBY		
Ogleby	Thos	171
OLIVER		
Oliver	William Frederick	56
Oliver	William Frederick	56
OREAR		
Orear	Benjamin F.	146

Fauquier County, Virginia's Clerks Loose Papers: A Guide to the Records 1759-1919

NAME INDEX

Surname	Given Name	pg #
OREAR (Cont.)		
Orear	Dolphus	146
Orear	Eliza	146
Orear	Levina Ann	146
OWENS		
Owens	Cuthbert	162
Owens	Mason	104
Owens	Thomas	180
PALMER		
Palmer	Joseph	98, 99
PAYNE		
Payne	Francis	66, 69, 70
Payne	Richard	13
PEAKE		
Peake	John	129
PENDLETON		
Pendleton	Edmond	129
Pendleton	George	139
Pendleton	Henry	101
Pendleton	James A.	13
PENQUITE		
Penquite	Mary	180
PEYTON		
Peyton	Chandler	160
Peyton	Charles	90
Peyton	Yelverton	158
PHILIPS		
Philips	Moses	171
PICKERALL		
Pickerall	Levi	145
PICKET		
Picket	W^m	150
PICKETT		
Pickett	Charles	54
Pickett	James	145, 162
Pickett	John	121
Pickett	Sanford	140
Pickett	William	115, 166

NAME INDEX

Surname	Given Name	pg #
PICKETT (Cont.)		
Pickett	W^m	102
POPE		
Pope	Benjamin	159
PORTER		
Porter	Thomas	13, 34
Porter	Thos	150
POWELL		
Powell	John	81
PRICE		
Price	Andrew	146
Price	Nalls	66
PRIMM		
Primm	John	152
PURCELL		
Purcell	George	81
RANDALL		
Randall	Geo.	171
Randall	John	171
Randall	Rich^d	171
RANDOLPH		
Randolph	Thomas M.	82
RANSDELL		
Ransdell	Wharton	153
RATLIF		
Ratlif	Zefiniah	172
READE		
Reade	John	171
READISH		
Readish	Joseph	25, 29
RECTOR		
Rector	John (Lt.)	81
REDGRAVES		
Redgraves	Simon	144

Fauquier County, Virginia's Clerks Loose Papers: A Guide to the Records 1759-1919

NAME INDEX

Surname	Given Name	pg #
Reid		
Reid	Hiram C.	139
RENNO		
Renno	Page	173
RICKETTS		
Ricketts	William S.	139
RIDLEY		
Ridley	John	175, 178
RIXEY		
Rixey	Richard	16, 18
Rixey	Rich^d	171
ROACH		
Roach	Thos	41
ROBINSON		
Robinson	Benjamin	42
Robinson	James	171
Robinson	John Senr	171
Robinson	William	171
ROCKINGBAUGH		
Rockingbaugh	Jacob	176
RODES		
Rodes	David	160
ROLEY		
Roley	Ben	172
ROOKWOOD		
Rookwood	Hiram (Lt.)	81
ROTH		
Roth	Ritty	146
ROUTT		
Routt	James	95
RUSIE		
Rusie	Michael	108
RUST		
Rust	Peter C.	64
Rust	Samuel	63

NAME INDEX

Surname	Given Name	pg #
SALLARD		
Sallard	Rebecca	160
SAMPSON		
Sampson	Alexander	136
SAUNDERS		
Saunders	Robert	140
SCRURRY		
Scrurry	Jno.	84
SEBASTIAN		
Sebastian	Joseph	93
SETTLE		
Settle	Joel	171
Settle	John	90
SHACKELFORD		
Shackelford	Benj^m	171
Shackelford	Captain	171
SHADRACK		
Shadrack	Eliza	158
Shadrack	John	158
SHADRICK		
Shadrick	Thomas	4
SHARPLESS		
Sharpless	W^m	146
SHAVER		
Shaver	Geo.	171
Shaver	John	171
SHAY		
Shay	Mary	180
SHEARMAN		
Shearman	John	139
Shearman	Maria	139
SHEPHERD		
Shepherd	Ann	84
Shepherd	Jno.	84
Shepherd	W^m	84

Fauquier County, Virginia's Clerks Loose Papers: A Guide to the Records 1759-1919

NAME INDEX

Surname	Given Name	pg #
SHIP		
Ship	John	169
SHIPE		
Shipe	J. R.	152
SHIPP		
Shipp	Betsey	152
SHULTZ		
Shultz	Benjamin	152
SHUMATE		
Shumate	J.	169
Shumate	John	171
Shumate	Jos.	135
SIDEBOTTOM		
Sidebottom	Sam	139
SILMAN		
Silman	Rich^d	41
SINCLAIR		
Sinclair	George	104
Sinclair	Isaac	162
Sinclair	William	104
SKINKER		
Skinker	Samuel	4
SLAVES		
	Aaron	51
	Abby	51
	Addison	169
	Andrew	169
	Banger	169
	Ben	156
	Bess	169
	Boatswain	169
	Brister	169
	Caesar	169
	Caesar	169
	Cate	169
	Cate	169
	Charles	156, 169
	China	169
	Clary	156
	Conner	169

NAME INDEX

Surname	Given Name	pg #
SLAVES (Cont.)		
	Crafford	153
	Cumbo	156
	Cuttena	169
	David	156
	Diana	169
	Dick	169
	Doll	169
	Dolly	146
	Frank	156
	George	169
	Guy	169
	Guy	169
	Hanah	169
	Hannah	156
	Harper	169
	Harrison	169
	Jack	169
	Jacob	156
	James	153, 169
	Jane	169
	Jenny	156, 169
	Jeoffery	169
	Joan	169
	Joseph	156
	Judah	156
	Kingston	156
	Kitty	156
	Lewis	156
	Lucy	169
	Lydia	156
	Manuel	156
	Margery	169
	Margt.	169
	Mary	153
	Max	169
	Moll	169
	Moses	169
	Nanny	153, 169
	Nell	169
	Nell	169
	Parson	169
	Patience	156
	Pegg	169
	Peter	153, 169
	Phillis	156, 169
	Phillis	169
	Phillis	169
	Punch	169

Fauquier County, Virginia's Clerks Loose Papers: A Guide to the Records 1759-1919

NAME INDEX

Surname	Given Name	pg #
SLAVES (Cont.)		
Ratliff		169
Robert		51
Rose		156
Sampson		156
Sarah		153, 169
Sarah		169
Sawney		169
Scipio		156
Susanah		169
Tom		156, 169
Tom		169
Warner		169
Will		153, 169
Wisser		169
SMALLWOOD		
Smallwood	Sarah	139
SMITH		
Smith	Alex^r	169
Smith	Jarriott	171
Smith	John	171
Smith	John	171
Smith	John A. W.	120
Smith	Lewis	41
Smith	Mary	171
Smith	Nicholas	140
Smith	Rebecca	176
Smith	Thomas	135
Smith	Thomas	135
Smith	Weathers	104
Smith	William	156, 171
Smith	William Junr	171
SNYDER		
Snyder	Henry	171
SPILLER		
Spiller	Jeremiah	91
SPILMAN		
Spilman	Jacob	25, 176
STADLER		
Stadler	Jacob	176
STANTON		
Stanton	William	129

NAME INDEX

Surname	Given Name	pg #
STEPHENSON		
Stephenson	Catharine	52
STEVENSON		
Stevenson	James	61, 71
STIGGERS		
Stiggers	Sarah	146
STIGLER		
Stigler	George W.	53
STINSON		
Stinson	Toliver	13
STONE		
Stone	John	61, 71
Stone	W^m	96
STRANGE		
Strange	William	117
STRINGFELLOW		
Stringfellow	R.	96
STUART		
Stuart	Alexander	84
Stuart	William Junr	42
SULLIVAN		
Sullivan	Patrick	113
Sullivan	Warner (Ensign)	82
SUTTON		
Sutton	William	102
SWAN		
Swan	Charles	78
TANNER		
Tanner	Dorothy	84
TAYLOR		
Taylor	Benjamin	83
Taylor	Evan	66
Taylor	Isaac	169
Taylor	Rich^d	115

Fauquier County, Virginia's Clerks Loose Papers: A Guide to the Records 1759-1919

NAME INDEX

Surname	Given Name	pg #
THARP		
Tharp	Andrew J.	146
Tharp	Elizabeth	146
THATCHER		
Thatcher	Hanna	84
THOMPSON		
Thompson	Elizabeth	66
Thompson	Jesse	171
THORNBERRY		
Thornberry	Mary	146
Thornberry	Samuel	64
THRELKELD		
Threlkeld	Mary	175
Threlkeld	William	175
TIMBERS		
Timbers	Elijah	54
TOMLIN		
Tomlin	John	12
TOOMEY		
Toomey	Elisth	84
TUCKER		
Tucker	W^m	84
TULLOS		
Tullos	Joshua	99
TULLOSS		
Tulloss	Joshua	169
Tulloss	Rodham	99, 169
Tulloss	Rodham Jr.	169
TURNER		
Turner	Charles	139
Turner	Harry	3
Turner	Henry	143
Turner	John	129, 135
TYDINGS		
Tydings	Richard	11, 14, 16

NAME INDEX

Surname	Given Name	pg #
VAUGHAN		
Vaughan	**Zachariah**	**144**
VERONE		
Verone	Joseph	129
WADKINS		
Wadkins	Elijah	139
Wadkins	Hannah	139
Wadkins	Matthew	139
WAGGONER		
Waggoner	Peter	154
WALDEN		
Walden	John	66
WALLER		
Waller	Charles	61
Waller	John	64
WARD		
Ward	Berkeley	15
WASHINGTON		
Washington	Augustine	1, 3, 4, 8, 148, 152
Washington	George	1, 3, 4, 5, 152
Washington	Lawrence	3, 4
Washington	Martha	3, 4
WATERS		
Waters	John	68
WATSON		
Watson	Margaret	144
WAUGH		
Waugh	Mary	4
WEAVER		
Weaver	Joseph	51
Weaver	Samuel	51
Weaver	Tilman	14, 129
WEEDON		
Weedon	George	65
WELCH		
Welch	Joseph	4

Fauquier County, Virginia's Clerks Loose Papers: A Guide to the Records 1759-1919

NAME INDEX

Surname	Given Name	pg #
WELSH (Cont.)		
Welch	Sarah	4
Welsh	Alexander	176
Welsh	James	25
Welsh	Joseph	62
Welsh	Sarah	62
WHEATLEY		
Wheatley	William	171
WHEELER		
Wheeler	Catharine	176
WHITE		
White	Mitchel	180
White	Wilson	180
WHITING		
Whiting	Thomas	104, 162
WHITNEY		
Whitney	Betty	56
WIGFIELD		
Wigfield	Thos	171
WILLIAMS		
Williams	Joe	176
WILLIS		
Willis	Mary	140
WILLSON		
Willson	Willis	84
WINDHAM		
Windham	Mary	84
WINDSOR		
Windsor	Caty	180
WINN		
Winn	Minor	90, 175
WITHASON		
Withason	Celia	144

NAME INDEX

Surname	Given Name	pg #
WITHERS		
Withers	Daniel	97, 120
Withers	James	129, 171
Withers	James O.	13
Withers	John	172
Withers	Thornton	125
Withers	William	91, 144, 150
WOODSIDES		
Woodsides	Clara	23
Woodsides	Elizabeth	23
Woodsides	John	93
Woodsides	Mary	23
Woodsides	Sarah	23
Woodsides	William	23
WOOLINGHAM		
Woolingham	Polly	139
Woolingham	Washington	13, 139
WRIGHT		
Wright	James	129
Wright	John	116, 158
Wright	William	140
YEATMAN		
Yeatman	Henry L.	64
YOUNG		
Young	Original	15, 16, 159

Other Heritage Books by Joan W. Peters:

Abstracts of Fauquier County, Virginia Birth Records, 1853–1896

Being of Sound Mind: An Index to the Probate Records in Fauquier County, Virginia's Clerk's Loose Papers and Superior and Circuit Court Papers, 1759–1919

Fauquier County, Virginia's Clerk's Loose Papers: A Guide to the Records, 1759–1919

Military Records, Certificates of Service, Discharge, Heirs, and Pensions Declarations and Schedules from the Fauquier County, Virginia Court Minute Books, 1784–1840

Military Records, Patriotic Service, and Public Service Claims from the Fauquier County, Virginia Court Minute Books, 1759–1784

Military Records, Pension Applications, Heirs at Law and Civil War Military Records from the Fauquier County, Virginia Court Minute Books, 1840–1904

Neglected and Forgotten: Fauquier County, Virginia French and Indian War, Revolutionary War and War of 1812 Veterans

Prince William County, Virginia General Index to Wills, 1734–1951

Prince William County, Virginia Patriots and Pensioners, 1752–1856 Military Records from the Prince William County, Virginia Minute and Order Books and Other Source Records

The Tax Man Cometh—Land and Property in Colonial Fauquier County, Virginia: Tax Lists from the Fauquier County Court Clerk's Loose Papers, 1759–1782

The Third Virginia Regiment of Foot, 1776–1778, with Flags Flying and Drums Beating Volume One: A History

The Third Virginia Regiment of Foot, 1776–1778, with Flags Flying and Drums Beating Volume Two: Biographies

www.ingramcontent.com/pod-product-compliance
Lightning Source LLC
Chambersburg PA
CBHW080549230426
43663CB00015B/2767